American History
in the Making

American History in the Making

Daily Events That Helped Form a Country

Mike Henry

ROWMAN & LITTLEFIELD
Lanham • Boulder • New York • London

Published by Rowman & Littlefield
An imprint of The Rowman & Littlefield Publishing Group, Inc.
4501 Forbes Boulevard, Suite 200, Lanham, Maryland 20706
www.rowman.com

86-90 Paul Street, London EC2A 4NE

British Library Cataloguing in Publication Information Available

Library of Congress Cataloging-in-Publication Data

Names: Henry, Mike, 1952- author.
    Title: American history in the making : daily events that helped form a
       country / Mike Henry.
    Other titles: Daily events that helped form a country
    Description: Lanham : Rowman & Littlefield, [2023] | Includes
       bibliographical references. | Summary: "This book gives out a fun
       historical fact for each day of the year"-- Provided by publisher.
    Identifiers: LCCN 2022060309 (print) | LCCN 2022060310 (ebook) | ISBN
       9781475869903 (cloth) | ISBN 9781475869910 (paperback) | ISBN
    9781475869927 (epub)
    Subjects: LCSH: United States--History--Chronology. | United
       States--History--Anecdotes.
    Classification: LCC E174.5 .H46 2023 (print) | LCC E174.5 (ebook) | DDC
       973--dc23/eng/20230105
    LC record available at https://lccn.loc.gov/2022060309
    LC ebook record available at https://lccn.loc.gov/2022060310

Contents

Preface

Greetings once again. News is made every day and after an undetermined time, those items that were once classified as current events become a part of the past. At that point, we refer to them as history.

The big stories that made headlines or led off the evening newscasts are usually known by most and become a part of the history books as time moves along. Each day there are stories that promote debate and play a role in the decision-making process for citizens.

However, when one begins to explore beyond the main items, there are elements that played a key role in a story that got pushed to the back burner.

Behind the signatures of the Founding Fathers are interesting backstories that have been mostly ignored. These records of the past have helped us understand the foundation of the country. There are also other instances where this has happened.

As an example, President John F. Kennedy was assassinated on Friday, November 22, 1963. Many people already know this, but he wasn't the only well-known person to meet his maker on that day.

In addition to JFK, three other persons of accomplishment made the news cycle's obituary list that day. In Los Angeles, the 69-year-old famed author Aldous Huxley died of cancer. He is best known for writing the popular futuristic novel *Brave New World.*

Another well-known writer, C. S. Lewis, died from the effects of nephritis in Oxford, England. The 64-year-old composed many works including *The Chronicles of Narnia* which also became a major motion picture. Finally, William R. Titterton, who was also a British author and penned the biography *G.K. Chesterton: A Portrait*, died at age 84.

History is full of examples where there are important stories that took place which coincided with a landmark event. There is no shortage of items worth mentioning that have been overshadowed by other aspects of history.

This book is about those events with one dedicated to each day of the year that it took place. The United States doesn't have a prolonged period of history like some other countries, although for a nation that has been around for fewer years, the events are interesting, exciting, and can often bring a smile.

Enjoy.

JANUARY

JANUARY 1

HAPPY NEW YEAR!

The president often receives gifts, most of which usually end up in a museum or library. On New Year's Day 1802, president Thomas Jefferson received a gift of a mammoth cheese wheel that measured more than four feet in diameter, thirteen feet in circumference, and seventeen inches in thickness. Once cured, it weighed 1,235 pounds.

But Jefferson isn't the only commander in chief to sample the cheese. In 1835, Andrew Jackson was presented a similar gift from dairy farmer and colonel Thomas S. Meacham of Sandy Creek, New York, that was four feet in diameter and two feet thick, weighing nearly 1,400 pounds, and was wrapped in a giant belt that bore the patriotic inscription, "The Union, it must be Preserved." Like Jackson, Meacham was a veteran of the War of 1812.

In 1837, Old Hickory's second term was drawing to a conclusion, and he wasn't about to haul a two-year-old mountain of cheese with him back to his home in Tennessee. At that point, he decided to make the oversized dairy product a snack for the people during his last public reception at the White House. The gathering's 10,000 visitors attacked the wheel of the tasty food with such fervor that the entire thing was gone within two hours.

JANUARY 2

DR. PEMBERTON'S MAGIC MEDICINE

Georgia became the nation's fourth state on January 2, 1788. It is located in the southeastern region of the country and partially sits on the Atlantic Ocean. It is also the home of the world's largest-selling soft drink. Coca-Cola, aka Coke, sells about $47 billion worth of their popular beverage, but how did the well-recognized soda get its start?

In April 1865, lieutenant colonel John Pemberton of the Confederate Army was wounded during the Civil War. He was a pharmacist by trade and after returning home to Columbus, Georgia, he began working on painkillers that could serve people, like himself, who were hurt in combat.

In some of his experiments, Dr. Pemberton mixed coca, syrup with carbonated water, and the kola nut along with other ingredients to make his formula. He then decided to sell the creation as a drink rather than a medicine.

In 1897, Coca-Cola became the first company to use coupons. They hired salesmen to distribute them in Atlanta for a free sample. The company hoped that people would try the drink, enjoy it, and then purchase it.

Today, visitors to Georgia's capital city can learn more about the product by visiting the World of Coca-Cola which houses a number of interesting items inside its museum.

JANUARY 3

WHEN THEY CALLED THE DOME THEIR HOME

Ground was broken on this day in 1962 for the construction of Houston's Astrodome which opened in 1965. It was the world's first indoor stadium and played host to sporting events, concerts, political conventions, and other attractions.

However, as the years passed and the wear and tear took hold on Texas' grand edifice, by 2005, Houston's professional baseball and football teams had moved to newer facilities.

But in August (2005) at 40+ years of age, the old Astrodome took on a new role as it became the temporary home for 25,000 residents of New Orleans who were displaced by Hurricane Katrina. The stadium, where boxing champion Muhammad Ali fought on four occasions in the 1960s and 1970s, was used for three weeks while the refugees were relocated to other facilities.

It wasn't the Astrodome's first dealings with a hurricane situation. On August 18, 1983, Hurricane Alicia roared through Houston with winds topping 80 mph as it crossed the city. Doubters had claimed that the roof would never stand up to hurricane conditions but the stadium survived with hardly a scratch.

Unfortunately the same couldn't be said for New Orleans' Superdome which took a direct hit from Katrina and saw extensive damage. It was closed for 13 months in 2005–2006.

JANUARY 4

SPUD STORIES

There are many foods that are made from potatoes—like French fries, potato chips, and potato cakes, just to name a few. There are actually dozens more different dishes and recipes that are made from the earth-rooted vegetable but one state has become famous for growing the best spuds (the common nickname for potatoes). That would be Idaho.

Potatoes were not introduced in Idaho by a farmer but by a minister from New York named Henry Spalding. In 1837, he enlisted their aid and taught the local Native Americans to farm the crop in order to provide food for themselves rather than relying exclusively on hunting and foraging.

However, the most famous man in the "Gem State" when it comes to potatoes is J. R. Simplot who was born on this day in 1909. He and one of his scientists, Ray Dunlap, created frozen French fries which are ubiquitous in today's restaurants. They became so popular that it made Mr. Simplot a billionaire.

Today, potatoes are grown in thirty states, but Idaho produces more than any of the others, although the largest potato ever grown wasn't in Idaho. It was produced in 2010 by Peter Glazebrook in his home garden in England, and weighed an amazing 11 pounds!

JANUARY 5

HOW THE GRIEF STOLE CHRISTMAS

In 1972, Joe Biden defeated Republican incumbent J. Caleb Boggs to become the junior US senator from Delaware. He was the only Democrat willing to challenge Boggs.

With a minimal amount of campaign funds on hand, the political newcomer was given no chance of winning. In fact, eight months before the election, Biden trailed Boggs by a nearly insurmountable 30 percentage points, but with assets like his energy, an attractive young family, and the ability to connect with voters, he was able to cross the finish line with 50.5 percent of the vote.

At the time of his election, the Wilmington resident was still just twenty-nine years old, but he reached the constitutionally required age of thirty before he was sworn into office.

On December 18, 1972, just days before he was to be sworn in, Biden's wife Nealia and infant daughter Naomi "Amy" were both killed in a traffic accident in Hockessin, Delaware. Their sons, Hunter and Beau, were seriously injured in the wreck when the family vehicle was struck by a tractor-trailer. Contrary to some news reports, investigators found that alcohol didn't play a role in the crash.

The accident changed Biden's perspective about being a member of the exclusive legislative body. However, Senate Majority Leader Mike Mansfield (D-MT) persuaded him to give it a try for six months. Thus, on this day in 1973, Joe Biden became the junior US senator from Delaware. He took the oath in the hospital room of his four-year-old son Beau in Wilmington just weeks after the tragic car wreck.

It was the beginning of a political career that endured for decades as Biden was reelected to six terms as a US senator (1978, 1984, 1990, 1996, 2002, and 2008); he served two terms as vice president in 2009 and 2013; and in 2020, he was elected as the nation's oldest president at 78 years of age.

JANUARY 6

THE CASE FOR FELIX

When it comes to the history of slavery in America, one of the most famous events took place in 1857. That was the Dred Scott v. Sandford Supreme Court case in which a slave, Dred Scott, tried to sue for his freedom on the grounds that his owner had moved him into to the free territory of Wisconsin and the state of Illinois. The ruling went against Scott on a 7–2 vote in what is often considered one of the worst Supreme Court decisions in American history.

However, Scott wasn't the first slave to use political and legal avenues to seek emancipation. Decades earlier, on this day in 1773, an African American slave named Felix delivered a written request to the Massachusetts General Court. In his document, he asked to end slavery and simply signed it "Felix."

As the years progressed, enslaved African Americans filed petitions throughout the colonies in other places like New Hampshire and Connecticut. When the Massachusetts state constitution was adopted on October 25, 1780, it stated, "All men are born free and equal, and have certain natural, essential, and unalienable rights."

Ten years after Felix delivered that first petition, another Massachusetts slave named Quock Walker sued for his freedom. His lawyers argued that the new constitution forbade his bondage.

In 1783, state Supreme Judicial Court Justice William Cushing ruled slavery contradicted the constitution's statement that "men are born free and equal" which effectively ended slavery in Massachusetts. Dred Scott was born sixteen years later in Virginia.

JANUARY 7

BIGGER THAN DEATH, LARGER THAN LIFE

Nikola Tesla died on this day in 1943. He was one of the world's most renowned scientists but when he passed, the Austrian native was alone and in debt, residing on the 33rd floor of the Hotel New Yorker. Tesla was eighty-six years old and had been living in small hotel rooms for decades.

Among those who had provided financial support in the past was multi-millionaire John Jacob Astor who died during the sinking of *Titanic* in 1912. Tesla's cause of death was due to coronary thrombosis. He had been working on a treasure trove of creations that included items featuring "wireless communication." He also hinted at a powerful weapon called Tesla's Death Ray, which would harness a beam of metal ions hurtling along at 270,000 miles per hour.

While inventors like Edison, Ford, and Marconi were often spotlighted in the media, the world gradually withdrew from the experiments of Tesla. By 1912, his behavior became more erratic as he was increasingly compulsive: he counted his steps, insisted on having eighteen napkins on the table, and obsessed about cleanliness as well as the numbers 3, 6, and 9. The scientist became further alienated, spending more time with his rooftop pigeons rather than other humans for companionship.

Upon his demise, representatives from the federal government ransacked Tesla's room and confiscated multiple files for examination. Three weeks after his death, they tasked MIT scientist John G. Trump—former president Donald Trump's uncle—with evaluating Tesla's papers.

In July 2003, Martin Eberhard and Marc Tarpenning named their new company Tesla Motors to honor the great researcher. They specialized in building electric and clean energy vehicles.

In 2004, Elon Musk became a major investor and CEO of Tesla Motors and was the world's richest person for several years.

JANUARY 8

BUSHUSURU . . . NOT GODZILLA!

On this day in 1992, prime minister Kiichi Miyazawa of Japan was hosting a dinner for president George H. W. Bush during a state visit. Bush, who was sixty-seven at the time, appeared to be in fine health, having played doubles tennis with Emperor Akihito and his son that morning.

However, during the dinner, Bush suddenly fell ill. He leaned over before falling to his side, vomiting into the lap of his host, the prime minister. The president then fainted as his wife Barbara, along with aides and members of the Secret Service, swiftly tended to him. He was revived within moments and was able to leave the dinner under his own power, apologizing for the incident.

Doctors later stated that the former World War II pilot had suffered from acute gastroenteritis but felt fine after taking an anti-nausea drug. He resumed his normal schedule the following afternoon. Nonetheless, the incident was the lead story on the news shows and provided fresh material for late-night television comedians.

Tonight Show host Johnny Carson took advantage of the opportunity and chimed in that evening to a national audience, "The president got some more bad news: Japan also bars the import of Kaopectate."

Fortunately, he fared much better than one of his predecessors with the same malady. In 1850, president Zachary Taylor, a former war hero, died just hours after eating a bowl of cherries and drinking a glass of milk. Doctors cited the cause of death as gastroenteritis.

The episode gave wake to a new term in the Japanese lexicon—the colloquial phrase bushusuru, which roughly translates to "to pull a Bush," became a popular slang term for vomiting.

JANUARY 9

THE FIRST BURGER

Connecticut became the fifth state on January 9, 1788. It is located in the New England region of the country and was one of the original thirteen colonies. But most people don't associate it with the birthplace of hamburgers.

Who invented the famous sandwich? There are many stories about cooks who have taken credit for the creation of the burger. But in Connecticut, they believe that the first true hamburger was made by Louis Lassen.

He owned a small restaurant called Louis' Lunch with only enough room for a few chairs. It was located in the town of New Haven, the home of Yale University. It is claimed that one day in 1900, a local businessman went to Louis' place for his afternoon meal but told the owner that he couldn't stay and needed something that he could eat on the go.

At that point, Louis took some ground streak trimmings and placed them between two pieces of toast. The customer was satisfied and went on his way, but the restaurant's boss knew that he had discovered a special item that could be added to his menu.

Louis' Lunch restaurant is now more than one hundred years old and is run by his great-grandson Jeff. They only sell one main item, the original burger on toast that started it all over a century ago. It's even cooked the same way in antique cast iron gas stoves that were made in 1898.

While some may continue to argue about the burger's creation, in 2000, the Library of Congress in Washington, DC, certified that Louis Lassen served the country's first hamburger sandwich.

JANUARY 10

UP IN SMOKE

The United States Census is a national survey conducted every ten years to enumerate the population for taxation and political representation. However, like any large-scale program, there have been bumps in the road along the way.

Early census records from several states including Delaware, Georgia, Kentucky, New Jersey, Tennessee, and Virginia have been lost to history. No one knows exactly what happened to them but the prevailing theory holds that they were destroyed when British forces set fire to Washington, DC, during the War of 1812.

Problems continued on this day in 1921 when a fire in the basement of the US Department of Commerce building in the nation's capital destroyed more than 99 percent of the 1890 census records. Some of the information that was saved pertained to Union veterans of the Civil War.

JANUARY 11

NOT SO FAST

The Confederate States of America was made up of a group of eleven southern sovereignties that left the Union. Among that contingent was Alabama, which changed sides on January 11, 1861. However, that wasn't its first secession.

It didn't take long for counties in northern Alabama and eastern Tennessee to attempt to exit the Confederacy and rejoin the United States. The citizens of Winston County, Alabama, declared themselves the Republic of Winston and defied Confederate authority. The area had been known as a longtime Yankee stronghold with many residents enlisted in the US Army.

Among the populace of Winston County were between 8,000 and 10,000 deserters from the Confederate forces.

JANUARY 12

REGULAR or DECAF?

When amateur and professional prospectors headed to California in search of gold in 1848, the results were mixed. A few ambitious individuals were fortunate enough to locate enough of the precious metal to change their lives forever.

Others got rich without the assistance of any shovels or pans. Perhaps the most renown of the lot was Levi Strauss, who became wealthy because he made a new type of durable work pant; however, there were those less well known who also prospered.

William H. Bovee worked as a clerk in his uncle's boot and shoe shop in Sandusky, Ohio. He then returned to his birthplace of New York City where he was employed at Hope Mills, one of the leading coffee and spice companies. On this day in 1849, Bovee and his wife joined the ever growing horde going west to be a part of the gold rush.

Following his long journey, the young man opened the first coffee-roasting plant in San Francisco known as the Pioneer Steam Coffee and Spice Mills company. It was there that he met and hired brothers Edward, Henry, and James Folger. The business produced the first roast coffee available anywhere in Northern California and was also the first to commercialize and mass produce java.

Bovee sold his company to the Folger brothers in 1859 who renamed it as their own. He went on to serve as Mayor of Oakland in 1863 and 1864 before passing away in 1894 at the age of 70.

In 1969, James Folger's great-granddaughter Abigail was murdered in Los Angeles, along with six others, by members of the Charles Manson gang in a highly publicized crime. She was a graduate of Harvard University and the heiress to the Folger Coffee fortune.

Folgers was the leading brand of regular ground coffee in the United States in 2020 exceeding sales in excess of $1 billion, double that of its nearest competitor.

JANUARY 13

THE MOUSE IN THE HOUSE

Mickey Mouse, a comic strip created by animator Walt Disney, debuted on January 13, 1930. It ran until July 29, 1995.

By 1931, the cartoon was published in sixty newspapers in the United States, as well as those in twenty other countries. By 1940, the characters began appearing in *Disney's Comics and Stories.* Over the years, Mickey became the centerpiece of many of the company's projects such as books, television, theme parks, and movies.

JANUARY 14

UP IN THE CLOUDS

On this day in 1943 during World War II, president Franklin D. Roosevelt journeyed from Miami, Florida, to Morocco to meet with British prime minister Winston Churchill, becoming the first American chief executive to travel overseas by airplane.

But FDR wasn't the initial member of his family to take to the sky. On October 11, 1910, his cousin Theodore Roosevelt became the first US president to fly in an airplane. The craft, which was built by the Wright brothers, was piloted by Arch Hoxsey and stayed airborne for four minutes at Kinloch Field in St. Louis.

Theodore was a lover of adventure. Among his other thrill-seeking escapades were leading the charge up Kettle Hill during the Spanish-American War and participating in big game hunting.

JANUARY 15

ANOTHER TRAGEDY FOR THE KING FAMILY

Dr. Martin Luther King Jr. was born on this day in 1929. In 1983, president Ronald Reagan signed the bill into law recognizing his birth as a national holiday.

It is well known that Dr. King was the victim of an assassin's bullet in 1968. However, many don't realize that he wasn't the only person in his family to be struck down by a gunman.

On June 30, 1974, his mother 69-year-old Alberta Williams King was playing the organ during a Sunday service at Atlanta's Ebenezer Baptist Church where her son had preached numerous sermons about peace and nonviolence. It was then that 23-year-old Marcus Wayne Chenault Jr. rose from the front pew, drew two pistols, and began firing.

Rounds from Chenault's weapon struck Mrs. King, church deacon Edward Boykin, and congregation member Jimmie Mitchell. She and Boykin were both pronounced dead at the hospital. The attack occurred less than 100 yards from where Dr. King is buried.

The deranged gunman said that Christians were his enemy and that he had received divine instructions to kill King's father, who was also in the congregation, but murdered his mother because she was an easier target. After being found guilty, Chenault received the death penalty although his sentence was later changed to life imprisonment, due in part to the King family's opposition to capital punishment.

In 1995, Chenault died of a stroke while in prison.

JANUARY 16

A FULL SINGLE SHOT IN A CLEAN GLASS

When the United States government decided to put the clamps on hardcore drinking, rumors circulated there was no limit that American lawmakers wouldn't go beyond to make their point, including intentionally poisoning shipments of liquor during Prohibition.

Historical facts can sometimes get lost in the legal jungle when truth, as they say, often tends to be stranger than fiction. At first, those claims took on a conspiratorial tone; yet, as bizarre as it sounds, the government once came up with the misguided idea of using poisoned spirits to get people to stop drinking booze!

In an ultimate example of illogicalness, this meant that the public was in danger from those they had voted into office to protect them. While it could never be proven that the government had directly tampered with the alcohol supply, it did take steps to ensure that toxic chemicals were included in various industrial alcohols.

Such chemicals were commonly converted into beverages for adults during the era of the Constitution's Eighteenth Amendment, a reality of which officials were aware.

The Volstead Act, officially the National Prohibition Act, became the law of the land on this day in 1920.

For over a decade, the United States barred the production and sale of drinking certain alcoholic beverages in what became known as the Prohibition era.

One of the worst incidents took place on New Year's Eve 1927 where forty-one people died at New York's Bellevue Hospital from alcohol-related poisonings. It was not uncommon for the drinking public to overdo it when it came to indulgence in dangerous industrial strength methanol, otherwise known as wood alcohol, which was legal but an extremely unsafe poison not meant for human consumption.

JANUARY 17

HERE'S TO YOU, MR. PRESIDENT

Prohibition, aka the Volstead Act, was a nationwide constitutional ban on the production, importation, transportation, and sale of certain alcoholic beverages from 1920 to 1933. As the Eighteenth Amendment to its Constitution, the new law touched off a crime wave like none ever seen in the United States.

But not everyone was on board with the sweeping changes. Not even the man at the top.

Publicly, president Herbert Hoover supported Prohibition although he was known for visiting the Belgian Embassy in Washington, DC, for cocktails as the premises was considered foreign soil, thus making it legal to drink there. A person of wealth, the chief executive also owned an extensive wine collection and was known to enjoy a good martini. Prohibition started on this day in 1920.

JANUARY 18

WHERE IT BEGAN

The Centers for Disease Control and Prevention took samples on this date in 2019 in Washington state to conduct tests, two days later reporting the first US laboratory–confirmed case of COVID-19 in the United States.

It marked the beginning of a yearslong pandemic.

JANUARY 19

SNOW? IN FLORIDA?

On January 19, 1977, snow fell in South Florida for the first time in recorded history. Residents and visitors were both surprised and thrilled at the phenomenon and local newspapers ran headlines that were nearly as big as those for major national or world events. News of president Jimmy Carter's inauguration was pushed to the area for secondary stories.

The snow came on the heels of a strong arctic cold front which moved rapidly down the Florida peninsula from late on January 18 through the predawn hours of January 19. Tampa measured .20 inches and Plant City, east of Tampa, received up to 2 inches of the white stuff.

The extended duration of freezing temperatures devastated the agricultural community in South Florida with estimated losses of $350 million statewide and over $100 million in Dade County alone. Skinned fruits such as tangerines, tangelos, and temple oranges were almost totally destroyed, as were tender vegetables such as beans, corn, tomatoes, and squash. A total of thirty-five counties in Florida were declared disaster areas.

JANUARY 20

NOT JUST A POLITICIAN

On January 20, 2021, 78-year-old Joe Biden was sworn in as the forty-sixth president of the United States. Throughout his lifetime, he has spent more than a half-century as a politician.

Many decades ago in 1969, just after graduating from Syracuse University law school, the future commander in chief practiced law, first as a public defender and also with a local law firm headed by a politically active Democrat. Since criminal law did not pay well, he supplemented his income by managing properties.

The following year Biden entered politics and his ascension from a law office to the Oval Office is a rather common move. Of the nation's forty-six presidents, twenty-six were lawyers.

JANUARY 21

THE SNOW IN THE BAY

San Francisco has its share of weather. There are many sunny days but it also has its allotment of rain and many mornings begin with a thick layer of fog. But for those looking for snow, they have to travel about 200 miles to the beautiful slopes at Lake Tahoe.

However, old-timers who were residing by the Bay on this day in 1962 were part of a rare occurrence as snow fell in the area and accumulated to about 3 inches in Daly City and San Francisco. This was the heaviest local snowfall since 1887.

JANUARY 22

SMOKE SIGNALS

In 1908, temperance groups were busy imparting their views on society and attempting to influence the behavior of its citizens. Such groups could be found in big cities along with small towns and, in most cases, were enumerating the various evils of the turn-of-the-century's array of bad habits.

One such demonstration of the attempt to control conduct took place on this day in 1908 when New York City police arrested Katie Mulcahey for violating the new Sullivan Ordinance, a municipal law passed one day earlier by the board of aldermen barring women from smoking in public places. Temperance organizations applauded the action while the majority of the city's residents sided with the accused. Angry women held rallies proclaiming they should have all the rights that men were afforded, including the choice to smoke a cigarette wherever they wanted.

A district judge fined Mulcahey $5 for her offense, which she refused to pay, lecturing the court's authority figure, "I've got just as much right to smoke as you have . . . No man shall dictate to me."

Soon afterward, lawyers reviewed the wording of the new law and noticed that it did not mention a fine or punishment for public smoking. Mulcahey was released the next day after being the first and only person cited for breaking Sullivan's mandate. Two weeks later, the mayor of New York City, George B. McClellan Jr., the son of the well-known Civil War Union general, vetoed the law and it was stricken from the books.

Today, it is illegal for both men and women to smoke in most public areas of NYC.

JANUARY 23

TRUTH IN NUMBERS

From the mid-1960s until the early 1970s, rarely did a week pass where there wasn't a protest of events surrounding the Vietnam War. Most of these took place on college campuses and in large cities, as groups of mainly young people loudly voiced their disagreements over the policies of the Johnson and Nixon administrations regarding the conflict in Southeast Asia.

On this day in 1973, president Richard Nixon announced that an accord had been reached to end the Vietnam War. During a televised speech, he stated that the agreement would "end the war and bring peace with honor."

The accord didn't last and it took another two years of fighting to officially end the conflict.

JANUARY 24

GET YOUR KICKS ON ROUTE 66

Before the federal government built the interstate highway system, cross-country drivers traveled along the legendary road known as Route 66. It was established in 1926 and ran for 2,448 miles from Chicago to Los Angeles.

Author John Steinbeck drove the entire throughway with his wife Carol in September 1937 as research for his masterpiece *The Grapes of Wrath*. The couple bought a car in Chicago after returning from Europe. During their journey, they saw firsthand the cavalcades of migrants making their way to California during the Dust Bowl in search of work.

The novel was published in 1939 and won the National Book Award and the Pulitzer Prize for Fiction (both in 1940). It was made into an award-winning film and cited prominently when Steinbeck was presented with the Nobel Prize for Literature in 1962.

Upon the novel's release some twenty-three years prior, copies were burned by the East St. Louis (IL) Public Library and barred from the Buffalo (NY) Public Library because "vulgar words" were used. It was also banned in Kansas City (MO) and Kern County (CA) where much of the story takes place.

The Grapes of Wrath's 1939 release took place six years after book burnings began in Nazi Germany. Interestingly, even though the storyline focuses on a farm family from Oklahoma, the Steinbecks didn't spend any of their research time in the Sooner State.

The film version of Steinbeck's classic starred Henry Fonda and premiered on this day in 1940 in New York City.

JANUARY 25

JUST HANGING AROUND

There are many forms of execution but, until the 1890s, hanging was the primary method of carrying out the death penalty in the United States. Over the years, officials have employed electrocution and the gas chamber, intended as a more humane process of capital punishment.

Perhaps one of the most spectacular hanging scenes of all time took place on July 7, 1865, in Washington, DC. Four of the conspirators who took part in the Lincoln assassination were lynched simultaneously by order of the federal government in the courtyard of Fort McNair. It was a warm day and one of the convicted, Mary Surratt, requested that her executioners hold a parasol over her to prevent the condemned woman from getting sunburned before she was killed. The final request was granted.

Today, all thirty-two states that have the death penalty employ lethal injection, although hanging remained as an alternative method of execution in two states until New Hampshire ended the practice in 2015, which left Washington's inmates the last to have the option of going to the gallows.

It was on this day in 1996 that Billy Bailey became to be the last convict to be hanged in the United States. He had murdered an elderly Delaware couple in 1979. "The First State" had carried out its initial execution in September 1662 but hadn't employed the rope of finality in fifty years.

A few weeks before the sentence was to be carried out, prison officials from Delaware needed advice on the proper procedure so they traveled to meet with officials at the Washington State Penitentiary in Walla Walla where a hanging had been performed in 1994. They returned home with the information that was needed.

Apparently, the instructions were concise as the time of death on January 25, 1996, was announced as 12:15 a.m.

JANUARY 26

THE MUSIC OF THE NIGHT

At the Majestic Theatre on Broadway in New York City, history is made eight times per week. That is because it is the home venue of the district's longest running play, *The Phantom of the Opera*.

The production, written by Andrew Lloyd Webber, opened on Broadway on January 26, 1988. It had premiered in London fifteen months earlier.

Going into 2023, more than 13,000 performances had taken place at the Majestic, which does not include the touring companies that perform it on stages throughout the world.

The Majestic Theatre opened on March 28, 1927.

JANUARY 27

KEEPING COOL

In 1802, a versatile person who was a cabinetmaker, engineer, and farmer named Thomas Moore needed a way to transport butter from Georgetown in Washington, DC, to his home some 30 miles away in Montgomery County, Maryland, which led to the creation of the ice box.

The device started out with an oval cedar tub utilizing a tin chamber on its interior. Moore placed ice in gaps between the wood and the tin walls and finally insulated his creation with rabbit fur along the exterior.

In 1802, he invited president Thomas Jefferson to his home to view his invention, which he called a refrigeratory. Always inquisitive, especially when it came to food and its preparation, the chief executive made the short journey to Moore's dwelling. During his visit, the well-traveled Virginian sketched a picture of Moore's invention onto his invitation.

It was on this day in 1803, that Thomas Moore received a patent for his device that became the forerunner to the modern-day refrigerator. It was signed by President Jefferson who also bought one the following year for his Monticello estate.

JANUARY 28

PITTSBURGH'S BRIDGE IS FALLING DOWN

On this day in 2022, president Joe Biden was preparing to give a speech in Pittsburgh.

At about 7:00 a.m., the 447-foot-long bridge on Forbes Avenue caved in, leaving a mass of twisted metal and concrete rubble along with ten people injured, but amazingly there were no deaths. Rescue crews had to rappel 150 feet down the hillside to reach some of the injured. The busy crossing was used by 15,000 drivers daily and was forty-nine years old.

Pittsburgh is known as the "City of Bridges" and boasts 446 overpasses—more than any other city in the world. It's history also includes its growth as a titan of the steel industry in the nineteenth century.

The collapse took place about four miles from where the president was scheduled to speak. The topic of his address? The nation's crumbling infrastructure problem.

JANUARY 29

A DANGEROUS JOB

Just like the other forty-nine states, Arkansas elects members to the US House of Representatives. But like so many others, that too can be a dangerous job.

In September 1868, Thomas C. Hindman, who had served in Congress prior to the Civil War, was killed by unknown assailants who fired through the parlor window of his home in Helena, Arkansas, as he was reading his newspaper. His assassin was never found.

A month after Hindman's murder, another Arkansas Congressman James M. Hinds was assassinated during an ambush when he was shot by a member of the Ku Klux Klan.

In 1888, John Middleton Clayton ran to represent Arkansas' second congressional district in the US House. His opponent was incumbent Clifton R. Breckinridge. The election became one of the most fraudulent in the state's history.

Clayton lost the election by a narrow margin of 846 out of over 34,000 votes cast. However, in one incident in Conway County, four masked and armed white men stormed into a predominately black voting precinct and, at gunpoint, stole the ballot box that contained a large majority of votes for Clayton.

Losing under such circumstances, Clayton decided to contest the election and went to the town of Plumerville to start an investigation into the matter. On the evening of January 29, 1889, an unknown assailant shot through the window to the room where he was staying at a local boardinghouse, killing the challenger instantly.

The deceased Clayton was later declared the winner of the election and Breckinridge was removed from office with the seat being declared vacant. Clayton's assassin was never found.

JANUARY 30

THE CHOSEN ONE

Happy birthday to former United States vice president Dick Cheney who was born on this day in 1941. During a political career that began in 1969, he held an array of positions including the second seat in the Executive Branch, Secretary of Defense, and White House Chief of Staff among others.

In July 2000, Cheney supervised the vice presidential search for potential Republican nominee and Texas governor George W. Bush. The candidate examined the research and came to the conclusion that Cheney was best suited for the job. Bush made the offer, which was quickly accepted. In truth, stories circulated throughout the nation's capital that the agreement between the men had been struck weeks earlier.

The pair served two complete terms together, battling against the terrorists on 9/11 and those in the Iraq War.

JANUARY 31

HAM IT UP

By this day in 1961, no human being had ever gone into space. The United States and the Soviet Union were in a two-country competition referred to as the space race, but before either of the world powers could send a human being into the great beyond, they experimented with animals.

The first of these flights took place on June 11, 1948, carrying a rhesus monkey named Albert, who was anesthetized and sedated before being launched 39 miles above Earth's surface. Unfortunately, the first primate in space died of suffocation during the flight which had originated from White Sands, New Mexico.

For the rocket scientists in both camps, it was a case of back to the space-flight drawing board. The two Cold War adversaries ramped up their efforts to put the first person into space.

On January 2, 1961, six chimpanzees were brought to Cape Canaveral, Florida, where they went through evaluations as candidates for a future test flight. At the end of the month on this day, one of those chimps who was simply known as Number 65 was loaded into a *Mercury-Redstone 2* spacecraft for a 16-minute flight. He traveled 157 miles above the Earth becoming the first hominid to go into space.

However, the biggest news was that he returned alive! The capsule splashed down in the Atlantic Ocean and was recovered by the USS *Donner* later that day. The first chimpanzee in space was given the name "Ham" once he had successfully completed his mission, because NASA believed that it would be bad publicity if a "named" chimp burned up in the atmosphere or otherwise died as a result of mission failure.

The following week, Ham appeared on the cover of one of the most widely read publications, *LIFE Magazine*, which usually featured world leaders, celebrities, and star athletes.

A little more than three months later, on May 5, 1961, Alan Shepard became the first American human being launched into space and, thanks in large part to the missions of Ham and his predecessors, Shepard also returned home safely and eventually flew to the Moon in 1971.

In 1963, Ham was retired to the National Zoological Park in Washington, DC, where he remained a popular attraction.. He died twenty years later at the relatively young age of 26 (most live to about 40) and some of his remains were buried in front of the International Space Hall of Fame at the New Mexico Museum of Space History in Alamogordo, New Mexico.

FEBRUARY

I bet after seeing us, George Washington would sue us for calling him "father."

—Will Rogers

FEBRUARY 1

RIKERS TO THE RESCUE

Rikers Island is a 400-plus-acre landfill located in New York City's East River between Queens and the Bronx. It is home to one of the world's largest correctional and mental institutions which has been the subject of many books and movies.

However, on this day in 1957, Rikers went from being a correctional lockup to a massive first responder unit. At 6:01 p.m., Northeast Airlines Flight 823 lifted off from nearby LaGuardia Airport bound for Miami, Florida, when it crashed shortly after departure. The aircraft was a Douglas DC-6, a four-engine propeller model.

The original takeoff time had been scheduled for 2:45 p.m. but delays due to snowfall pushed getaway back to 6:01 p.m. After the more than three-hour delay, the plane went airborne with a nearly full complement of 95 passengers and 6 crew members.

Just seconds after takeoff, the airliner flew over Rikers but the DC-6's altitude was insufficient to clear the upcoming bank of trees in its path. It crashed, coming to rest about 1,500 feet from the point of first impact. The duration of the flight from takeoff to collision was only about 60 seconds but resulted in 20 fatalities and 78 injuries among the passengers. There were no fatalities among the crew.

Shortly after the accident, Rikers Island prison personnel and trustees (inmates on good behavior who had earned additional privileges) ran to the scene to assist survivors. As a result of their actions, of the 57 inmates who

21

assisted with the rescue effort, 30 were released and 16 received six-month sentence reductions by the NYC parole board. Governor W. Averell Harriman also granted eight additional prisoners eligibility for immediate release. A follow-up investigation cited pilot error as the cause for the crash.

FEBRUARY 2

DETROIT DYNASTY

Like most major metropolises, Detroit has produced its fair share of famous people. One of the names that the locals know well may not be as recognized outside the state of Michigan but, since the days of the Great Depression, voters in and around Motown have become familiar with this family.

Over the years, the Dingells have evolved as fixtures on Michigan's political front, especially at election time. They have dominated their district congressional races for decades, vanquishing one challenger after another.

It all began in 1932 when Detroit native John Dingell Sr. decided to run for the local seat in the US House of Representatives. He grew up working in the newspaper business and eventually became a printer at the *Detroit Free Press.* He also helped organize a union.

That was an election year and Dingell Sr. was voted in as a Democrat from the newly formed 15th district in west Detroit. He was reelected eleven times and served until his death in 1955 at the age of 61.

A special election was called for by governor G. Mennen Williams to fill the remainder of Dingell's term. On December 13, 1955, two months after the representative's death, the electorate spoke and John Dingell Jr., who was born on this day in 1926, took over the Congressional seat previously held by his father. He was a 29-year-old lawyer with no experience as an elected official but that soon changed.

Dingell Jr. went on to become the longest-serving member of Congress in history at 59 years and 21 days. He outlasted redistricting on three occasions and served under eleven presidents (approximately one quarter of all who have held the office). He won his first full term in 1956 and was reelected 29 times, including runs in 1988 and 2006 without a Republican opponent.

The representative retired on January 3, 2015, after serving 21,571 days in Congress but that didn't mean that the Dingells were through with the House.

In November 2014, Dingell Jr.'s wife Debbie ran and won the seat that had been held by her husband. She was reelected in 2016, 2018, 2020, and 2022. Like her spouse, she entered the House with no prior political experience.

John Dingell Jr. died in 2019 at the age of 92.

The three Dingells have represented the southeastern Michigan area for 90 consecutive years (as of 2023).

FEBRUARY 3

GIVING AND RECEIVING

In November 1867, British author Charles Dickens began a six-month tour of the major east coast cities doing personal readings of his classic works. Among his most famous writings is his masterpiece, A Christmas Carol.

On February 3, 1868, he conducted a presentation at Carroll Hall in Washington, DC. Among those in the audience was president Andrew Johnson.

Four days later, he was the chief executive's guest at the White House. The fact that Johnson admired the great writer's works should come as no surprise as he had no formal education and couldn't read until he was a young man. Thus, the opportunity to meet the renowned author was extra special for the president.

But the joy was short lived as he was impeached by Congress three weeks after his meeting with Dickens. The writer stayed in the United States for five months and gave 76 performances for which he earned $228,000, an incredible amount of money for that era. Johnson was equally fortunate as the following May, he was acquitted of the charges leveled against him by the Senate.

FEBRUARY 4

THERE WILL ALWAYS BE ONLY ONE

On this day in 1792, George Washington was living the politician's dream as he was elected to a second term as US president in a vote of the Electoral College. It was the second time that he had been chosen unanimously, an accomplishment that would be unheard of today.

But history was almost repeated in 1820 until William Plumer, an elector from New Hampshire, a former US senator, and state governor, cast his ballot for his longtime friend secretary of state John Quincy Adams over the incumbent James Monroe who was running unopposed. He was partial to Adams and didn't come away impressed by the president's first-term performance, stating that he cast his vote to, "protest against the wasteful extravagance of the Monroe Administration."

When he left office in March 1825, President Monroe, who had served under General Washington during the Revolutionary War, exited the White

House carrying a piece of shrapnel in his shoulder from the Battle of Trenton which remained there for the rest of his life.

FEBRUARY 5

LET'S GO TO THE MOVIES

Henry Renno Heyl was an engineer from Philadelphia who was also an inventor. He is best remembered for presenting two public exhibitions of thirty-two moving pictures with his Phasmatrope, a device using sixteen photographs arranged around the edge of a revolving disk which were moved intermittently. There were three disks, each with an individual subject: (1) a couple dancing a waltz; (2) a Japanese acrobat making a steep jump; and (3) a brief speech by a political cartoon character known as Brother Jonathan, a forerunner to Uncle Sam.

Heyl's moving pictures were exhibited on two occasions. The first was on this day in 1870 before an audience of 1,500 at the Philadelphia Academy of Music during a church gathering. There were three showings of the Phasmatrope, each one using a different disk. Since there was no sound, the "Uncle Sam" disk was accompanied by a live lecturer who delivered the address and in the other featuring the dancers (Heyl was the male lead), it was synchronized with a 40-piece orchestra playing a waltz.

The next demonstration, which is believed to be the final presentation, took place on March 16 at Philadelphia's Franklin Institute.

FEBRUARY 6

A FIGHT IN THE NIGHT

The most infamous floor brawl in the history of the US House of Representatives erupted as members debated the Kansas Territory's pro-slavery Lecompton Constitution late into the night of February 5–6, 1858. Shortly before 2:00 a.m., Pennsylvania Republican Galusha Grow and South Carolina Democrat Laurence Keitt exchanged insults that quickly evolved into punches.

"In an instant, the House was in the greatest possible confusion," the *Congressional Globe* reported. More than thirty members joined the fracas.

Afterward, the melee dissolved into a chorus of laughs and jeers, but the regional nature of the fight powerfully symbolized the nation's divisions over slavery and states' rights.

FEBRUARY 7

NOTHING RUNS LIKE A DEERE

Happy Birthday to John Deere who was born on this day in 1804 in Rutland, Vermont.

In 1837, he invented the steel walking plow. It became the backbone of the multibillion-dollar company specializing in construction, farm, and lawn equipment that still bears his name today.

The saga began when he curved a broken steel sawmill blade that let the soil slide off the plow. In 1863, Deere created the Hawkeye Cultivator, the company's first implement adapted for riding. It was an important addition, as all of this era's Deere tractors have comfortable seats, although it never received the accolades of the one that started it all, the old steel plow.

FEBRUARY 8

MY ENEMY IS MY FRIEND

Happy Birthday to Civil War hero William Tecumseh Sherman who was born on this day in 1820. Much is written about generals and their exploits during battle but quite often, when the shooting stops, so do their stories. However, that doesn't apply to all of them.

In early April 1865, Sherman was relentlessly pursuing Confederate general Joseph E. Johnston through North Carolina.

Realizing the inevitable with his men tired of fighting and on the brink of total desertion, Johnston signed the surrender of his soldiers to Sherman on April 26, 1865, which included a statement by the Virginia native declaring that he would never again take up arms against the United States. It completed the second largest surrender of Confederate soldiers.

After the war, Sherman's battlefield accomplishments made him a national celebrity and a potential presidential candidate in 1884 which he turned down. In 1888, after returning to Virginia, Johnston was elected to the US House of Representatives where he served one term but remained in political life as commissioner of railroads in the Grover Cleveland administration. During the postwar years, he became a close friend with none other than his one-time adversary William T. Sherman.

After a military career filled with headlines and accolades, Sherman died in New York City on Valentine's Day, February 14, 1891. He was buried a week later in St. Louis, next to his wife, during a four-hour funeral that included a procession of 12,000 soldiers, veterans, and notables marching along a seven-mile path from downtown to Calvary Cemetery.

Among the pallbearers was none other but the Union general's former nemesis turned ally, Joseph Johnston. While preparing for the funeral, the one-time Confederate officer had caught a cold that turned into pneumonia. He died a month later.

FEBRUARY 9

ALMOST TRUE

There are a number of skyscrapers in Chicago. One of those is the Field Building (now the Bank of America Building) which opened in 1934. It was designated a Chicago Landmark on February 9, 1994.

The structure was said to be the first high-rise to use structural steel in its frame. It is also noted as the first tall building to be supported, both inside and out, by a fireproof metal frame.

However, this may not be entirely correct as the Ditherington Flax Mill was built as a fireproof metal framed building in Shrewsbury, Shropshire, England, in 1796. It is as tall as a modern five-story building and is still standing today.

In December 2004, fire swept through the 29th and 30th floors of the Bank of America Building. It was later revealed that the 43-story structure did not have a fire suppression system.

FEBRUARY 10

COMING AND GOING

Anaheim, California demonstrates a quintessential example of turning travelers into treasure. In 2019, tourism contributed $144.9 billion to the city's account. Two years later, that amount dropped to $97.4 billion due to COVID-19 restrictions which closed many attractions—still a substantial amount but not up to Anaheim's lofty standards.

The city's cash cow, as it has been since it opened in 1955, is Disneyland. It was closed from March 13, 2020, until April 30, 2021. During the same period, the Los Angeles Angels baseball team's fan attendance was restricted due to the virus, as were crowds at the Honda Center, the local arena that seats nearly 18,000 for hockey, basketball, concerts, and other events, many of which were canceled. Other attractions also experienced low turnout totals.

Those factors explain Anaheim's revenue setbacks during the pandemic. But it wasn't the first time that taxes played a role in the city's makeup.

Anaheim was incorporated as a city on this day in 1870, but the tax burden was too great for the people to handle, so two years later it was unincorporated. However, it was reincorporated by an act of legislature on March 18, 1878.

FEBRUARY 11

ONE MORE TIME . . . READY . . . AIM . . .

At the time of his duel with Alexander Hamilton, Aaron Burr held the office of vice president. But Burr isn't the only VP to shoot someone while serving in that capacity.

On February 11, 2006, sitting vice president Dick Cheney accidentally shot Harry Whittington, a 78-year-old Texas attorney, while participating in a quail hunt on a ranch in Kenedy County, Texas. Three days later, Whittington suffered a minor heart attack due to the shot pellets lodged in or near his heart. He was released from the hospital a few days later. President Bush was not present when the shooting occurred.

FEBRUARY 12

THE RIGHT TIME

Happy birthday to Peter Cooper who was born on this day in 1791. He was an inventor who designed and built the first American steam locomotive, the Tom Thumb.

In 1876, he was nominated to be the presidential candidate of the Greenback Party. At the age of 85, he is the oldest nominee of a US political organization. The election was won by Republican Rutherford B. Hayes who was thirty years younger than Cooper.

FEBRUARY 13

STAND BACK!

More than a few who have served in the executive branch of government have fancied themselves as pretty good golfers. Unfortunately, like many of the things that a politician claims, this is also not always true.

A good example of this took place on this day in 1971 when vice president Spiro Agnew was playing at the Bob Hope Desert Classic in Palm Springs, California. He was part of a Pro-Am foursome that included Hope, baseball great Willie Mays, and pro golfer Doug Sanders.

As the round got underway, Agnew's first tee shot sliced into the crowd striking a 66-year-old man and his wife. After taking some time to visit with them and apologize to the couple, the VP returned to the tee box but again shanked his shot into the gallery, hitting another woman in the ankle; she had to be sent to the hospital for X-rays.

Agnew's golf skills somewhat mirrored his political competence. In 1973, he was forced to resign the office when it was revealed that he had accepted bribes totaling more than $100,000 when he was governor of Maryland. That was worse than a double bogey.

FEBRUARY 14

A TALE OF TWO MRS. ROOSEVELTS

In most cases, Valentine's Day is a time to celebrate being with a person's significant other. For that, Theodore and Alice Hathaway Lee Roosevelt of New York City had much to enjoy as their first child, a daughter, had been born two days earlier in 1884.

But Alice suffered from Bright's disease, a kidney ailment that often proved fatal. The malady coupled with complications from the child's birth marked the downfall of the 22-year-old mother. She died just 48 hours after giving birth. It was the same disease that claimed the life of former president Chester Arthur in 1886.

But Alice wasn't the only member of the family to be visited by the Grim Reaper that day. Just eleven hours earlier in the same house, Roosevelt's mother, 48-year-old Martha "Mittie" Bulloch Roosevelt, died of typhoid fever.

This double tragedy greatly affected T. R. At the time, he was an assemblyman in the New York State Legislature. Roosevelt returned there for a few months before making a temporary career and life change. Leaving his infant daughter in the capable hands of his older sister Bamie, the future president headed west to Medora, North Dakota, for the next few years where he lived and worked as a rancher.

FEBRUARY 15

WHAT ABOUT THE *MAINE*?

On this day in 1898 at 9:40 a.m., the American battleship USS *Maine* was blown up in Cuba's Havana Harbor. The event marked the US entrance into the Spanish-American War. The act was used to inspire young patriots into battle with a bold decree, "Remember the *Maine*!"

Congress, which had already authorized the use of armed force, formally declared war on Spain on April 25.

In regard to time, as wars go, this one was short. Following a few weeks of skirmishes, the sides agreed to stop fighting on August 12, 1898, which was followed by the signing of the latest version of the Treaty of Paris on December 19, 1898. This was the second treaty that involved the United States and the twenty-seventh overall. As part of the pact, Cuba gained its independence while America took control of Guam, Puerto Rico, and the Philippine Islands as territories for $20 million.

However, there remains one important question about the war after more than a century . . . who blew up the *Maine*? There has been no shortage of investigations or theories as to what happened to the battleship that was anchored in Havana Harbor. The fact is that no one has ever established an exact cause of the explosion or determined who was responsible.

FEBRUARY 16

DANGER ON THE SLOPES

Some people get to a certain point in life and elect to alter their career path. The reasons are varied, but quite often it is because they aren't having the success that they had hoped for in their current job.

But that's not why Sonny Bono took a different road in 1988 at age 53, in fact, it was quite the opposite. In the 1960s and 1970s, he and his wife Cher formed one of the most successful rock music duos in the world. He had experienced the fame of being a singer, actor, and songwriter. His string of hits included: "I Got You Babe," "The Beat Goes On," and "Baby Don't Go."

The couple also starred in a one-hour weekly variety show on CBS which remained in the Top 20 of the weekly ratings during its four year run. But that all ended in 1974 when the Bonos announced that they were getting divorced. Cher continued on as a concert soloist and movie actress while Sonny, who was born on this day in 1935, moved to Palm Springs and dabbled in television guest appearances.

In 1988, the celebrity entrepreneur ran for mayor and won. This was about the same time that actor Clint Eastwood was concluding a two-year term as the mayor of Carmel, California.

In 1986, Bono married Mary Whitaker and they had two children. He remained as mayor until 1992 and three years later, to the surprise of many, was elected to the US House of Representatives as a Republican. But on January 5, 1998, the congressman was killed when he collided with a tree during a skiing accident in California. He was sixty-two years old and his wife was chosen to fill the remainder of his term.

Bono's manner of death wasn't a first for someone with ties to politics. Just a week earlier, Michael Kennedy, the son of former attorney general and presidential candidate Robert Kennedy and nephew of president John F. Kennedy, died when he skied into a tree in Aspen, Colorado. He was thirty-nine years old.

FEBRUARY 17

REQUEST DENIED

Inaugurations are times for celebration while the nation's work usually becomes secondary for that day.

Among the participants in Theodore Roosevelt's inaugural parade of 1905 were six Indian chiefs, who were decorated in traditional headgear with painted faces as they rode horses along Pennsylvania Avenue. They included the celebrated Comanche leader Quanah Parker; Buckskin Charlie from the Ute; Hollow Horn Bear and American Horse of the Lakota; along with Little Plume from the Blackfoot Nation.

Not lost among the group was perhaps the best known of them all. Over time, he had led his people through raids and warfare and, in 1886, was eventually captured by the US military and held as a prisoner of war. After years of movement by the government, he was finally relocated to Fort Sill, Oklahoma (Indian Territory at the time), but yearned to return to his home territory in Arizona; he was none other than the well-known Apache warrior Geronimo.

Over the years, the stories from his past had catapulted him to celebrity status. It was common for the government to put him on display at major events where he was often greeted by slurs and other insults from those who carried a long-standing hatred of Native Americans. Many citizens remained bitter toward the tribes over what had taken place with George Custer's troops at the Battle of the Little Bighorn some twenty-nine years earlier.

It was Geronimo's hope to meet with Roosevelt while in the nation's capital to persuade him to let his people return to their home in Arizona.

Following the parade, the two men met but the president was not in a giving mood as an interpreter told Geronimo, "When you lived in Arizona, you had a bad heart and killed many of my people. . . . We will have to wait and see how you act."

Geronimo was returned to Fort Sill where, four years later (February 17, 1909), he was thrown from his horse and died of pneumonia a few days afterward. At the time, he was still a prisoner of the United States. On his deathbed, the respected medicine man is said to have told his nephew, "I should never have surrendered. I should have fought until I was the last man alive."

FEBRUARY 18

DOGS, TRAINS, AND WHISKEY

Dave Stone passed away on this day in 2004 at the age of 85. He joined radio station KSEL in Lubbock, Texas, in 1946 and became a country DJ host a year later.

In 1953, he put KDAV radio on the air in Lubbock, Texas, programming it exclusively with country music.

Stone gave hometown star Buddy Holly his first radio exposure on KDAV's *Sunday Party*, a live local show. In January 1955, he booked Elvis Presley and paid a reputed $75 for one of his first headlining appearances. Dave Stone was inducted into the Country Music DJ Hall of Fame in 1999 after retiring that same year.

FEBRUARY 19

NOW, TARZAN MAKE WAR!

The character Tarzan was one of the most popular movie heroes of the 1930s and 1940s, so it was only natural that when World War II broke out, the man from the jungle would be headed for a showdown against the Nazis on theater screens across the world.

On this day in 1943, Metro-Goldwyn-Mayer released *Tarzan Triumphs* where the ape man wearing his trademark loincloth, portrayed by former Olympic swimming champion Johnny Weissmuller, took on the Third Reich. Prior to the big fight scene where Tarzan and his comrades kill off a few dozen German soldiers, crowds in the movie houses went wild when Weissmuller looked into the camera and uttered the film's famous line, "Now, Tarzan make war!"

In the final scene, the scriptwriters took a last jab at the German dictator as Cheeta the chimpanzee is mistaken by Nazi officers to be Hitler.

FEBRUARY 20

PUT DOWN YOUR SWORDS

During the presidential campaign of 1992, Democrat challenger Bill Clinton criticized his opponent Republican George H. W. Bush when he stated, "President Bush says this election is about trust and character and judgment. He has seriously called into question those issues and now has to answer your questions on all."

But after Clinton left office in 2001, the two former rivals became close friends. They teamed up to lead relief efforts for the 2005 Asian tsunami raising $10 million in funds for nations like Indonesia, Thailand, Sri Lanka, and the Maldives, the four countries visited by the two former presidents during their tour of region in February. The pair performed a similar effort in Louisiana for the victims of Hurricane Katrina the following year.

In October 2006, Bush sent a message to Clinton which said, "This note is to simply let you know that I so appreciated your words about our relationship, about our friendship. It was from your heart—and I hope you know I feel the same way."

When the former World War II fighter pilot died in 2018, among those sitting in the front row at the memorial service was his one-time political adversary turned friend, Bill Clinton.

FEBRUARY 21

IF YOU BUILD IT . . . THEY WON'T BE THERE!

The United States is laden with well-known structures from sea to shining sea. However, several of those who were responsible for these famous works never lived to see the finished product, notably a certain landmark in the nation's capital.

Perhaps no project was more slowed by delays than the Washington Monument. Construction of the obelisk that was to be a tribute to the Father of the Country began in 1848, but was halted from 1854 to 1877 due to a lack of funds. Much of that money was used to fight the war between the states during that period. However, construction resumed in 1879 and the dedication finally took place on February 21, 1885 (George Washington's 153rd birthday).

Not only was Washington not in attendance at the ceremony but neither was the monument's architect Robert Mills. He had died back in 1855.

FEBRUARY 22

HAPPY BIRTHDAY PRESIDENT WASHINGTON

The nation's first president, George Washington, was born on this day in 1732.

The adoption of the Declaration of Independence took place on July 4, 1776. It is considered to be the country's most historic day but for General Washington, the triumphal spirit of that date must have been tempered by some bitter memories.

On that day, exactly twenty-two years earlier in 1754, the strapping, twenty-two-year-old militia commander surrendered to an enemy for the first and only time in his career. That low point came at the Battle of Fort Necessity during the French and Indian War. Following the submission, Washington signed a murder confession.

FEBRUARY 23

GET A JOB

It's not unusual to leave a job and get a new one. That is unless you were the President of the United States, which is exactly what John Quincy Adams did in 1831 after he departed the White House. However, he didn't have to travel very far for his new position. In fact, he was pretty familiar with his latest place of employment since it was the US Capitol Building.

Before being elected president in 1824, Adams had served as a US senator from Massachusetts in the same famous confines. For his new job, he took a seat in the other congressional chamber as a member of the House of Representatives. Subsequently, it would be the place where his life came to a dramatic conclusion.

On February 23, 1846, the 78-year-old Adams rose from his House seat to address a matter pertaining to the Mexican-American War. The former president immediately collapsed suffering a massive cerebral hemorrhage. He was taken to the Speaker's Room where he died two days later.

FEBRUARY 24

READY . . . AIM . . .

The most famous duel in the nation's history took place between Aaron Burr and Alexander Hamilton.

Over the years, there were other faceoffs of note. One of those was the not-so-famous Graves-Cilley duel. On February 24, 1838, congressman William Jordan Graves, a Whig from the state of Kentucky, fatally shot Maine congressman Jonathan Cilley in a duel.

Graves approached Cilley with a letter at the behest of a newspaper editor, James Webb, who was incensed about a bribery accusation Cilley had made on the House floor. Cilley refused to accept the letter which Graves interpreted as a direct insult to his character and, in turn, challenged Cilley to a duel. In an ironic twist, neither man had any known grievance with the other prior to the incident.

The duel went beyond the customary two rounds, resulting in Cilley's death in the third round. While many demanded that action be taken against Graves, the only punishment he received was a censure.

After some much-heated debate, a bill was passed in the US Senate by a vote of 34–1 that would ban duels within the District of Columbia. While this measure failed in the House, the next year (February 20, 1839), a bill was finally passed through both bodies and became law.

FEBRUARY 25

THE TAX MAN COMETH

On this day in 1919, Oregon placed a 1¢ per gallon tax on gasoline becoming the first US state to levy such a charge. It is also one of two states, New Jersey is the other, where citizens are not allowed to pump their own gasoline.

FEBRUARY 26

CHANGE THE SONG

The First Amendment came under a serious challenge for an usual reason on this day in 1954. Representative Ruth Thompson (R-MI) introduced a bill to prohibit the distribution of "obscene, lewd, lascivious or filthy" language as it pertained to songs, recordings, or other items that were capable of producing sound. The proposal was a reaction to the lyrics of certain rock-n-roll tunes and how they were presented by entertainers like Elvis Presley.

Thompson's measure was meant to take a legislative bite out of, what was presumed to be, risqué performing. It included penalties punishable by five years' imprisonment and a $5,000 fine!

Thompson wasn't a radical crackpot looking to make a political name for herself. Before becoming the first woman from Michigan to be voted into the US House of Representatives, she had been a practicing attorney and a judge. All were notable accomplishments for a woman of her era. She served three terms in Congress from 1951 to 1957.

However, what the representative had hoped would be landmark law never materialized as it failed to pass. Elvis and the other forefathers of rock music were free to sing on. As for the 70-year-old Thompson, her song ended in August 1956 as she was defeated for reelection in the Republican primary when she narrowly lost to Robert Paul Griffin who won her former seat in the general election and years later went on to serve in the US Senate.

FEBRUARY 27

LIKE FATHER, LIKE SON

On February 27, 1991, George H. W. Bush reached an approval rating of 89 percent that coincided with the US victory in the Gulf War. That record stood for a decade until his son, George W. Bush, garnered a 92 percent favorable grade after the 9/11 attacks.

But fame was fleeting as W. found out when his rating dropped to 25 percent (the third lowest of any president) in 2008 due to a major recession. The story wasn't much better for the elder Bush who was defeated in his 1992 reelection bid.

FEBRUARY 28

WISCONSIN TO THE RESCUE

Harriet Tubman is one of the legendary figures of the Civil War era. As a "conductor" on the Underground Railroad, she was able to lead hundreds of slaves out of the South and across the Mason-Dixon line to freedom.

After the war, Tubman's life began to take a more normal course. In 1869, she married a battlefield veteran and, five years, later they adopted a baby girl named Gertie. The family resided at Harriet's home in Auburn, New York, which she had purchased in 1858 from William Seward, Abraham Lincoln's secretary of state during the war. The house had served as a stop along the Underground Railroad.

While her war efforts had been successful, from a financial aspect, her own road was rough. In 1873, Tubman was the victim of a swindle which, coupled with personal debts that included her property, placed the well-known liberator in a bind for cash.

In an effort to help Tubman regain some control of her fiscal situation, in June 1874, US congressman Gerry W. Hazelton of Wisconsin introduced a bill (H.R. 3786) hoping to assist the woman known as, "Moses."

The proposed measure would provide Tubman $2,000 for her service to the Union Army as a scout, nurse, and spy. Even though the effort was sincere, the bill was defeated in a House vote.

However, overwhelming public support for Tubman led Congress to pass and, on this day in 1899, president William McKinley to sign H.R. 4982 into law, which "authorized an increase of Tubman's pension to twenty dollars per month for her service as a nurse."

In the end, one of the country's most accomplished civil rights icons had finally won the battle begun by a congressman from Wisconsin twenty-five years earlier.

FEBRUARY 29

HAVE A COKE AND A SMILE

There have been a number of historic cases that have been heard by the Supreme Court, but not all could be classified as setting a new precedent. On February 29, 1916, the justices heard arguments in the United States v. Forty Barrels and Twenty Kegs of Coca-Cola, a federal lawsuit under which the government unsuccessfully attempted to force the Coca-Cola Company to remove caffeine from its famous beverage.

Also, Happy Leap Day.

MARCH

History is the story of events, with praise or blame.

—Cotton Mather, New England Puritan clergyman and writer

MARCH 1

MEGA MONEY AND NOT

Charlie Chaplin was one of the biggest movie stars of all time. In 1916, he was earning an astounding $10,000 per week! By comparison, president Woodrow Wilson's salary was $75,000 a year when the average American made $708 for twelve months of work.

On March 1, 1978 (just three months following his death), Chaplin's corpse was stolen by a small group of Swiss mechanics in an attempt to extort money from his family. The plot failed, the robbers were captured, and the remains were recovered eleven weeks later near Lake Geneva. His body was reburied under two meters of concrete to prevent further attempts.

Chaplin was also a cofounder of United Artists Digital Studios in Hollywood.

MARCH 2

SEUSS I AM!

Happy birthday to Theodor Seuss Geisel who was born on this day in 1904. He was better known to the world by his pen name, Dr. Seuss, and was one of the most successful children's book authors of all-time.

Geisel's best-known works included *The Cat in the Hat* (1957); *How the Grinch Stole Christmas!* (1957); and *Green Eggs and Ham* (1960). He had no children of his own, saying of youngsters, "You have 'em; I'll entertain 'em."

Was Dr. Seuss a real doctor? That answer is determined by the reader as Geisel was awarded an honorary doctorate of Humane Letters (L.H.D.) from Whittier College, Richard Nixon's alma mater, in 1980. He also studied at Oxford in the 1920s.

While Geisel's collection is filled with award winners and best sellers, not all of his books made a splash on the literary market. During his career, Dr. Seuss had seventeen manuscripts rejected by his publisher.

MARCH 3

FAMILIAR FACES IN NEW PLACES

One of America's most enduring monuments is that of the four images that were carved near the peak of Mount Rushmore in South Dakota. They are composed of the spectacular 60-foot likenesses of George Washington, Abraham Lincoln, Thomas Jefferson, and Theodore Roosevelt which are annually seen by 3 million visitors. But few realize that none of the statues of those four former presidents were part of the original plan.

The initial proposal highlighted rugged heroes and trailblazers such as Lewis and Clark, Buffalo Bill Cody, and the Chief Red Cloud. But those designs were altered when the organizers went to Washington, DC, seeking financial assistance from the government.

After long negotiations involving a congressional delegation and president Calvin Coolidge, the project received approval on this day in 1925.

MARCH 4

THE WAR AT HOME

In 1918, many researchers believed that the first cases of the outbreak of the Spanish flu pandemic were recorded in Haskell County, Kansas, where young men were being hospitalized for severe flu-like symptoms. A local doctor sent a report to the Public Health Service, but it was ignored.

On March 4, an outbreak happened at Fort Riley with as many as 500 soldiers hospitalized within a week. After a month, the number of patients dwindled and it seemed like the worst was over.

From there, many of the infected soldiers were sent to Europe to help fight in World War I. While on the front, the malady mutated and spread from the soldiers on the battlefield to the civilian population of the war-torn continent and proceeded around the world. Few areas on earth remained unaffected, although Antarctica had no recorded deaths.

By October, twenty-four countries reported cases of influenza. The majority of victims during this pandemic ranged from age 20 to 40 and typically had been healthy individuals, although pregnant women were among the most vulnerable.

Another wave of the contagion returned in the spring of 1919 that many believed to be a more virulent strain. It hit quickly, killing some in just hours. However, by the end of spring the number of influenza patients dropped so that official bans were lifted in cities and states as people resumed their regular routines like school, church, and other activities where crowds gathered. Since the outbreak occurred during World War I, its toll was often overshadowed by the conflict on the battlefields.

Every known remedy of the day was tried including quinine tablets, bleeding, castor oil, digitalis, morphine, enemas, aspirin, tobacco, hot baths, cold baths, iron tonics, and expectorants of pine tar. But none were very effective.

Deaths rose again and many locations were closed to public assemblages. Newly enacted ordinances made it illegal to spit, cough, or sneeze in public—with threat of $500 fines in New York City. When people went out, they wore required gauze masks over their nose and mouth, often soaked in camphor or other medicinal substances.

The pandemic of 1918–1919 was believed to be responsible for an estimated 17.4 million deaths worldwide, although there is no official tally. The influenza led to 675,000 deaths in the United States, about equal to all during the Civil War, and caused twice the number of casualties for the U.S. during World War I (both killed and wounded) which totaled nearly 323,000.

MARCH 5

POUR ME ANOTHER ONE

Throughout history, the country's leaders have exercised various modes and methods of utilizing their free time. During the 1850s, president James Buchanan would use his Sunday ride as an excuse to visit the Jacob Baer distillery in the nation's capital where he would pick up a ten-gallon cask of "Old J.B. Whiskey." The chief executive would usually begin his partaking with cognac and conclude the evening with old rye. It was not unusual for two or three bottles to be consumed during one sitting.

The commander in chief's resistance to alcohol's effects was so astonishing that it drew commentaries from journalists in their newspaper columns. But the one-term president didn't just sit around swilling spirits. For exercise, he walked for an hour every day along Pennsylvania Avenue.

MARCH 6

THEY CALL IT KARMA

General Antonio López de Santa Anna, the leader of the Mexican forces is best known for his role in the fight against Texas independence and his actions at the battles of the Alamo (March 6, 1836) and San Jacinto (April 21, 1836). Unknown to most, he was also a big proponent of chicle, the principal ingredient in the traditional recipe for chewing gum. It is made from the sap of the sapodilla tree which is native to Mexico and Central America.

After his years on the battlefield, Santa Anna returned to Mexico where he served as president but fell upon hard times and, in a stroke of irony, was eventually driven into exile and to the cradle of his old enemy—the United States.

In 1869, the former military commander was visiting inventor Thomas Adams at his home in Staten Island, New York. Santa Anna recommended that chicle might be used as a cheap substitute in reducing the cost of producing rubber products like boots, toys, and tires. He told Adams that he could easily supply him with ample amounts of the sap and believed that both of them could become rich. Although Adams worked diligently for a year to find a way of transforming chicle into a satisfactory rubber substitute, all of his best efforts were in vain.

The inventor was about to dump his remaining supply of chicle into the East River but instead, elected to use it to make a batch of chewing gum. Adams offered it for sale to local storekeepers who were soon selling out of their allotments. Sales were so brisk that it was impossible to keep up with all of the arriving orders, which led to his invention of a chewing gum manufacturing machine for which he received the patent in 1871.

Adams went on to attain great wealth from his inventions in the chewing gum industry. But the story wasn't the same for Santa Anna who never saw the riches that he had dreamed. In 1874, he was granted amnesty and allowed to return to Mexico where he died two years later.

MARCH 7

FOR MY NEXT NUMBER . . .

Due to problems during his second term, it was often overlooked that Richard Nixon was a respectable pianist. The longtime political figure composed a piece titled "Richard Nixon Piano Concerto #1" which he played on the prime-time TV show, *The Jack Paar Program*, in 1963.

On March 7, 1974, Nixon once again tickled the ivory keys by accompanying entertainer and singer Pearl Bailey in a performance at the White House. That was followed on March 16 in Nashville where he played "God Bless America" on stage at the Grand Ole Opry.

However, five months later, the piano went quiet as Richard Nixon became the only president to resign the office.

MARCH 8

LISTENING TO THE SUPREMES

At one time, Abraham Lincoln had been a pretty well-known lawyer in Illinois. During his years in practice, he handled nearly 5,000 cases. Most were simple matters, often related to disputes over a debt or promissory notes, but they comprised the bread and butter of his clientele.

About 400 cases were argued before the state's highest legal body, the Illinois Supreme Court. Also of note were more than 300 cases that he and his partners tried before the federal courts. Most of these were at the district and circuit levels sitting in Springfield and Chicago. Yet he also worked on six cases that went to the US Supreme Court.

Of those, Lincoln's only appearance before the nation's highest legal body came on March 7 and 8, 1849, in the case of *Lewis v. Lewis*. The matter had to do with the statute of limitations of Illinois in its application to a lawsuit brought by Lincoln's client Thomas Lewis. The court decided against him with the majority opinion rendered by Chief Justice Roger B. Taney.

Taney was sympathetic toward the Confederate states and their plight. In 1857, a few years after the *Lewis* case, the judicial official voted against Dred Scott, a slave who was seeking his freedom.

Taney died on October 12, 1864, while still serving as chief justice as he had never resigned. That left the choice of his replacement to the person who was serving as president of the United States at the time of his death, who had also argued before the Taney Court when he was a country lawyer from Illinois—Abraham Lincoln.

MARCH 9

ONE DOOR CLOSES . . .

Happy birthday to Leland Stanford who was born on this day in 1824. He was one of the original members of the "Big Four" along with Collis Huntington, Mark Hopkins, and Charles Crocker who developed the Transcontinental

Railroad. He was also the founder of the university in Palo Alto, California, that bears his family name.

Stanford didn't come from affluence, in fact he was raised on family farms. In 1845, he earned a law degree and joined a practice in Albany, New York, where he met his future wife Jane.

From there, Stanford went west, ending up in Port Washington, Wisconsin, where he became a lawyer and newspaper publisher. That was until 1852 when a fire destroyed his office and law library.

At that point, he joined his five brothers who were running a store for miners in Placer County, California. As the business grew, so did his personal wealth. It provided him an opportunity to become a key investor in the Central Pacific Railroad and the formation of the "Big Four."

In 1869, when the Transcontinental Railroad was completed, Stanford and his associates had prospered and were some $54 million richer, and it all began because of a fire years earlier over 2,000 miles away.

MARCH 10

LET'S HAVE A WORD

Throughout history, a number of names have been associated with a particular item—for example, Edison and the light bulb or Bell and the telephone.

When it comes to the dictionary, Americans most often link Noah Webster to the classic word finder. He was a lexicographer from Connecticut who, in 1806, published his debut edition, *A Compendious Dictionary of the English Language*. It was Webster's first but not the initial offering by an American writer.

Samuel Johnson Jr. was a Guilford, Connecticut, schoolteacher who was born on this day in 1757. He was the author of the first English dictionary compiled by an American, "A school dictionary: being a compendium of the latest and most improved dictionaries." It was printed in New Haven (CT) in 1798.

Although, for all that he accomplished, the man of words is sometimes overlooked because of his British counterpart who wrote a 40,000 word dictionary that was published in 1755. His name was also Samuel Johnson and even though the two were both lexicographers, they were not related.

MARCH 11

CLOSE CALL

Accidents do happen but usually are not as spectacular as the one that took place on this day in 1958. Known as the 1958 Mars Bluff B-47 nuclear weapon loss incident, it occurred in Florence County, South Carolina, when a series of mishaps on board an Air Force B-47 carrying an atomic weapon resulted in the emergency pin getting dislodged.

The device broke free, falling through the plane's floor and nosediving 14,000 feet through the sky to the turf of the Palmetto State. There was no nuclear detonation although six people were injured by the explosion of the bomb's conventional device.

The impact damaged several buildings and created a crater 75-feet across and 35-feet deep. The injured parties sued the government and were collectively awarded $54,000.

MARCH 12

THE ONE AND ONLY

Happy Birthday to American naval officer, aviator, aeronautical engineer, test pilot, and astronaut Wally Schirra who was born on this day in 1923. While others like John Glenn and Neil Armstrong may have received more press coverage, the naval pilot served in both the World War II and Korean conflicts along with making history in space.

Schirra was one of the original seven astronauts chosen for Project Mercury in NASA's first effort to put humans into the great beyond. He flew the six-orbit, nine-hour Mercury-Atlas 8 mission on October 3, 1962, becoming the fifth American, and the ninth human, to ride a rocket into space. In addition, he was the only astronaut to fly in the Mercury, Gemini, and Apollo missions.

MARCH 13

SELF TAUGHT IS SELF MADE

Clyde Tombaugh was born into a farm family in 1906 in Streator, Illinois. He had hoped to attend college but those dreams were quashed when a hailstorm ruined his family's crops.

Starting in 1926 and without formal training, he built several telescopes with lenses and mirrors by himself. He sent drawings of his views of Jupiter and Mars to the Lowell Observatory at Flagstaff, Arizona, which offered him a job where he worked from 1929 to 1945.

However, it was on this day in 1930 that Tombaugh made history when he discovered Pluto, making him the first American to discover a planet. Even more impressive was the fact that he had achieved so much without attaining a college degree!

Following his discovery, the self-taught scientist earned his bachelor's and master's degrees in astronomy from the University of Kansas in 1936 and 1938. In 1980, he was inducted into the International Space Hall of Fame.

MARCH 14

HOOSIERS IN HIGH PLACES

The United States has seen forty-six presidents take the oath over a span of two-plus centuries. The state that produced the most chief executives is Virginia with eight. Close behind is Ohio with seven.

That information is pretty common but what about the person who is just a heartbeat away from the top job? There's little surprise that, with its large population, New York has turned out 11 vice presidents, which leads the list. However, the runner-up might raise an eyebrow as Indiana, which is best known for farming and a major automobile race, has sent six men to the nation's capital even though it ranks as just the seventeenth-most populous state.

The Hoosiers who turned VP include Schuyler Colfax (took office in 1869), Thomas Hendricks (1885), Charles W. Fairbanks (1905), Thomas R. Marshall (1913), Dan Quayle (1989), and Mike Pence (2017). Three others from Indiana were nominated for vice president but lost in the general election during those years.

Marshall was born on this day in 1854 but didn't believe that being vice president was a major event. He served two terms under Woodrow Wilson (1913–1921) and said, "Once there were two brothers: one ran away to sea, the other was elected vice president. Nothing was ever heard from either of them again."

MARCH 15

THE HOMECOMING

After eight years away commanding troops during the Revolutionary War, and then another eight serving two-terms as the nation's first president,

George Washington permanently returned to his home at Mount Vernon (VA) on this day in 1797.

The estate was very profitable with numerous crops grown and livestock raised. One of the most successful moneymakers was Washington's on-site whiskey distillery, which he built upon his homecoming and soon became a significant part of his business holdings. Like everything else around the property, it was big with five stills that churned out about 11,000 gallons of alcohol per year using corn and rye. With sales of $7,500 in 1799, it was the country's largest distillery at the time.

In addition to liquor, the former general also had a fishery, a meat processing facility, a gristmill, a blacksmith shop, and a textile production as well as his lucrative crop plantation. It's no wonder why he was one of the wealthiest men of his era, although he had little time to enjoy the fruits of his labor; the "Father of Our Country" passed away in 1799.

MARCH 16

THE THREE-FOR-ONE SPECIAL

On November 8, 1904, the voters of Colorado went to the polls to elect a new governor. The state had been wracked by continuous miners' strikes, violence, and bouts of political corruption for years. When it was over, Democratic nominee and former two-time governor Alva Adams defeated incumbent Republican James Hamilton Peabody with 50.64% of the vote.

There were accusations of fraud from both sides but the shenanigans didn't stop there. The scandal included an episode where Juan Montez, the election clerk of Huerfano County, jumped out of a moving train. He was en route from Denver to Walsenburg with orders from the court to bring back one of the ballot boxes that had been used in the most recent election.

Montez had already failed to previously produce the ballot box and the legislature wanted to be sure that it was brought back this time so a sheriff was sent along to escort him. But not long after the train left the station, the clerk jumped off and tried to flee. He was captured and promptly charged with election fraud.

The Huerfano County ballot box was eventually recovered but an investigation revealed that it was completely empty. It didn't even have a poll book inside. Apparently the official bin hadn't been used during the election and, as a result, all the ballots cast in the precinct were not official and had to be rejected.

Adams took office for three months but was replaced by Peabody on this day in 1905 under the condition that he'd have 24 hours to resign. Things then moved quickly as Peabody stepped down and Republican lieutenant governor Jesse F. MacDonald was sworn in to the top office that same day, resulting in the only period where the state had three governors during the same 24-hour period. MacDonald went on to serve only one term as governor and neither Adams nor Peabody ever served in that capacity again.

MARCH 17

TURN LEFT WHEN YOU SEE THE WATER

Happy Birthday to frontiersman James Bridger who entered the world on this day in 1804. As a young man, he joined other mountaineers who roamed the western region of North America. While trapping in late 1824, Bridger reached what he believed to be the Pacific Ocean.

However, what he had actually discovered was the Great Salt Lake. Experts are not sure if he was alone when he came upon the massive body of water; even though he didn't really know where he was, historians decided to credit Bridger with the find.

Afterward, it was discovered that the lake known as America's Dead Sea contained between 4.5 and 4.9 billion tons of dissolved salt. The areas with the highest salt content are nearly nine times saltier than those found in the ocean.

MARCH 18

THE BOSTON BURGLERS

A number of historical events have taken place in Boston. But for art lovers, the act that happened on March 18, 1990, at the city's Isabella Stewart Gardner Museum was like a dagger being plunged into their communal heart. The largest art theft in world history occurred when thieves stole thirteen pieces, collectively worth more $500 million.

The works that were taken included Vermeer's *The Concert*, which is the most valuable stolen painting in the world; two works of Rembrandt—*Christ In The Storm On The Sea Of Galilee* (his only known seascape) and *A Lady And Gentleman In Black*; a Rembrandt self-portrait etching; Manet's *Chez Tortoni*; two paintings and three drawings by Edgar Degas; Flinck's *Landscape With Obelisk*; an Shang Dynasty Gu; and a finial that once stood atop a flag from Napoleon's army.

The Vermeer, one of only thirty-four known works by the artist in existence, may be worth as much as $250 million, and is so famous that it is unsalable on the open market, which means the thieves may have had to destroy the very treasures they stole in order to conceal their crime. None of the items has ever been recovered and a reward of $10 million is still being offered for information leading to their return.

MARCH 19

SAME TIME, SAME PLACE

There were a number of ships lost by both sides during the Civil War. One of those was on March 19, 1863, when the Confederate cruiser SS *Georgiana* was destroyed on her maiden voyage. The wreck was discovered near Charleston, South Carolina, on the same day and month, exactly 102 years later by then 18-year-old diver and adventurer E. Lee Spence.

It wasn't Spence's only Civil War discovery as, in 1970, he located the remains of the Confederate submarine *H. L. Hunley*.

MARCH 20

WELCOME TO KENTUCKY

Happy anniversary to brothers Frank and Jesse James who pulled off their first bank robbery outside of their home state of Missouri on this day in 1868. It was then that six members of the James-Younger Gang rode into Russellville, Kentucky, and proceeded to make a gunpoint withdrawal at the Nimrod Long Banking Company.

After approaching the counter, fellow robber Cole Younger ordered bank president Nimrod Long to give him all of the money on hand. Meanwhile, the James brothers made the other employees put the cash in a wheat sack and after it was full, they rode away from the small town depository firing their pistols in the air.

At that instant, Long ran to the back door where another bank employee fired a shot at the departing thieves but instead accidentally hit his boss. By good luck, the wound was minor.

The amount snagged in the heist ranged in estimates from $9,000 to as high as $14,000. It was the first of Frank and Jesse's twenty bank robberies that took place in nine different states.

MARCH 21

RED ROOM RUMBLE

A bizarre and disturbing episode shattered the peace of president Benjamin Harrison's term in the White House on the evening of March 21, 1891. Its resolution showcased the heroism of Washington, DC, police and, according to others, the president himself.

Policeman "Big" John Kenny—a veteran officer and former cavalryman who had fought violent criminals on the city streets and now patrolled the executive mansion—was making his rounds at 8:00 p.m. when he heard a jarring crash on the South Portico. Racing into the Red Room, Kenny discovered a burly young man wearing only "a pair of pants and a blue balbriggan undershirt" busily engaged in smashing through the window.

President Harrison, who had been dining upstairs with guests, heard the noise and, according to some reporters, arrived in time to witness the fracas. The intruder—later identified as Harry Martin, stepson of North Carolina senator Zebulon Vance—lunged out of Kenny's grasp, whereupon the 57-year-old chief executive allegedly "deftly struck out with his right hand and landed a stunning blow between the eyes of young Martin."

"Mr. Harrison then calmly re-entered the Red Room and, cutting away the cord which was used in draping a curtain, brought it out and proceeded to tie the hands of the maniac like an old jack tar"—so much so that the officers found it nearly impossible to remove the cord later that evening.

Martin had made a bad choice because in addition to being heavily guarded, President Harrison was a veteran of the Civil War who had taken part in several major battles which meant he knew a few things about being in a fight.

MARCH 22

SETTING THE STANDARD

On this day in 1933, president Franklin Roosevelt signed the Cullen-Harrison Act into law which legalized the sale of beer in the United States with an alcohol content of 3.2% (by weight) and wine of similarly low alcohol volume. Upon signing the legislation, Roosevelt made his famous remark, "I think this would be a good time for a beer."

While Congress is often accused of not taking certain matters seriously, they had passed the new law through both houses in the previous 48 hours. It was seen as the last major action against Prohibition.

However, that's not to say that no one could get a drink in Washington, DC, since the Volstead Act was instituted in 1920. It was originally hoped that the nation's capital would serve as the model for dry cities across the country, but it ended up being one of its worst offenders with more than 3,000 illegal speakeasies where many of the best customers were the same lawmakers who had voted for the teetotaling measure.

But Congress didn't have to go far to find a drink as they employed their own bootleggers, most notably George Cassiday, better known as The Man in the Green Hat (now immortalized by a locally made gin). He roamed the halls of the US Capitol building, personally delivering booze to his favorite customers.

MARCH 23

GIVE ME LIBERTY AND SOME KIDS TOO!

On this day in 1775, founding father Patrick Henry gave one of history's most recognized speeches that included the famous line, " Give me liberty or give me death."

The address was made during the Second Virginia Convention at Richmond's St. John's Church and warned of the upcoming conflict with the British Empire.

In its early years as a nation, Henry had more kids than there were states. He married his first wife Sarah Shelton in 1754. They had six children together before she died in 1775.

Two years later, the patriot spokesman wed Dorothea Dandridge, cousin of future First Lady Martha Washington, in 1777. Together. they had eleven little Americans.

MARCH 24

THOU SHALT EAT CHILI

Governor P. H. Bell of Texas granted William Davis and wife Margaret an area of 3,150 acres of land where the town of McKinney now stands. The residential area is located north of Dallas in Collin County.

Davis and his family had a little log cabin on the property in 1848 when the county seat was moved to the future community. He and his wife donated 120 acres to the new location to be used as a townsite.

Frank and Jesse James were two of the most famous outlaws of the Old West. The pair engaged in a number of holdups that included banks, stagecoaches, and trains. Because they were constantly on the run, the brothers were always looking for a place to hide out.

One of their favorite hideouts became McKinney where their cousin Tuck Hill, a mule trader, resided. They freely mingled with the local townspeople and attended Sunday services at the First Christian Church. Jesse even refused to rob the local bank because he liked the chili that was served at his favorite café.

Today, Frank and Jesse are long gone but McKinney is one of the fastest-growing communities in the nation where one can still get a good bowl of chili.

MARCH 25

IT'S ALL IN THE CLOTHES

Zoot Suit, the first Chicano theatrical production on Broadway in New York, debuted on this day in 1979. From there, Universal Studios converted the stage play into the first feature-length film in history to be written, performed, and directed by Hispanics.

Zoot Suit had originally shattered all box office records when it premiered on stage on July 28, 1978, in Los Angeles. Close to a half-million people saw the production over the course of a year—originally in its sold-out run in Hollywood before heading to Broadway.

MARCH 26

FIRST AID

The United States has long been recognized for the massive amount of foreign aid that it delivers each year, contributing billions to other nations. But where did it all begin?

The first foreign aid bill, approved by the United States Congress, was in May 1812 for Venezuela. They appropriated $50,000 (equal to $ 1.1 million in 2022) for relief following an earthquake. It is estimated that 20,000 people were killed in the shaker centered near Caracas on March 26.

MARCH 27

A FIXER UPPER

In 1947, after almost 150 years of existence, the White House was in danger of internal and physical collapse. One day, while president Harry S. Truman took a bath upstairs, a great Blue Room chandelier threatened to crash down on his wife, Bess, and her guests from the Daughters of the American Revolution. The president made a typical joke that he might have unexpectedly dropped through the ceiling in his birthday suit onto the ladies gathered below, and he confessed that the incident made him nervous. The upstairs floor, he noted, "sagged and moved like a ship at sea."

The following year, his daughter Margaret's piano broke through the floor of the family quarters. In August 1948, Truman recorded in his diary that with his wife away, he had been "moved into the Lincoln Room—for safety—imagine that!"

That November, after the president won a full term over Republican challenger Thomas E. Dewey, the First Family was whisked across Pennsylvania Avenue to reside in Blair House, the official presidential guest quarters. At that point, Truman examined his options. Tearing down the White House had been seriously considered, but it was decided to gut the interior and leave the exterior walls standing. The mansion was budgeted for a $5.4 million renovation.

"It perhaps would be more economical from a purely financial standpoint to raze the building and rebuild completely," Truman admitted. "In doing so, however, there would be destroyed a building of tremendous historical significance in the growth of the Nation."

Harry Truman and his family finally moved back into the White House on this day in 1952.

MARCH 28

A HERO NAMED RECKLESS

The Battle for Outpost Vegas took place from March 26–30, 1953, during the Korean War. One of the heroes was an American who had been raised in South Korea.

During the five days of fighting, the US combat trooper made fifty-one trips from the ammunition supply point to the firing sites; 95 percent of the time without assistance. A total of 386 rounds of ammunition accounting for nearly five tons was walked over 35 miles through open rice paddies and up steep mountains through enemy fire.

On return trips, the recruit would carry wounded soldiers down the mountain to safety before returning with another load of ammo. Even though the Marine was wounded twice, the mission was completed.

For those many acts of heroism, the soldier was awarded two Purple Hearts, a Marine Corps Good Conduct Medal, a Presidential Unit Citation with bronze star, the National Defense Service Medal, a Korean Service Medal, the United Nations Korea Medal, a Navy Unit Commendation, and a Republic of Korea Presidential Unit Citation. This was in addition to being promoted to the rank of sergeant.

The war hero was a chestnut mare named Reckless who had been bought from a Korean stable boy in 1952. She was beloved by the soldiers and became a national celebrity after the war. She was buried with full military honors following her death in 1968.

MARCH 29

THE OTHER GUNFIGHT

The most famous showdown in the history of the Old West, the Gunfight at the O.K. Corral, took place in Tombstone, Arizona. However, it wasn't the biggest—not even in the southwestern region.

That distinction falls to a dispute that was mislabeled as the Pleasant Valley War. It was America's bloodiest range battle, fought across the high-grazing lands below the Mogollon Rim. Like the O.K. Corral, it began as a dispute between two families—the Grahams and the Tewksburys—but eventually included friends, neighbors, and other interested parties such as hired gunmen.

On this day in 1884, John Graham filed a felony complaint against the Tewksbury brothers (Ed and John) for altering brands on sixty-two head of cattle which was tantamount to rustling. It was the final act that triggered the bloody altercation between the factions.

After years of further disputes, fighting, and death, the war finally ended, not due to either side's effort to seek a peaceful resolution but because, in reality, there was nobody who had been involved who was left to kill.

In 1892, Ed Tewksbury gunned down Tom Graham on the streets of Tempe. He was not convicted of any crime and Tom's departure meant that there were no more Grahams left to fight. Estimates claimed that the Pleasant Valley War claimed between twenty and fifty lives.

Although, Ed Tewksbury's was not among them. He died of a stroke in Globe, Arizona, on April 21, 1904, at the age of 46.

MARCH 30

WHO'S IN CHARGE?

On March 30, 1981, there seemed to be some confusion among the nation's top government officials as to who was in charge?

That afternoon, President Ronald Reagan was undergoing emergency surgery at George Washington University Hospital following an assassination attempt. At the same time, a press conference was underway in the White House press room. A reporter asked deputy press secretary Larry Speakes who was running the government, to which Speakes responded, "I cannot answer that question at this time."

Upon hearing Speakes' remark, secretary of state Alexander Haig scribbled out a note which was passed to the press secretary, ordering him to leave the dais immediately. Moments later, the former army general entered the briefing room, where he made the following statement: "Constitutionally, gentlemen, you have the president, the vice president and the secretary of state, in that order."

Perhaps Secretary Haig was never taught, back in high school, that the secretary of state is not second in the line of succession but fourth, after the vice president (who at the time was George H. W. Bush); Speaker of the House (at the time, Tip O'Neill); and the president pro tempore of the Senate (at the time, Strom Thurmond).

However, Vice President Bush was en route in the air over Texas and had no means of secure voice communications from his aircraft.

Meanwhile at G.W.U. Hospital, as the president was being taken into surgery, he looked at his doctors and said, "Please tell me you're all Republicans." Among those on the surgical team that helped save his life was Dr. Joseph Giordano, a liberal Democrat.

MARCH 31

BEFORE TOMBSTONE, THERE WAS THAT MESS IN MISSOURI

Wyatt Earp was a true legend of the Old West and is best remembered for his role in the Gunfight at the O.K. Corral. While his reputation as a legendary lawman is unquestioned, Earp was also a man who was known to cross the line to make the law fit his own agenda.

One of those actions centered around the filing of a $200 lawsuit against him on March 14, 1871, by officials in Barton County (MO) for failure to deliver license fees collected for use in funding schools. At the time, Earp was the constable for the town of Lamar. The action was eventually vacated when it was determined that he had left the state.

Two weeks later on this day, a second lawsuit was filed against Earp by a man named James Cromwell who alleged that the law officer had falsified court documents referring to the amount of money that he had collected from Cromwell to satisfy a judgment.

A summons was issued for Wyatt Earp to appear before the court on April 5, 1871, but it was returned unserved as the respondent could not be located within the county. Earp's personal property that he had left behind was confiscated to satisfy the obligation.

APRIL

If you think you have it tough, read history books.

—Bill Maher, television personality

APRIL 1

SMOKED OUT

On this day in 1970, president Richard Nixon signed the Public Health Cigarette Smoking Act into law as an effort to limit the practice of smoking. It required a stronger health warning on cigarette packages, saying "Warning: The Surgeon General Has Determined that Cigarette Smoking Is Dangerous to Your Health." It also banned cigarette advertisements on American radio and television.

Today, almost every American facility is a smoke-free area. Those bans have increased in recent years but, contrary to popular belief, they aren't new and not part of any of the US Congress' doings.

Centuries ago, when many colonists were growing tobacco, some had already begun to restrict its use but not for health reasons. In 1632, Massachusetts became wary of the fire danger from smoldering butts; as a result, it banned outdoor smoking. Connecticut followed suit in 1647 when it dictated that citizens could only smoke once a day. In the 1680s, Philadelphia joined in with a ban on smoking on the city's streets. All the while, tobacco remained the major export for the colonists, making many farmers wealthy.

As laws were relaxed over the following decades, a growing number of citizens could be seen lighting up wherever and whenever they desired. However, in 1990, the city of San Luis Obispo, California, became the first municipality in the world to restrict indoor smoking in certain areas. Five years later, the Golden State took the action a step further as it enacted the first statewide smoking ban.

APRIL 2

THE REAL GREAT DEBATERS

On Christmas Day, 2007, the motion picture *The Great Debaters* premiered nationwide starring Academy Award recipients Denzel Washington and Forest Whitaker.

The film is set in 1935 in the depths of the Great Depression and tells the story of a visionary professor/coach Melvin Tolson and the successful debating team he founded at little Wiley College in Marshall, Texas.

Tolson arrived on the Wiley campus in 1924 and took the 1930–1931 academic year off to do graduate work at Columbia University. Upon his return, he pitted his young competitors against some of the best debate squads at the university level.

In 1934, Tolson took his team on a goodwill tour through the Southwest. Their extended 5,000 mile sojourn included the University of New Mexico, the University of California at Oakland, and San Francisco State Teachers College.

The highlight of the pilgrimage took place on this night in 1935, before an audience of 2,200 anxious spectators at the University of Southern California's Bovard Auditorium in downtown Los Angeles. The setting could have been intimidating since the speech department at USC was larger than the entire Wiley College. Not to be ignored was the fact that the Trojans were also the defending national champions.

That evening proved to be a double victory for the Wiley debaters. They defeated the top team in the land but also influenced a future star.

In the audience that April night was Hamilton Boswell who had graduated from a Los Angeles high school. He was so impressed with Coach Tolson's team performance that he decided to leave the bright lights of L.A. and enroll at the obscure little Texas college. He, like so many, went on to become one of Wiley's standout debaters.

APRIL 3

YOUTH WILL BE SERVED

The minimum age for military enlistment during World War II was seventeen. But that didn't stop Calvin Graham from Canton, Texas who, at age 12, became the youngest US serviceman enlisting after the attack on Pearl Harbor. He was born on this day in 1930.

Graham, while serving in the US Navy, was wounded at the Battle of Guadalcanal and awarded the Purple Heart and the Bronze Star. He was eventually given a dishonorable discharge for lying about his age, which was later changed to honorable and his military benefits were restored by an act of Congress. When Calvin turned seventeen, he enlisted in the Marine Corps where he served for three years.

APRIL 4

CAN YOU TAKE ME UPTOWN?

Gertrude Jeannette died on this day in 2018 at the age of 103 at her home in Harlem, New York. In 1935, she became the first woman to get a license to drive a motorcycle in New York City and followed up on that accomplishment in 1942 when she took and passed the cab driver's test, making her the first female taxi driver in the Big Apple.

However, not all of Ms. Jeannette's exploits took place while operating a motor vehicle. Among her additional talents was the fact that she wrote five plays, worked as a director, appeared in three stage productions including the Broadway theater along with acting in six motion pictures. She acted into her eighties and retired from theater directing at the age of 98.

APRIL 5

A WILD GOOSE CHASE

General George S. Patton rose to legendary status in December 1944 when he and the Third Army advanced 100 miles in 48 hours overcoming inclement weather to relieve the 101st Airborne at Bastogne, Belgium, during the Battle of the Bulge. But the hard-talking tank commander came under sharp criticism months later when he ordered the liberation of a prison camp where his son-in-law was being held.

In March 1945, just weeks before the German surrender, Patton sent the Fourth Armored Division to Stalag 13 near Hammelburg, Germany. Although the general never admitted it, the true objective of the mission was to free his son-in-law lieutenant colonel John Knight Waters.

However, the plan was a disaster as from the 314 troop unit, 9 were killed; 33 were wounded; 16 were reported as missing; and all 57 of their vehicles were destroyed. Waters was among those wounded inside the camp.

The POW facility was liberated by the 14th US Armored Division on April 5, 1945—just a few days after the failed attempt.

Patton denied publicly and to Waters directly that the raid was planned to facilitate his family member's release. His longtime friend and commanding officer general Omar Bradley called the mission "a wild goose chase that ended in disaster."

APRIL 6

WEDDING BELL BLUES

On this day in 1896, 62-year-old former president Benjamin Harrison married Mary Scott Lord Dimmick, the widowed 37-year-old niece and former secretary of his deceased first wife, Caroline. Originally, a music teacher, Caroline had served as First Lady from 1889 until her death from tuberculosis in 1892.

Harrison's second wedding was held at St. Thomas Protestant Episcopal Church in New York City but while many dignitaries attended the nuptials, what was evident was who wasn't there. The former chief executive's two adult children, Russell, forty-one years old at the time, and his sister Mary (Mamie) McKee, thirty-eight, disapproved of the union and did not attend the ceremony. Benjamin and Mary had one child together, Elizabeth (February 21, 1897–December 26, 1955).

APRIL 7

THE END OF AN ERA

On this day in 1957, a trolley from the privately owned Queensborough Bridge Line crossed the span for the last time, ending a century and a quarter of streetcar history in New York City.

The community's first trolley made its maiden run on November 14, 1832. The line was an improvement over horse-drawn coaches called "omnibuses" which consisted of two horse-drawn cars built by John Stephenson, a local coach maker, with a capacity of 40 passengers each. Those first versions of streetcars attained a speed of about 12 miles an hour, charged 25 cents, and ran every 15 minutes.

By 1922, the city's network of about 500 miles of trolley track moved a billion passengers a year. Over time, the popular people carriers were nudged out by the subway system, city buses, taxis, and other means of transportation.

APRIL 8

OVER AND OVER AGAIN

There is that old proverb that said, "Lightning never strikes twice in the same place." However, one might understand if the residents of Codell in western Kansas don't agree with that well-known saying. The town located in Rooks County had never been struck by a tornado until May 20, 1916, when a twister roared through their tiny community.

A year later to the exact day, on May 20, 1917, Codell was hit a second time. On May 20, 1918, it was struck on the same date for the third consecutive year. The 1918 tornado was the most destructive, killing ten people and damaging a large part of the community.

The town has not been hit since but that may not seem that unusual to the folks who live in Wethersfield, Connecticut. On this day in 1971, a meteorite weighing 350 grams (about three-quarters of a pound) struck a house in their town. Only eleven years later, November 8, 1982, a second house in the same community was also hit by a meteorite, this one weighing 2,760 grams (about six pounds). Wethersfield is only 12.4 square miles in area.

APRIL 9

WHERE IS SENATOR LEWIS?

His name was James Hamilton Lewis and his resume is impressive. Having grown up in Augusta (GA) after the Civil War, he became a lawyer, a soldier, a diplomat, a US congressional representative and a member of the US Senate. Lewis graduated from the University of Virginia, then went into law.

He served in the Spanish-American War, moved to Seattle, ran for Congress, and won. The House member then relocated to Chicago where he ran for the US Senate seat and won again, becoming one of the few politicians to be sent to Capitol Hill from two different states.

So when Lewis died on this day in 1939, the 75-year-old senator was honored in the US Capitol with all of the trappings that one would expect before being entombed in a fashionable mausoleum near Arlington National Cemetery. That's where the story should have concluded, but it didn't.

The mausoleum ran into financial problems, plus it became the target of vandals. In one incident during the 1970s, intruders pried off grates and gained entrance where caskets were forced open and other acts of destruction took place. The mausoleum structure was later demolished and those interred there were removed to other cemeteries.

However, there was never any report about Senator Lewis, perhaps because someone may have overlooked the remains of the former lawmaker. Federal archives indicate that the Lewis crypt was empty when the move took place, and might have been empty for quite some time.

APRIL 10

CAN YOU HEAR ME NOW?

Cincinnati's *Enquirer* is one of the nation's oldest newspapers. Its first issue debuted on April 10, 1841.

A local patron who made his own fair share of news was Charles Henry Turner. He was born in 1867 in the Queen City and earned his BS (1891) and MS (1892) degrees from the University of Cincinnati along with a PhD (1907) from the University of Chicago. He was the first African American to earn a doctorate from that institution.

Turner became a noted authority on the behavior of insects, proving that they modify their actions as a result of experience. The scientist became equally known for his commitment to civil rights and for his attempts to overcome racial barriers in American academia.

APRIL 11

YOU'RE FIRED!

It was on this day in 1951 that US president Harry S. Truman relieved General of the Army Douglas MacArthur of his commands after he made public statements which contradicted the administration's policies. The action set off a contentious relationship between the two men leading to MacArthur's retirement from the military after fifty-two years of service and many awards including the Medal of Honor.

From there, the former battlefield commander settled into a life of luxury at New York City's Waldorf Astoria Hotel where he and his wife Jean occupied a multiroom suite on the 37th floor. But the hard feelings between the general and his former boss didn't stop at the hotel's doors.

During a trip to NYC the following year, Truman was booked into the Waldorf where most presidents usually stayed. He resided in a suite on the 32nd floor, five flights below the former World War II hero.

Orders from the management to the staff during the stay was that the pair was to be kept clear of one another at all times and they were.

APRIL 12

THREE'S A CROWD

In 1976, Steve Jobs and Steve Wozniak formed Apple Computer. But many were not aware that there was a third partner, Ronald Wayne. On April 12, 1976, Wayne made the costly mistake of selling his share of the fledgling partnership for just $2,300! He needed the cash to pay off some personal and business debts.

In 2011, Jobs died leaving an estate with an estimated net worth of $7 billion. Wozniak's wealth is believed to be more than $100 million.

APRIL 13

DEAR MR. FORD

On April 13, 1934, Henry Ford received a letter from the notorious gangster Clyde Barrow. He praised the auto maker's product saying, "I have driven Fords exclusively when I could get away with one."

A month later, Ford received another endorsement. This testimonial was from "Public Enemy No. 1" John Dillinger who wrote, "Dear Mr. Ford—I want to thank you for building the Ford V-8 as fast and as sturdy a car as you did, otherwise I would not have gotten away from the coppers in that Wisconsin, Minnesota, case. Yours till I have the pleasure of seeing you— John Dillinger."

But the two gangsters met their fates just weeks afterward. Barrow, along with his criminal partner Bonnie Parker, was killed on May 23, 1934. They were ambushed by lawmen while riding in a Ford V-8. Meanwhile, Dillinger could have used a getaway car on July 22, 1934, when FBI agents gunned him down as he walked through an alley next to the Biograph Theater in Chicago.

APRIL 14

THIS IS YOUR LUCKY DAY

On April 14, 1912, the British luxury liner RMS *Titanic* struck an iceberg at 11:40 p.m. (ship's time) on her maiden voyage while crossing the North Atlantic. By 2:20 a.m., the ship that was termed "unsinkable" had gone under, carrying 1,502 of its 2,228 passengers and crew to their deaths. The remains of what had been the largest vessel afloat rested at the bottom of the sea for the next seventy-three years until it was discovered in 1985 by Dr. Robert Ballard.

However, there's another aspect to this tragic tale that could have had an even greater impact, not only on the history of the United States but other countries as well. There are a number of prominent individuals of that era who were scheduled to be aboard the ill-fated floating palace but, for one reason or another, they all missed the embarkation. Here are some familiar names who were not aboard *Titanic*:

Seventy-four-year-old American J. P. Morgan was scheduled to be in his personal suite on the private promenade deck. One of his many companies (US Steel, General Electric, and AT&T among others) was International Mercantile Marine of which White Star Lines, the owner of *Titanic*, was a subsidiary.

However, the powerful businessman was on a European holiday and chose to remain at the French resort in Aix-les-Bains. In addition, another well-known name was forgoing the journey as Alfred Vanderbilt of the famous railroad family elected to alter his travel agenda. Milton S. Hershey, the founder and chairman of Hershey Chocolate, and his wife Catherine had been booked on *Titanic* but were forced to return early to Pennsylvania due to a business matter. Today, the deposit check of $300.00 that Milton wrote to White Star Lines for his suite resides at the Hershey Community Archives.

Not so lucky was the aforementioned Alfred Vanderbilt who previously missed being on board *Titanic* but was one of the 128 Americans who died three years later on RMS *Lusitania*. But for those who did actually miss the boat, that was truly their lucky day.

APRIL 15

IT'S ALWAYS ANOTHER TAX

Anyone who has ever paid federal income tax realizes the significance of April 15. When the tax overhaul of 1954 took place, that became the nation's new date when payment was due. That's because, like most aspects of the country, the tax system has its own history.

On August 5, 1861, president Abraham Lincoln imposed the first federal income tax by signing the Revenue Act. Strapped for cash to pursue the Civil War, Lincoln and Congress agreed to impose a 3 percent fee on annual incomes over $800.

The latest law was an expansion of the first US income tax established under the previous Revenue Act of 1861. It was designed to provide additional funds in the war against the Confederate states.

Congress repealed Lincoln's mandate in 1871 which was replaced by the Sixteenth Amendment that was ratified in 1913.

Also, April 15th has not always been the filing deadline. March 1st was the original date.

APRIL 16

THE SLEEPING SENTINEL

When the Civil War broke out in 1861, 21-year-old William Scott and his three brothers wasted little time enlisting in the Union Army. Like most of his peers, the farm boy from Groton, Vermont, was enthusiastic but had no idea of what lay ahead.

In the early hours of September 1, Scott was standing watch. Three men were assigned to a post, rotating turns on two-hour shifts while the other two soldiers slept.

When it was discovered that the private had dozed off at his post, he was charged with sleeping on duty—a capital offense. Three days later, colonel Breed Hyde ordered Scott to be executed by firing squad.

With haste, the condemned man's colleagues put forth a petition drive that included 191 signatures asking for leniency. The document made its way across the Potomac to the White House under the direction of Reverend Moses Parmelee, the regiment's chaplain and the petition's author. It is believed that it was taken to President Lincoln by Lucius Eugene Chittenden, a Vermonter who was the register of the treasury.

Lincoln was informed that Scott had stayed awake the previous night to help care for a sick soldier. With the war just getting underway and the Union troops still trying to acclimate themselves to its harsh conditions, the last thing that the new president needed was malcontent within the ranks. He issued a pardon to the private which went over well with the troops and the public.

Seven months later on this day in 1862, Scott went from near execution to hero status when he was killed during a charge at a battle at Lee's Mill, Virginia. He was buried in Yorktown and was one of about forty Vermont soldiers who died that day. None of the four Scott brothers survived the war.

APRIL 17

LET'S GO FISHING

On this day in 1961, 1,400 Cuban exiles launched what became a botched invasion at the Bay of Pigs on the south coast of Cuba. It was an attempt by the US government to overthrow the regime of Fidel Castro. The invasion force was depending on information provided by the CIA to secure their landing position.

But, the agency's class reports showing that the area was an unpopulated beach was years out of date. In reality, the bay was Castro's favorite fishing ground where he was building a home for himself. Thus it was constantly patrolled by the Cuban military. As a result, all of the Cubans who were involved were either captured or killed.

APRIL 18

NO DEGREE? NO PROBLEM.

Happy Birthday to Clarence Darrow who was born on this day in 1857. He is widely recognized as America's most renown defense attorney. Among his most famous cases were Leopold and Loeb along with the Scopes Monkey Trial.

Darrow attended Allegheny College followed by the University of Michigan Law School. He left Allegheny after one year without graduating.

In 1873, at age 16, he began a three-year stint teaching school in his hometown of Kinsman, Ohio. It was around that time that Darrow began studying law on his own under the direction of an attorney and was urged by his family, after his third year as a classroom instructor, to enroll in law school. However, like his previous college, he lasted only one year at Michigan, opting to apprentice at an actual law office in Youngstown, Ohio.

When Darrow felt that he was ready, he took the Ohio bar exam and passed. The 21-year-old law school dropout was admitted to the Ohio bar in 1878 and began practicing a year later in Youngstown. From there, the self-made litigator garnered headlines taking on some of history's most high-profile cases.

In 2009, the man who never earned a college degree was inducted into the National Trial Lawyers Hall of Fame's inaugural class.

APRIL 19

THE EVIL AMONG US

Former Desert Storm veteran Timothy McVeigh, aka the Oklahoma City Bomber, was put to death by lethal injection on June 11, 2001, for killing 168 people when he bombed the Alfred P. Murrah Federal Building on this day in 1995.

He remains the only terrorist to be executed by the federal government. His victims included men, women, along with nineteen children. McVeigh's lawless act also destroyed several blocks of the city's downtown area.

APRIL 20

THE VOYAGE OF NO RETURN

RMS *Titanic* was popular and remains so even though it never completed its maiden voyage. However, many potential passengers had already booked their trips when the giant ship struck an iceberg and sank to the bottom of the Atlantic.

Had that not taken place, the vessel's return to Plymouth, England, would have departed from Pier 59 at the White Star Pier on New York City's North River on Saturday April 20, 1912. Just as had taken place for the original journey, the guest list for the second trip was filled with big names from all areas of society including Henry Adams, a descendant of presidents John and John Quincy Adams; John Alden Dix, the sitting governor of New York; Nobel Prize–winner Guglielmo Marconi; Frank Seiberling, the founder of Goodyear Tire and Rubber; along with J. C. Penney, who started the famous department store chain that still bears his name.

APRIL 21

A MUST READ

In a math class, students are taught that a century is comprised of one hundred years. But who knew that some readers would wait a century for the release of a book?

Mark Twain had specified that his autobiography remain unpublished for that period following his death, to ensure that he felt free to speak his "whole frank mind."

The author passed away on April 21, 1910. According to his wishes, his 736-page work was released as mandated a hundred years later in November 2010 and, like so many of his other works, was an immediate best seller.

APRIL 22

NOT JUST ANOTHER RICH GUY

On April 25, 1892, William Backhouse Astor Jr. died. With his passing, his son, 28-year-old John Jacob "Jack" Astor IV, was now in charge of the family business thus making him the world's wealthiest person.

He continued to develop the family's holdings in the New York real estate market, concentrating on luxury hotels. In 1897, he built the Astoria adjacent to his cousin William's Waldorf Hotel which today is the world famous Waldorf-Astoria. In 1993, the complex was designated as a National Historic Landmark.

While he was showing gains for the family account, Astor was not a workaholic as he found ample time to pursue his personal interests. He wrote a science fiction novel, *A Journey in Other Worlds: A Romance of the Future* about space travel and life on other planets. The creative work was published in 1894 prior to the writings of H. G. Wells. His enthusiasm for science led to his acquiring several patents in the late 1890s.

In 1912, Astor and his new wife Madeleine decided to return home from their European honeymoon on the maiden voyage of the White Star Line's newest vessel, *Titanic*. After the liner struck an iceberg, Astor's wife and unborn child were placed in a lifeboat but all of the money in the world couldn't help the husband and father on that cold morning. It was somewhat ironic that the family fortune, which had been built through shipping, was going to claim its wealthiest descendant's existence as the final moments of *Titanic* ticked away.

After the sinking, the cable ship *Mackay-Bennett* began the grizzly task of rounding up bodies. Among the haul of April 22 were the remains of Jack Astor, found floating in the frigid North Atlantic. The millionaire was identified by the initials sewn onto the label of his jacket.

APRIL 23

SOLD BY EDISON

Thomas Edison's first projected motion pictures made their US debut on the night of April 23, 1906. The location was Koster and Bial's Music Hall in New York City. It is no longer there, having been replaced by a Macy's department store.

So, who ran the projector that evening? As expected, it was Edison himself.

Like so many who accomplished outstanding achievements in other fields, the noted inventor was not as proficient as a businessman. On March 30, 1918, Thomas A. Edison, Inc. sold its movie studio and plant to the Lincoln and Parker Film Company of Massachusetts for $150,000 cash and $200,000 in common and preferred stock. Edison once said, "My main purpose in life is to make enough money to create ever more inventions."

APRIL 24

FRUITS AND VEGETABLES

The Supreme Court is the nation's highest judicial body. Since its first gathering in 1790, the justices have ruled on some of the nation's most historic cases such as the *Dred Scott v. Sandford*; *Miranda v. Arizona*; *Roe v. Wade*; and *Plessy v. Ferguson*. But not every verdict from litigation can be termed a "landmark decision."

In 1883, president Chester Arthur signed the Tariff Act of March 3, 1883, requiring a tax be paid on imported vegetables but not fruit. Among those were tomatoes which, from a botanical standpoint, were considered to be fruit.

John Nix, a produce seller from New York City, stepped forward to take on the US government. The case was submitted to the Court on April 24, 1892. During the trial, the arguments included reading the definitions of both a fruit and a vegetable from several dictionaries and bringing in botanists to declare the true identity of the tomato. Customs agents countered this, claiming that the words "fruit" and "vegetable" had no legal significance, and while it may have been technically a fruit, it was commonly considered a vegetable.

The decision was announced on May 10, 1893, by a unanimous 9–0 decision ruling that, for legal purposes, a tomato shall be considered a vegetable.

APRIL 25

DEJA VU . . . ALMOST

RMS *Titanic* sank after hitting a massive iceberg in the dark of night.

On this evening in 1935, a ship named the *Titanian*, carrying coal from Newcastle to Canada, almost suffered the same fate as its well-known predecessor when encountering an iceberg in the same area of the North Atlantic.

Luckily, crewman William Reeves had a premonition of the impending disaster and yelled, "Danger ahead!" to the navigator, thus saving his ship from the disaster that had doomed the ill-fated British liner two decades earlier. So, how did he know? Perhaps because Reeves was born on April 15, 1912 . . . the day *Titanic* sank.

APRIL 26

A PIRATE'S TALE

President Kennedy's youngest surviving child was his son, John Jr. In 1984, he was working as a diver and spotted a pair of 300-year-old cannons belonging to the pirate ship *Whydah*, which sank in a storm off Wellfleet, Massachusetts, on April 26, 1717.

Though archaeologists dismissed the idea, treasure hunter Barry Clifford proved the former president's son's claim and the recovery of artifacts from the ship has been ongoing.

Many of the recovered pieces from the *Whydah* haul have been seen on traveling exhibits throughout the United States. In 1999, Kennedy Jr. was killed in a plane crash only about 80 miles from where he discovered the artifacts.

APRIL 27

NOT SO FAST, MR. PRESIDENT!

Happy birthday to the eighteenth president of the United States, Ulysses S. Grant who was born on this day in 1822. He was a man who was always in a hurry to get where he was going, which was evident by the way his troops moved across the southern states during the Civil War, but that practice extended beyond the battlefield.

On April 11, 1866, almost exactly a year to the day that the South surrendered to the North, Union hero Grant was cited for riding his horse above the speed limit in Washington, DC. He had been warned for the same offense one day earlier. Officer William West escorted the country's idol to the police station where he paid a $20 fine.

On July 1, Grant repeated the scenario and once again paid the standard penalty. Years later, the chief executive admitted that he had been arrested at least twenty-five times for speeding.

However, Grant wasn't the only bad driver in the saddle. In 1853, president Franklin Pierce was coming home from drinking at a friend's house when he struck an old woman with his carriage. Police stopped and arrested him but when they discovered his identity, they let him go.

In 1958, Congress passed the Former Presidents Act which, among other things, forbids current and former chief executives from driving and they are not allowed to go anywhere alone. Happy Motoring!

APRIL 28

WE BID YOU ADIEU

A happy birthday to James Monroe who was born on this day in 1758. At the age of 18, he was among those who patriotically crossed the Delaware with George Washington but a few hours later was almost killed by gunfire during the Battle of Trenton.

Years later, Monroe found himself working alongside the commander in chief. In 1794, hoping to find a way to avoid war with France, Washington appointed Monroe as his minister (ambassador) to America's one-time ally. However, the men disagreed over items in the Jay Treaty which eventually led to his dismissal. It wasn't the first time that the politicians couldn't find some common ground on a major issue.

Fortunately, cooler heads prevailed and a conflict was avoided. But it wasn't the end of the road for the ousted ambassador.

Many years after Washington's departure, his former lieutenant was able to locate other employment as he was elected to the first of two terms as president in 1816.

APRIL 29

THE TALE OF WILLIE, TRIGGER, AND THE IRS

Happy Birthday to country-and-western singing legend Willie Nelson who was born on this day in 1933 in Abbott, Texas. Throughout a long singing/ songwriting career, he has been bestowed with every major award from his industry including induction into the Country Music Hall of Fame (1993); the Kennedy Center Honors (1998); and the Gershwin Prize, along with the lifetime achievement award from the Library of Congress (2015).

As opposed to many musicians who use multiple instruments during their concerts, appearances, and recording sessions, the bandanna-wearing Texan is widely known for using just one guitar when he's on stage which has become nearly as famous as the artist himself.

He named it Trigger after the horse that belonged to western movie star Roy Rogers. Nelson and his stringed sidekick have become synonymous with each other over the decades, but there was an instance where it appeared that the pair might be permanently separated.

That close call was in 1993 when the entertainer ran into a problem with the IRS after it was discovered that he owed more than $16 million in back taxes. Fearing that Trigger might be seized as part of the agency's collection haul, Nelson put his daughter along with the guitar on a plane to Maui, Hawaii. Once there, she took it to her father's manager's home where it remained hidden for two years until the debt was paid.

Since then, the pair have been seen live by millions of fans across the world. That would explain his affection for Trigger since the two of them have been together longer than Willie has with any of his four wives.

APRIL 30

THE FIRST THANKSGIVING

Thanksgiving is the traditional US holiday that celebrates the early period when the young territory was settled by Europeans who came in search of a new life. In many households, it is annually recognized with a large meal of traditional favorites, family gatherings, and viewing football on television.

However, there were several days that were recognized as Thanksgiving before the one we currently observe. In 1941, president Franklin D. Roosevelt signed a law establishing the fourth Thursday in November as the official federal Thanksgiving Day holiday.

Prior to Congress' action, there were other days that took up the slack. George Washington and Abraham Lincoln each declared a day of Thanksgiving, which followed the most famous event of the same name that took place in 1621 with the Pilgrims showing their gratefulness for being able to survive the rugged New England winter.

But like so many others, the group from the *Mayflower* had to take a backseat when it came to attendance at something referred to as Thanksgiving.

During a time of explorers and conquerors, an earlier version of a group of wanderers took some time to give thanks.

That day was celebrated by Spanish explorer Juan de Oñate and his expedition on April 30, 1598. A month earlier, Oñate's throng of 500 people, including soldiers, colonists, wives, and children along with about 7,000 head of livestock, was ready to cross the treacherous Chihuahuan Desert located on today's US-Mexican border.

Almost from the beginning of the fifty-day march, nature challenged the Spaniards. The journey got underway with seven consecutive days of rain adding to the difficulty of travel. The wanderers then had to endure the dry weather. On one occasion, a chance rain shower saved the parched colonists.

Finally, for the last five days of the march before reaching the Rio Grande, the expedition ran out of both food and water, forcing the men, women, and children to seek roots and other scarce desert vegetation to eat. Both animals and humans almost went mad with thirst before the party reached water. Two horses drank until their stomachs burst, and two others drowned in the river in their haste to consume as much water as possible.

The Rio Grande became the salvation of the expedition. After recuperating for ten days, Oñate ordered a day of thanksgiving for the survival of the expedition. Included in the event was a feast, supplied with game by the Spaniards and with fish by the natives of the region. A mass was said by the Franciscan missionaries traveling with the group. And finally, Oñate read La Toma—a declaration proclaiming that the land north of the Rio Grande had become the possession of King Philip II of Spain.

MAY

I'm the only person of distinction who has ever had a depression named for him.

—President Herbert Hoover

MAY 1

BUILDING BY THE NUMBERS

The Empire State Building opened on May 1, 1931. At the time of its completion, it was the tallest building in the world at 1,250 feet. Amazingly, it was built in just 18 months at a cost of $40.9 million providing thousands of jobs during the Great Depression.

It has also played an important part in several hit movies including *King Kong* (1933) and *Sleepless in Seattle* (1993). However, records are made to be broken.

In 1966, construction began in New York City on the World Trade Center's twin towers. The following year, Moscow's Ostankino Radio Tower succeeded the Empire State Building as the tallest freestanding structure in the world.

In 1970, after thirty-nine years, the Empire State surrendered its position as the world's tallest building, when the WTC's North Tower, which was still-under-construction, surpassed it on October 19 and topped out on December 23, 1970, at 1,362 feet.

In December 1975, the observation deck was opened on the 110th floor of the Twin Towers, significantly higher than the 86th floor observatory on the Empire State Building.

On September 11, 2001, terrorists used two airliners to destroy the matching skyscrapers. Their elimination made the Empire State Building, once again, the tallest property in New York City but only the second-tallest in the Americas after the Sears (later Willis) Tower in Chicago.

However, the Empire State Building's position as NYC's tallest structure was short-lived. The WTC's successor was One World Trade Center, also known as the Freedom Tower, topping out on April 30, 2012, at a record 1,368 feet. While the Empire State went up in eighteen months, things took a bit longer for the Freedom Tower as it took eight years to complete!

MAY 2

FAMILY TIES

On May 2, 2011, a team of US Navy SEALs killed terrorist Osama bin Laden in Pakistan. But not everyone in the family was out to destroy the United States. Osama's niece, Wafah Dufour bin Laden, earned a master's degree in law from Columbia University. She currently lives in New York City and is an aspiring recording artist and model.

MAY 3

OLD MAN RIVER

Happy birthday to John B. Meachum who was born on this day in 1789. He was an African American minister, businessman, and educator.

After he was ordained in 1825, Reverend Meachum constructed a separate building on the same site for his church and school, which he called "The Candle Tallow School."

In 1847, as a slave state, Missouri banned all education for Black citizens. In response, Meachum took a bold step and moved his classes to a nearby steamboat in the middle of the Mississippi River, which was beyond the jurisdiction of Missouri law. He provided the water-worthy campus with a library, desks, and chairs, calling it the Floating Freedom School.

Meachum published a pamphlet, "An Address to All of the Colored Citizens of the United States," in which he emphasized the importance of collective unity and self-respect. He said that Black people needed to receive practical, hands-on education so they could support themselves after emancipation. John Berry Meachum died at his pulpit on February 19, 1854.

MAY 4

SHARING THE WEALTH

The Great Depression of the late 1920s and early 1930s was difficult for many Americans, whether they were living in the big cities or in the countryside. A third of the nation was out of work while another large share was struggling financially.

During this time, Alphonse was in his early thirties and already a successful businessman. He, his wife, and his son, who was deaf, lived in a comfortable but not opulent two-story home in the Park Manor neighborhood of Chicago.

However, what he saw each day with all of the hardship and men out of work disturbed him. In November 1930, the son of Italian immigrants started a soup kitchen that served breakfast, lunch, and dinner to an average of 2,200 hungry Chicagoans every day, where no second helpings were denied, no questions were asked, and no one was required to prove their need. Every day, the soup kitchen served 350 loaves of bread, 100 dozen rolls, 50 pounds of sugar, and 30 pounds of coffee at a cost of $300—a hefty sum for the time.

But while he was trying to help others, it was discovered that Alphonse had a problem of his own. In 1931, the government charged him with 22 counts of more than $200,000 of income tax evasion. Following a trial in November of that year, he was found guilty and sentenced to eleven years in federal prison. Many were surprised at the length of the punishment.

On this day in 1932, in a last-minute change of plans, Alphonse was taken by train from Chicago to the US penitentiary in Atlanta. He was originally scheduled to be incarcerated at Leavenworth, Kansas. Two years later, he was transferred to the maximum security lockup on Alcatraz Island.

Although it was believed that Alphonse may have been involved in more serious crimes such as the murders of dozens of individuals, the only case that the government could successfully make against him was tax fraud—he was never charged with anyone's death. After serving seven years behind bars, Alphonse "Al" Capone was released from prison in 1939.

MAY 5TH

REMEMBERING THE HEROES

The story of Memorial Day began in the summer of 1865, when Henry C. Welles, a prominent local druggist in Waterloo, New York, proposed a time to remember those who gave their lives for their country by placing flowers on their graves. The idea gained support from general John B. Murray. Murray, a Civil War hero, went to work with Welles to develop a more complete celebration plan.

On May 5, 1866, the village was decorated with flags at half mast, draped with evergreens and mourning black. Veterans, civic societies, and residents, led by General Murray, marched to the tone of martial music to the village's three cemeteries. One year later, the ceremonies were repeated and have been held annually ever since.

Ten months later, the State of New York recognized Waterloo by a proclamation officially designating the community as the birthplace of Memorial Day. Originally, the holiday was celebrated on May 30, regardless of the day of the week that it fell. In 1968, the Uniform Monday Holiday Bill was passed and as a result the day changed. It is now a federal holiday observed yearly on the last Monday of May.

MAY 6

THE OTHER HOOVER

Ike Hoover, no relation to the former president, was a 20-year-old electrician when he was sent to the White House on this day in 1891. He was there to help install the first electric lights and an electric bell system inside the mansion. At the time, no private building in the city had electricity, and the only government-owned building which did was the Bureau of Engraving and Printing.

Hoover was an employee of the Edison Electric Company. President Benjamin Harrison and the other members of the First Family were uncomfortable using the switches to run the devices, fearing that they could be electrocuted. At that point, the chief executive offered Hoover the newly created position of White House electrician, which he accepted. His primary duty was to turn the lights on and off.

In 1904, Hoover became an usher at the mansion. Five years later, he was made chief usher by president Theodore Roosevelt. If anyone knew what was going on at the White House, it was Ike Hoover who served ten different presidents over his 42-year tenure.

During one episode, he cited an incident in his autobiography where an intruder got near Roosevelt in the Red Room while carrying a loaded weapon before being arrested by the Secret Service. The individual had simply walked undetected into the nation's most famous home!

MAY 7

MY ESTEEMED COLLEAGUE

Over the years, citizens have come to expect less and less from their public officials. Although in most cases, they can usually rely on a certain amount of decorum to be displayed, especially when they're in the workplace.

However on May 7, 1947, the state capitol building in Oklahoma City took on the aura of the Old West as one elected officeholder attempted to settle a dispute with a gun. Sixty-four-year-old state senator Tom Anglin of Holdenville was standing next to the press table in the senate chamber when he was approached by his fellow lawmaker, state representative Jimie Scott, who hailed from the same town. Suddenly Scott, a 35-year-old ex-Marine, drew a .32-caliber revolver and fired two shots, one of which struck Anglin in the left hip.

In what resembled a showdown scene from a western movie, the wounded legislator then drew his own .25-caliber pistol, which he carried, but was unable to return fire as Scott fled the scene. The pistol-packing politico later surrendered while trying to hide in a nearby restroom. As news spread of the gunfight at the OK senate chamber, everyone started to wonder why it had happened?

A bettor's odds would be that the disagreement was about a woman, which it was, but not in the manner that one might have imagined. In addition to his elected office, Anglin was part of a law firm in Holdenville which had recently represented Scott's wife in a divorce action between the couple. Eleven days earlier, the 27-year-old woman was granted a final decree from the Hughes County politician and even though Anglin's law partner had actually handled the case, that fact didn't resonate with Scott in his quest for retribution.

His ex-wife stated that her former husband had been acting strange since returning from duty with the Marines during World War II. Anglin was taken to University Hospital and treated for a flesh wound before being released.

Senator Scott was arrested and booked at Oklahoma City's police head-quarters on charges of assault with intent to kill. He was later committed to a hospital following a sanity hearing. The case was later dismissed at Anglin's request.

Tom Anglin died in 1953, followed by Jimie Scott in 1994. No weapons were involved in either of their passings.

MAY 8

GONE BUT NOT FORGOTTEN

For those traveling through the state of Washington, one of its scenic high-lights is the majestic Mount Rainier located just 59 miles south-southeast of Seattle. It stands 14,411 feet and is the highest peak in the nation's forty-second state.

The mountain is a live volcano that was named by British captain George Vancouver on May 8, 1792, for his friend, then rear admiral Peter Rainier of the British Navy. During the American Revolution, he was severely wounded in 1778 while capturing an American ship.

Even with a mountain named in his honor, Rainier, who died in London in 1808, never visited America. Additionally, that peak is located in Washington, the state named after the commander of the army that he was fighting against.

MAY 9

GO DIRECTLY TO JAIL

Happy birthday to Lizzie Magie who was born on this day in 1866. With a background as a writer and feminist, in 1903, she created an activity called *The Landlord's Game* to illustrate the teachings of the progressive era economist Henry George.

That same year, Lizzie applied to the US Patent Office for a registration of her board game, which she received on January 5, 1904, and renewed in 1923.

In 1932 during the Great Depression, there were changes in store for the recreational activity. On one evening, Charles Darrow and his wife Esther Jones were dining with Lizzie and her husband Charles Todd at their Philadelphia home. After the meal, they introduced their guests to *The Landlord's Game* and they were impressed. So much so that by 1933, Darrow, who resided in Germantown, had secured the copyright for the game.

With the legalities taken care of, Darrow modified Lizzie's original design and, the following year, he presented the concept to executives at the famous game company Parker Brothers—but it was rejected. However, in 1935, he sold 5,000 homemade copies of the prototype through his own ingenuity to which Parker Brothers soon secured the rights.

Lizzie's share from her original invention was a paltry $500 while Darrow became history's first millionaire game designer.

The financially themed pastime is still around today with a slicker look and a different name. What was once *The Landlord's Game* is now known throughout the world as *Monopoly.*

MAY 10

SAVED BY A HANKIE

On May 10, 2005, while president George W. Bush was giving a speech at the Freedom Square in Tbilisi, Georgia, terrorist Vladimir Arutyunian threw a live Soviet-made RGD-5 hand grenade toward the podium where he was standing.

Also at the dais were Georgian president Mikhail Saakashvili, his wife, and First Lady Laura Bush, along with several officials. The grenade was live and had its pin pulled but did not explode because a red tartan handkerchief wrapped tightly around the weapon kept the firing pin from deploying.

Arutyunian was taken into custody in July 2005 as he killed an interior ministry agent while resisting arrest. He was convicted in January 2006 and given a life sentence.

MAY 11

BIGGER THAN EVER

On this day in 1911, the Supreme Court ruled that John D. Rockefeller's Standard Oil Company had become a monopoly and must be dissolved. It was eventually split into thirty-four different organizations.

Two of the businesses that emerged from that order were Jersey Standard and Socony. In 1963, Socony became Mobil and in 1972, Jersey Standard became Exxon.

In 1999, Exxon and Mobil merged for $73.7 billion. It meant that eighty-eight years after the nation's highest court ordered its breakup, two of the descendants of the original Rockefeller empire were rejoined to form the largest, non-state-owned energy firm as well as one of the largest publicly traded companies on Earth.

MAY 12

WE WON'T GO!

On this day in 1964, twelve protesters in New York City became the first known dissidents to publicly burn their draft cards as a challenge to the government's policies regarding the war in Vietnam.

Reports followed in 1972 that 206,000 persons had been delinquent from their draft boards during the entire war period. One year later, the draft was discontinued, although 18-year-old males were still required to register with Selective Service.

In 1977, president Jimmy Carter signed a general amnesty for all of those who had evaded the draft by fleeing the country, allowing them to return to the United States.

MAY 13

WHO'S THE BOSS?

On May 13, 1846, the US Congress declared war on Mexico at the request of president James K. Polk.

The conflict centered on the Republic of Texas, which opted to join the United States in late 1845 after establishing its independence from Mexico a decade earlier. The Mexican government considered the annexation of Texas an illegal act and, after several border skirmishes, the president called for a declaration of war.

Whenever nations go into battle, the best-known negotiators are usually dispatched to try to restore peace to the factions. At the time, future president James Buchanan was the secretary of state. He could have sent former president Martin Van Buren as the US representative in the matter but in a strange maneuver, in April 1847, Buchanan ordered Nicholas Trist to go to Mexico with the American victory on the horizon.

He was Buchanan's chief clerk, with his only other years of experience being that of serving as a diplomat in Cuba during the 1830s. It was evident that Trist lacked the experience for such a critical assignment.

Polk wanted the peace talks to take place in Washington, and sent orders to Mexico that Trist was recalled as the treaty negotiator. During the six weeks it took for the presidential orders to make their way to the fledgling diplomat, it was realized that he had a brief period to negotiate a treaty with the unstable government in Mexico.

Trist ignored the recall order and worked out terms that allowed the United States to buy California (north of the Baja Peninsula), as well as what amounted to half of Mexico's territory for $15 million (the same as the Louisiana Purchase).

On February 2, 1848, the Treaty of Guadalupe Hidalgo was signed in Mexico without President Polk's knowledge. When he found out, the chief executive was outraged not only at Trist's insubordination but that the treaty didn't cede more of Mexico's property to the United States.

On March 10, 1848, the Senate approved a treaty that led to California and much of the southwest joining the United States. But the man who negotiated the historic Treaty of Guadalupe Hidalgo was promptly fired upon his return to Washington and denied any salary payments earned during treaty negotiations.

As a consolation, Trist eventually received his back pay when he was appointed postmaster of Alexandria, Virginia, during the Grant administration. He died on February 11, 1874, as a forgotten figure from a significant moment in American history.

MAY 14

THE RACE FOR WISCONSIN

The race for space took center stage during the 1950s as the two superpowers (the United States and the Soviet Union) began the quest to conquer the great beyond. It didn't take long before all of the aspirations and fears of the new frontier were displayed on October 4, 1957, when the Soviets launched the first space satellite which they called *Sputnik*. The successful flight of the Russian spacecraft sent NASA and the Eisenhower administration into a panic. It would be another four months before the Americans could respond with their own space vehicle.

As the years passed, the rivalry continued. On this day in 1960, *Sputnik IV* took off from Balkanur, USSR, with a secret 7-ton payload including a life-size "dummy cosmonaut." It was scheduled to be a brief mission but five days later, there was an explosion when the reentry rockets were fired, sending the satellite drifting into the universe.

Sputnik IV wandered aimlessly through the wilderness of space until September 6, 1962, when it descended from the heavens toward Wisconsin. Most of the spacecraft burned up upon reentry—except for a 21-pound piece of the Soviet probe. It crashed into the corner of Park and Eighth streets in Manitowoc near the Rahr-West Art Museum in the early hours of the morning.

The small chunk of metal was discovered by two police officers but was still too hot to handle. They borrowed a Geiger counter from the local fire department to check for radioactive material and found it to be safe. Within hours, the 21-pound disk-shaped object was on its way to the Harvard–Smithsonian Center for Astrophysics for analysis and confirmation of its identity. As expected, it was all that remained of *Sputnik IV*.

MAY 15

IT'S EARTH DAY!

Happy birthday to Ira Einhorn who was born on this day in 1940. As a graduate student, he was the master of ceremonies for the first Earth Day celebration on April 22, 1970, at Philadelphia's Fairmount Park. Locally, Einhorn was known as an eccentric counterculture environmentalist and war protester who found comfort at any gathering where he could be the center of attention.

He met Holly Maddux in 1972. She was originally from Tyler, Texas, and was attending Bryn Mawr College, a liberal arts school just a few miles outside Philadelphia. Five years later, she informed the local hippie activist that their volatile relationship was over. She went to their apartment to retrieve her belongings and was never seen again.

Eighteen months afterward, on March 28, 1979, Maddux's decomposing corpse was found by police in a trunk stored in Einhorn's closet. After discovering the body, her former boyfriend told a police officer as he was being arrested, "You found what you found."

At the urging of his attorney—future US senator Arlen Specter—bail was set low, at just $40,000. That meant only $4,000 was needed to be free as he awaited trial. The cash was posted by a rich friend but just three days later, Einhorn was gone.

In 1981, just days before his murder trial was to begin, the suspect skipped bail and fled to Europe. He lived there for the next seventeen years and married a Swedish woman named Annika Flodin.

When Einhorn unlawfully fled the jurisdiction, it meant that he could be tried without being present in the courtroom, also known as absentia. After being found guilty, he was sentenced to life in prison without the possibility of parole.

There were sightings of Einhorn in such places as Ireland, England, Sweden, Denmark, and eventually France, where he was tracked down by Philadelphia investigators and arrested by that country's authorities in June 1997. Six months later, he was released when a French court originally denied the US extradition request.

That capture, where he spent most of time under house arrest, set off a long legal battle between the two countries over his custody. He was finally extradited to the United States in 2001.

The following year, he was given another trial, this time where he was present. At the conclusion of the one-month legal proceeding, the jury found him guilty and the following day, he was sentenced to a mandatory life term without the possibility of parole.

In 2020, the inmate died of natural causes.

MAY 16

THE BAD BLIMPS OF NEW JERSEY

On May 6, 1937, the most well-known crash of an airship took place when the German zeppelin *Hindenburg* caught fire while landing at Lakehurst, New Jersey. With just seconds remaining before landing, the craft exploded into flames killing thirty-six and injuring dozens more including captain Max Pruss. It was the sixty-third flight of that zeppelin.

At 804 feet long, the *Hindenburg* was the largest airship ever built. It wasn't the state's only crash nor the deadliest, but it was the first to be filmed as cameras were rolling at Lakehurst. A few days later, Depression-era audiences viewed the carnage from newsreels shown in movie theaters across America.

Unfortunately, the list of airship tragedies in and near New Jersey is long and devastating. They included at least seven fatal accidents including one that took place on this day in 1944 when ten of eleven crewmen were killed as airship *K-5* crashed into a hangar at Lakehurst during a training session.

MAY 17

THROW THE BUM OUT!

Before dawn on May 17, 1890, a US Navy cutter landed a party of armed sailors at Cedar Key, Florida. Their mission was to capture the enemy who, in this case, was the town's mayor William Cottrell. He had been ruling the community like an island dictator even forcing people he saw on the street to head-butt one another—at gunpoint.

Cottrell had made the mistake of roughing up the federal customs inspector, so president Benjamin Harrison sent the Navy to depose him. He evaded capture and fled but later died in a shootout with a sheriff in Alabama.

MAY 18

MOVING DAY

In 1945, San Francisco became the birthplace of the United Nations (UN) and wanted to continue as its regular home when its time as substitute host concluded. But the city by the bay wasn't the only prospect vying to be chosen as the international body witnessed some 250 locations in the United States that wished to become the UN's new permanent home.

In 1945–1946, representatives ranging from major cities to smaller communities in wide open spaces like the Black Hills of South Dakota had energetically promoted their own locales as the best and most sensible site for the new UN headquarters. The competition escalated into a sort of tournament atmosphere where destinations were eliminated as the list of possibilities were whittled down to an international version of a final four.

The quartet of last standers included the aforementioned San Francisco, along with Boston, Philadelphia, and New York City. Each brought its share of pluses and minuses to the table.

But New York entered the competition with something that no other city could match. Making the case for the Big Apple was the ultrapowerful and wealthy Rockefeller family. They first offered to have an international meeting complex built on the grounds of the 1939 World's Fair in Flushing Meadows–Corona Park in Queens. But the project failed to materialize.

Next, the family suggested their estate of Kykuit in the beautiful Hudson Valley, although the offer was rejected because the location was too isolated from Manhattan. The difference was about 120 miles from NYC and didn't offer the desired glamour and nightlife for officials.

Finally in December 1946, John D. Rockefeller Jr. purchased an 18-acre tract in the city's Turtle Bay section located on the East River for $8.5 million and donated it to the City of New York. The first task was clearing the area of the slums and slaughterhouses so as to allow the construction of the new UN nerve center to proceed. The removal of the elevated trains opened up the neighborhood for high-rise office buildings and condominiums.

The body officially vacated their temporary Long Island gathering locale at Nassau County's Lake Success on this day in 1951.

MAY 19

THE PRICE WAS NOT RIGHT

On a map, Alabama and Florida are neighbors in the southern region of the country. But over time, there were several attempts to annex the Florida Panhandle into the Yellowhammer State. In fact, there were at least nine legitimate efforts to rearrange the map starting in 1821.

When Florida became a state in 1845, there were still those who remained in favor of moving West Florida outside of the border. In 1868, following the Civil War, Alabama offered $1 million to purchase the area. The panhandle's voters approved the deal but eventually Alabama governor William H. Smith nixed it citing that the price became too high for the state's budget.

However, Smith's word wasn't the last on the subject as in 1869, a sale was almost made when the Alabama legislature sent three commissioners to Florida to propose cession. In response to their visitors, the Florida legislature authorized its governor to appoint a committee of its own to engage in dialogue on the topic. Thus, on this day in 1869, an agreement was signed by the parties calling for an election.

The deal provided that Alabama was to receive all of the country west of the Apalachicola River, including the lands belonging to the state of Florida in the area. In return, Alabama was to issue to Florida $1,000,000 in 8% bonds payable in thirty years. However, disagreements and negative publicity over the next five years eventually killed any hope of annexation.

The issue was revisited by the Alabama legislature. By 1901, they had increased the offer to $2 million and then upped it to $5 million in 1921. By that time, a political consensus couldn't be reached as most of the influential newspaper editors in the Florida Panhandle spoke out against annexation.

It was the only known instance where one American state attempted to buy another.

MAY 20

KEEP YOUR EYES ON THE PRIZE

In 1927, Charles Lindbergh made aviation history as the first individual pilot to successfully make a nonstop solo flight crossing the Atlantic Ocean going from New York to Paris. However, the ex–air mail deliveryman's first priority wasn't to get into the record book.

Like many fliers of his time, Lindbergh along with other pilots had their eyes on the coveted Orteig Prize. Established in 1919 by French-American hotelier, aviation enthusiast, and philanthropist Raymond Orteig, the $25,000 award was designated to the first person who could successfully navigate the 3,600 mile trip.

The initial offer of a $25,000 purse expired in 1924 without a winner. As such, Orteig extended the deadline another five years and, by 1926, nine teams came forward to formally accept the challenge. The amount of the award would be equal to nearly $400,000 today.

On this day in 1927, the Lone Eagle, as he was known, took off from Roosevelt Field on Long Island in a custom-built plane known as the *Spirit of St. Louis*. Some 33 hours later, he landed the aircraft at Le Bourget airfield in Paris.

The competition also had its share of tragedy. Of the nine fliers who attempted to make the crossing, six died in transit. Nevertheless, Lindbergh's success sparked a boom in aviation, and inspired many subsequent prizes.

MAY 21

HERE COMES SANTA CLAUS

The town of Santa Fe, Indiana, was established in 1854. Two years later, the community, which was composed mainly of German immigrants, was working to establish a post office but was refused as there was already a town by that name in the Hoosier State.

Local residents gathered at a nearby rural church on a December evening in 1955 with hopes of coming up with a new name for the community. Several were considered but when the adults heard their children playing outside and shouting, "Santa Claus, Santa Claus," the answer to their quest was solved.

The name was accepted by the postal authority and the Santa Claus, Indiana, Post Office was established on May 21, 1856. In 1914, James Martin, the town's fourteenth postmaster, began mailing response letters from Santa, at his own expense, to children who sent their Christmas wishes to Santa Claus, Indiana.

On August 3, 1946, the town opened Santa Claus Land, which became the first themed amusement park in the world. Before he was president, actor Ronald Reagan stopped by the tourist attraction in March 1955, just a few months before Disneyland opened.

MAY 22

GIVE ME A CALL SOMETIME

Alexander Graham Bell is credited with inventing the telephone. But on May 22, 1930, the US Senate, which had become exasperated with Bell's creation, passed a resolution without objection to remove all dial telephones in the Senate wing of the US Capitol and in the Senate office building.

The dissatisfaction stemmed from the fact that dial telephones were more difficult to operate than manual telephones.

One day before the scheduled removal of all dial phones, Maryland senator Millard Tydings offered a different resolution to give senators a choice, as some of the younger members actually preferred the dial phones. This move angered the anti-dialing old timers who immediately blocked the measure's consideration.

Finally, technology offered a solution. Although the Chesapeake and Potomac Telephone Company had pressed for the installation of an all-dial system, it acknowledged that it could provide the Senate with phones that worked both ways and an impending national crisis was averted.

Today, no member of Congress would ever be caught without their cell phone, or phones, nearby.

MAY 23

THE RANGER AND THE KING

Frank Hamer was a Texas Ranger from 1906 to 1948 who killed fifty-three people in the line of duty. The most famous of those came on May 23, 1934, when he and his posse ambushed gangsters Clyde Barrow and Bonnie Parker.

Always looking for justice to be served, at the outbreak of war in Europe in 1939, Hamer and forty-nine other retired Rangers offered their services to the King of England George VI, to help protect that country in the event of a Nazi invasion. The overture was turned down. Even though he was wounded seventeen times during his career, it was complications from a previous heat stroke that sent the Ranger to the last roundup in 1955 at age 71.

King George VI also displayed some grit as he remained for most of the war at Buckingham Palace, which was bombed nine times.

MAY 24

A HELPING HAND

Happy Birthday to England's Queen Victoria who was born on this day in 1819.

The United States has a proud history of helping nations in need. However, her royal highness came to the aid of America in a time of necessity. Following the Great Chicago Fire in October 1871, British citizens donated more than 8,000 books to help jump-start a new library for the city. Many prominent citizens from the Mother country contributed volumes including statesman Benjamin Disraeli; philosopher John Stuart Mill; and poet Alfred, Lord Tennyson.

But perhaps the most celebrated edition was a book that was sent to Chicago by the Queen herself, a biography of her late husband Prince Albert that featured a dedication bookplate and her signature.

It can still be viewed today in Special Collections at the Harold Washington Library Center. Victoria donated another book about Albert in 1884, while in 1972 Queen Elizabeth II celebrated the 100th anniversary of the first British donation with the gift of a lavishly illustrated volume about Buckingham Palace.

MAY 25

AN UNCONVENTIONAL CONVENTION

After eleven days of discussion and debate, the Constitutional Convention in Philadelphia struck a high point on this day in 1787 as representatives from seven states were in attendance which provided for a quorum.

What was also notable, in addition to those in the gathering, was who was not among those who had come together at Independence Hall. Declaration of Independence author Thomas Jefferson referred to the delegates as, "an assembly of demigods." Instead of being in Philadelphia, the connoisseur from Virginia was in Paris enjoying fine food and wine while serving as minister to France. Also, on the other side of the Atlantic was John Adams, who was performing his duties as minister to Great Britain.

Other major figures who were absent included some well-known patriots such as Samuel Adams, John Hancock, and Patrick Henry. Henry turned down an invitation to the conference because he said he "smelt a rat in Philadelphia, tending toward the monarchy."

MAY 26

HELLO AGAIN, OLD FRIEND

On this day in 1868, the Senate acquitted president Andrew Johnson and adjourned as a court of impeachment. Among those who voted to expel the chief executive during the proceedings was senator Hannibal Hamlin of Maine. He had been Lincoln's vice president during his first term but was dropped from the ticket in 1864 to make way for Johnson. Some felt that he got a measure of revenge by voting against his successor during the trial.

Seven years later in 1875, Johnson and Hamlin served together in the US Senate for five months prior to Johnson's death.

MAY 27

OPEN ANOTHER BUCKET

The Golden Gate Bridge opened on this day in 1937. It was the culmination of a project that was first discussed in 1872. Construction of the 4,200-foot crossover road was a four-year project.

Due to the San Francisco Bay's high salt content in the air, to keep the bridge from rusting, it is painted continuously. The ongoing task is a primary maintenance job where thirty-eight individuals apply more than 5,000 gallons of Sherwin-Williams Golden Gate Bridge International Orange paint to the bridge. It is a special blend that is not available in retail stores. The unique coating helps protect the steel from corrosion.

MAY 28

THE NEED FOR SPEED!

A speed limit took effect at dawn on this day in 1999, ending Montana's status as the last state in the nation without a posted daytime maximum ceiling. When Congress repealed the federal speed laws three-and-a-half years earlier, the Treasure State began operating under the so-called basic rule, a law requiring motorists to drive in a reasonable and prudent manner.

Support grew for restoring fixed limits after highway fatalities increased to 265 in 1997 (that was up from 198 the previous year). In December, the Montana Supreme Court declared the state's mandate to be unconstitutional due to its vague requirement to drive at "reasonable and proper" speeds. That led to the 1999 action where the legislature approved a speed limit of 75 mph on interstate highways and 70 mph during the day and 65 mph at night on most two-lane roads.

MAY 29

ALL THE GOLD IN CALIFORNIA

On May 29, 1848, *The Californian*, a newspaper published in San Francisco, had bold headlines about the discovery of gold some 130 miles away. Two weeks later, the weekly journal announced that it was ceasing publication because so many of its staff had departed to join the miners to seek their own fortunes.

MAY 30

HEY, WHERE'S VANPORT?

Imagine someone taking a test about the state of Oregon during World War II that included the question, "What is the state's second most populated community?"

Oregon's largest metro area, Portland, led the pack but which city was the runner-up in the 1940s? The obvious candidates included the current state capital, Salem; the home of the University of Oregon, Eugene; along with Corvallis, the town site of Oregon State University—three good guesses, but all are wrong.

Interestingly, the correct answer is Vanport. However, if you try finding it on a modern-day map, expect to come up empty-handed. That's because at 4:05 p.m. on May 30, 1948, a 200-foot section of a railroad berm holding back the mighty Columbia River collapsed during a flood. By nightfall, the city was under water, leaving 17,500 inhabitants homeless.

Vanport was a young town that began in August 1942 as a location to house workers while the wartime Kaiser Shipyard of Portland, Oregon, and Vancouver, Washington, provided hundreds of jobs to local employees. It was home to 40,000 people, about 40 percent of them were African American, making it Oregon's second-largest city at the time, behind Portland, and the largest public housing project in the nation.

After the war, there were more than 15,000 African Americans living in the Portland area, mostly in Vanport and other segregated housing districts. However, the community was susceptible to flooding, since it was built on reclaimed lowlands along the Columbia River.

At the time of the deluge, because of the Memorial Day holiday, many residents were away from their homes. That factor contributed to the lower loss of life than originally expected as only fifteen deaths occurred although the city was a total loss.

In addition to Portland State University, other sites that were later established in the area include Delta Park and the Portland International Raceway.

MAY 31

REDISCOVERED

In 1606, England's King James I granted a charter to a joint stock company to establish the Jamestown colony. It called for the creation of two emplacements. The other and lesser-known settlement, Popham, was in the northern region of what is today the state of Maine.

On this day in 1607, about 100 men and boys set sail for the northerly destination. Nearly three months later, the group landed on a wooded peninsula where the Kennebec River meets the Atlantic Ocean and began building Fort St. George. In December, with winter coming and food scarce, half of the colonists returned to England. The next fall, after erecting several buildings, the remaining forty-five visitors sailed home.

In 1888, Popham was rediscovered when a researcher happened upon a map of Fort St. George in the government archives in Madrid, Spain. It had been drawn and signed by Popham colonist John Hunt.

JUNE

Thomas Jefferson once said, "We should never judge a president by his age, only by his works." And ever since he told me that, I stopped worrying.

—Ronald Reagan

JUNE 1

THIS IS CNN!

Cable News Network (CNN) debuted on this day in 1980. It was the first 24-hour round-the-clock news network.

The station was the idea of cable television entrepreneur Ted Turner, a college dropout with no experience in broadcast journalism. But through his wheeling and dealing in the world of cable TV and radio, by 1979, he was worth an estimated $100 million.

Turner admitted that CNN came very close to not making it. In the network's first year, things were going so poorly, from a financial standpoint, that the visionary was called by bankers who were asking for their money back.

However, CNN became a history book on a television screen, providing in-depth coverage of such events as the assassination attempt on president Ronald Reagan, the explosions of space shuttles *Challenger* and *Columbia*, the Persian Gulf War, the Waco raid, the Oklahoma City bombing, and the 9/11 attacks. There was also an abundance of airtime given to major court trials like that of O. J. Simpson, and to mid-term and presidential elections, as well as sports and entertainment news.

In 1996, Turner sold most of his media empire, including CNN, to Time Warner for $7.5 billion.

JUNE 2

THE ACTUAL GREAT TRAIN ROBBERY

Most know Robert LeRoy Parker by his more famous moniker—Butch Cassidy. He and his gang of outlaws, referred to as the Wild Bunch made headlines across the Old West for pulling off several railway heists, but there was one that topped their others.

Originally known as the Wilcox Train Robbery, it took place in Wyoming on this day in 1899. The raid began in the early morning hours when several Wild Bunch members flagged down the first part of a two-section train operated by the Union Pacific Railroad. The bandits boarded the locomotive and ordered the engineer to cross a nearby bridge. As soon as the last car cleared the overpass, the outlaws dynamited the bridge, preventing any help for the victims to make their way from an approaching second train on the other side.

The robbers ordered the clerks in the express and mail cars to open their doors; they refused, at which point, they were blown away with explosives. In total, the gang made off with around $30,000 in unsigned banknotes before disappearing into the mountains. Their story later became the primary plot for the 1903 silent film classic, *The Great Train Robbery.*

JUNE 3

THE RANSOM PAID OFF

Whenever the creation of the first assembly line is discussed, the person who is often credited with its invention is the famous automaker Henry Ford. However, by the time that the new method of car production was helping build vehicles cheaper, faster, and on a larger scale, the use of the assembly line had already been in practice for twelve years.

Ransom Olds was born on this day in 1864 in Geneva, Ohio. By 1899, he and his backers had formed the Olds Motor Works in Lansing, Michigan. His design for a continuous assembly line was patented in 1901 and his company was the first to launch high-volume series-production cars on the market. However, instead of using conveyor belts, the raw body shells in his factory were transported on wooden pallets from one production stage to the next.

By 1904, sales of Oldsmobiles reached 5,000. It had previously taken a work crew a full day to put together one car but with the Olds assembly line, a vehicle could be built in less than two hours.

JUNE 4

WHERE DID THEY GO?

Iowa's Lake Red Rock is the state's largest recreational area with over 15,000 acres of water and 35,000 acres of land. It is located on the Des Moines River where the reservoir collects runoff and drainage from over 12,320 square miles from Iowa and southern Minnesota.

There is another aspect to the waterway that makes the area unique. The Red Rock Dam project was authorized under the Flood Control Acts of June 1938 and December 1944. In June 1944, the Senate Commerce Committee approved $15 million of the $1 billion national flood control program for a large dam.

In 1956, planning for the project began and on June 4, 1960, the ground-breaking ceremony was held. Over the years, six towns were submerged to make way for the lake. The remains of the communities of Red Rock, Cordova, Dunreath, Rousseau, Fifield, and Coalport lie beneath the water.

Each of the towns had been heavily damaged by floodwater prior to the dam construction, and it was decided that buying them out and flooding them over would be the most practical alternative.

On March 17, 1969, the dam went into operation and the permanent pool level of 725 feet was reached in three days due to the spring melt. When completed, the 6,300-acre dam was the largest man-made lake in Iowa.

JUNE 5

WRONG TURN

On June 5, 1968, US senator Robert Kennedy was feeling good and he had a right to be confident. Earlier in the evening, he had claimed victory in the California presidential primary election, giving him increasing momentum as the candidate to beat for the Democratic nomination. He was already setting his sights on the Illinois primary which was just a week away.

Kennedy had risen to prominence as attorney general in his brother's (president John F. Kennedy) administration from 1961 to 1963. In 1964, he was elected to the US Senate seat from New York.

That evening, he captured the Golden State's contest 46%–42% and, as the midnight hour approached on the west coast, he and his wife Ethel prepared to make their way to the podium to deliver his victory address. A large crowd had gathered in the ballroom of the Ambassador Hotel in Los Angeles, which served as the campaign headquarters, to hear RFK's victory speech.

At 12:10 a.m. PDT, Kennedy made his way to the microphone facing toward the robust crowd in the hotel's Embassy Room ballroom. He wrapped up the brief address by saying to the enthusiastic audience, "So my thanks to all of you, and now it's on to Chicago, and let's win there. Thank you very much."

It was at this point that events began to take an abnormal turn. Traditionally, when he concluded a speech, Kennedy would depart through the crowd shaking hands with supporters along the exit path. Former FBI agent Bill Barry, who served as the candidate's chief of security, had prepared for the usual departure route, but saw the candidate being led away to the kitchen area by the hotel's assistant maître d' Karl Uecker. Barry was normally very close to RFK whenever he was on the move but in the confusion of the moment, the two had become separated and Uecker now served as the senator's guide.

They soon entered the pantry area where Kennedy was greeted by members of the kitchen staff. Suddenly, a series of shots rang out in the confined area creating a chaotic scene as the entourage scattered away from the blast area. There were approximately eighty people in the room, six of them had been wounded, but the most seriously injured of the group was Robert Kennedy. He was laying on the floor, bleeding profusely, as officials began working on him. In the blink of an eye, it was November 1963 all over again.

Just a few feet away, a suspect was being subdued. He was a 24-year-old Palestinian immigrant named Sirhan Sirhan who had lived in the United States for twelve years. However, the slightly built assassin (5'4" and 120 pounds) was no match for his captors as he was immediately apprehended by 290-pound former professional football star Roosevelt Grier and Rafer Johnson, the 1960 Olympic decathlon gold medalist, both of whom were Kennedy supporters. During the scuffle, Uecker secured Sirhan's .22-caliber weapon.

Kennedy suffered three wounds including one to the brain which led to his death twenty-six hours later. As with his brother's assassination, there have been numerous theories about conspiracies and another gunman. But to this day, no one other than Sirhan has taken credit for the crime. In 2021, he was recommended for parole by the state's board after serving fifty-three years in prison. That proposal was denied by governor Gavin Newsom the following year.

If Kennedy had not exited through the kitchen area and had, in fact, become the Democratic nominee for president in 1968, who would he have faced in the general election? The same man that his brother defeated in 1960—Richard Nixon.

JUNE 6

THE BAYOU WAY FOR D-DAY!

This invasion of Europe, aka D-Day or Operation Overlord, took place on this day on the beaches of France in 1944. While the battle sites were European, there was definitely an influence from a state best known for jazz and gumbo.

US troops came ashore aboard landing craft boats that were originally designed for use in the Louisiana swamps.

Lumber businessman and former Nebraska National Guard infantry officer Andrew Higgins had a hard time extracting hardwood trees from the backwoods of the bayou. His early boats kept running aground in shallow waters, but he didn't give up and continued to improve the design over the next few decades.

The craft was exactly what the military needed for amphibious landings and he eventually secured a contract with the US government which purchased more than 20,000 of Higgins' Landing Craft Personnel (LCP) ships. His boats served in North Africa, Italy, Normandy, and the islands of the Pacific.

General Eisenhower once called Higgins "the man who won the war for us."

JUNE 7

HIS LUCKY DAY

On June 7, 1936, the high profile mobster Charles "Lucky" Luciano was convicted on 62 counts of compulsory prostitution. He was sentenced from 30 to 50 years in prison and had been prosecuted by US attorney, and future presidential candidate, Thomas E. Dewey.

But the government struck a deal with Luciano during World War II. In exchange for being moved to a more comfortable prison that was closer to New York City, the mob boss provided information to US military intelligence about his home island of Sicily in preparation for the upcoming invasion.

For his cooperation, in January 1946, Luciano was given a pardon with the caveat that he was to be deported back to Italy. He had served less than ten years of his original sentence. The governor reluctantly signed the agreement and the one-time crime boss returned home where he lived out most of his days until his death from a heart attack in 1962. So who was the governor who grudgingly signed Luciano's pardon? It was the man who had put him away a decade earlier as a federal prosecutor, Thomas E. Dewey.

JUNE 8

CALLING IT THE WAY THAT YOU SEE IT

Richard B. Fitzgibbon Jr. was a veteran of the United States Navy, having served during World War II. Following his discharge, he joined the newly formed United States Air Force, rising through the ranks to become a technical sergeant.

On June 8, 1956, Fitzgibbon was serving as part of the Military Assistance Advisory Group that was involved in training military personnel in South Vietnam. Many consider him to be the first American to lose his life in the Southeast Asian conflict.

However, Fitzgibbon was not killed in action but rather was murdered in Saigon by another American serviceman, staff sergeant Edward C. Clarke who had apparently been reprimanded for an incident during a flight that same day.

When he went off duty, the angry Clarke began drinking too much at a club on the base. Still upset, when he exited the establishment, the radio operator saw Fitzgibbon across the street and drew his sidearm.

Clarke shot his crew chief several times before fleeing the scene and exchanging fire with a Vietnamese police officer who was chasing him. During the pursuit, he jumped or fell to his death from a second-story balcony. Both men died in the incident.

In 1965, one of Fitzgibbon's sons, Marine lance corporal Richard B. Fitzgibbon III was also killed during the Vietnam War. Like his father, he is memorialized on the Vietnam Wall.

JUNE 9

NOT QUITE GOOD ENOUGH

Jonas Salk was a research scientist, but that wasn't good enough for Elmer Lindsay, a wealthy Manhattan dentist. That's because Jonas wanted to marry Lindsay's daughter Donna. The pair had spent a summer working together at a laboratory in Woods Hole, Massachusetts, and were ready to begin a life together.

The suitor made his intentions known but didn't make much headway. Lindsay eventually agreed to the marriage on two conditions: first, Salk had to wait until he could be listed as an official MD on the wedding invitations, and second, he must improve his "rather pedestrian status" by giving himself a middle name.

On June 8, 1939, Jonas graduated from the New York University's School of Medicine, which gave him the right to employ "MD" after his birth name. He also adopted the middle name of Edward to fulfill his soon-to-be father-in-law's marital prerequisites.

On this day in 1939, just one day after his graduation, Dr. Jonas E. Salk married Donna Lindsay, a master's candidate at the New York College of Social Work. The couple went on to have three sons, all of whom became doctors.

Whatever misgivings Dr. Lindsay may have had about his son-in-law disappeared in 1955 when it was announced that Dr. Salk and his research team developed a successful vaccine against the life threatening polio disease.

JUNE 10

UP AGAINST THE CLOCK

Carnegie Hall opened its doors in 1891. Its New York City location is the most famous musical palace in the United States featuring live performers from the genres of classical, jazz, country, rock, and everything in between. But there was a time when it appeared that the renown site might be down to its swan song.

After years of neglect and deterioration, by 1956, plans were being made to replace the celebrated entertainment edifice with a 44-story skyscraper. A final effort spearheaded by New York Philharmonic music director Leonard Bernstein, legendary violinist Isaac Stern, and philanthropist Jacob Kaplan to save the Carnegie went forward.

On June 10, 1960, the New York City Board of Estimate approved the purchase of Carnegie Hall for $5 million, with another $100,000 earmarked for improvements. Over the years, there were further restorations and in 1962, the grand old site was designated a National Historic Landmark, saving it for future generations of music lovers.

JUNE 11

SWEEPIN' DOWN THE PLAINS

June 11 is special for the citizens of Oklahoma. On that day in 1910, voters chose Oklahoma City as the state's permanent capital. It was also ninety-one years later to the day that the Oklahoma City Bomber Timothy James McVeigh was executed.

However, the entire case almost fell apart before attorneys were able to prosecute it. On the day of the crime, April 19, 1995, McVeigh was not originally arrested for his part in the bombing and nearly got away.

About 90 minutes after the explosion, he was taken into custody by Oklahoma Highway Patrol trooper Charlie Hanger a short distance from the small town of Billings, Oklahoma, after being pulled over for not having a license plate on his car. It was also discovered that he had no insurance and was carrying a concealed pistol and a knife.

At that point, he was taken about 30 minutes away to the Noble County Jail in Perry. Two days later, shortly before he was to be released on bail, the FBI contacted officials at the lockup to notify them about who their prisoner was and the crime that he was suspected of committing. A short while afterward, McVeigh was charged in the bombing and taken into federal custody.

JUNE 12

TEAR DOWN THIS WALL!

In 1936, Ron and his college friend Frank Mills, were en route to Hollywood to "become stars," and made a stopover in Fort Worth along the way. Mills decided to check out the local job market, and was offered a position with radio station KGKO and then one with WBAP.

Frank liked what he saw and stayed put working in the Dallas/Fort Worth television and radio markets for the next forty-one years before retiring. His buddy Ron opted to finish the journey to California by himself where he put together a successful acting career prior to being elected governor of the Golden State in 1966 and president of the United States in 1980.

Ron was none other than Ronald Reagan, who was speaking at the Brandenburg Gate of the Berlin Wall on June 12, 1987, challenged Soviet general secretary Mikhail Gorbachev to do away with his country's Communist government saying, "General Secretary Gorbachev, if you seek peace, if you seek prosperity for the Soviet Union and Eastern Europe, if you seek liberalization, come here to this gate! Mr. Gorbachev, open this gate! Mr. Gorbachev, tear down this wall!"

Many consider it his best and most famous speech.

JUNE 13

BLOODLINES

Confederate lieutenant general Nathan Bedford Forrest has been classified by some experts as the Civil War's most able cavalry commander. Even though he had twenty-nine horses shot from under him, the Tennessee native survived the conflict and later became one of the postwar leaders of the Ku Klux Klan.

On June 13, 1943, his great grandson Nathan Bedford Forrest III was killed in action while participating in a bombing raid over Germany, the first US general to be killed in action during World War II. He was posthumously awarded the Distinguished Service Cross (second only to the Medal of Honor) for staying with the controls of his B-17 bomber while his crew bailed out. The plane exploded before Forrest could follow them.

JUNE 14

SOME THINGS ARE ACTUALLY FREE

Eli Whitney's best known invention was the cotton gin, which made the process of cleaning the crop quicker so it was more readily available for market. It caused cotton's production in the south to skyrocket and made it the region's staple crop.

But Whitney's talents weren't limited to a single innovation. In 1798, four years after receiving his patent for the cotton gin, he opened an armory to produce muskets for the US government. On June 14 of that year, the inventor contracted to make 10,000 weapons to be delivered within 28 months at the cost of $134,000. Although he needed a little extra time to fill the order, he did complete the task within two years.

It was during that time that Whitney created the process of assembly using interchangeable parts, making the operation move more rapidly. By the time the War of 1812 rolled around, his factory at Hamden, Connecticut, was producing 1,000 to 2,000 muskets per year and since he never patented the method for interchangeable parts, other manufacturers adopted his process free of charge.

JUNE 15

THE PIG WAR

"The Pig War" was perhaps one of the most obscure but also ridiculous conflicts in history. The story began in 1846 when the Oregon Treaty was signed
between the United States and Great Britain. It was hoped that the settlement
would put to rest the long-standing border dispute between the two world
powers, specifically those relating to the land between the Rocky Mountains
and the Pacific coastline.

The document stated that the US/British border would be drawn at the 49th
parallel, a division which remains to this day.

By 1859, the British had a significant presence on San Juan Island, bol-
stered with the recent arrival of the Hudson's Bay Company. Meanwhile, a
contingent of between twenty and thirty Americans had also arrived on the
isle to make it their home.

Indications were that the settlers on both sides actually got along well.
However, this was not to last as on June 15, 1859, a pig belonging to British
citizen Charles Griffin accidentally wandered onto the land of Lyman Cutlar,
an American farmer. When Cutlar noticed the animal eating some of his potatoes, he became furious and then shot and killed the swine.

A petition requesting US military protection was received by the commander of the Department of Oregon. He sent a 66-man company of the US
ninth infantry to San Juan on July 27, 1859.

Upon hearing that news, the governor of British Columbia sent three
British warships to the area in retaliation. When word of the diplomatic mess
reached officials in Washington, DC, and London, both sides were shocked
that a dispute over a pig had grown into potential bloodshed involving 3 warships, 84 guns, and over 2,600 men.

The former enemies quickly began negotiations to quash the situation.
In 1872, an international commission led by Kaiser Wilhelm I of Germany
decided that the island should fall entirely under American control and, as
such, the dispute was finally laid to rest. Today, the San Juan Islands are part
of the state of Washington.

JUNE 16

RELAXING BY THE SEASHORE

Before there was television or the internet, people were in search of entertainment and many found ways to pass the hours by spending time at amusement parks which were often located near the seashore.

On this day in 1884, the first roller coaster in America opened at Coney Island in Brooklyn, New York. Known as a " switchback railway," it was the creation of LaMarcus Thompson, cost a nickel to ride, and soon became an instant success story as thousands of enthusiasts waited in long lines for an opportunity to ride the high rising tracks.

It wasn't comparable to the quick-paced cars that came along later, in fact, the top speed was just six miles per hour. But its popularity was without debate.

By the 1920s, Coney Island was reachable by subway and summer crowds swelled to more than a million visitors per day for rides, fun, and food. The area's most famous product is the world renown Nathan's Hot Dog which was invented at the island in 1867 by Charles Feltman. The company is famous not only for its franks but the nationally televised annual Fourth of July hot dog–eating contest.

JUNE 17

PULL UP A SEAT

On this day in 1775, the British won a costly victory at the Battle of Breed's Hill, aka Bunker Hill, as thousands watched the fighting take place. Individuals in the Boston area sat on rooftops, in trees, on church steeples, and atop the rigging of ships in the harbor to view the upstart colonial revolutionaries battle against the experienced British regulars.

It wasn't the last time that Americans viewed the ravages of a conflict as spectators. In 1861, at the start of the Civil War, curiosity seekers gathered at Manassas, Virginia, to take in the First Battle of Bull Run. Most of them viewed the fighting as they dined on picnic lunches.

JUNE 18

CHOICES

In October 1984, 23-year-old Ronnie Lee Gardner robbed a tavern in Salt Lake City while under the influence of cocaine. He shot and killed the bartender, getting away with less than $100. A few days later, the gunman attended his victim's funeral posing as a childhood friend.

Police apprehended Gardner three weeks afterward at the home of his cousin. He was tried for murder in April 1985 and attempted to escape from custody during the proceedings in a wild scene that resembled something from a movie.

A woman had slipped Gardner a gun while he was being taken to the courthouse from an underground parking area. A prison guard, who was escorting the inmate, shot him in the shoulder. Once inside, the bleeding suspect fatally shot attorney Michael Burdell and wounded bailiff Nick Kirk before being captured on the courthouse lawn. He was eventually convicted of aggravated capital murder for killing Burdell and sentenced to death.

The trial had been held in 1985 in Utah which allowed the convict to select his means of punishment between lethal injection or death by firing squad. The latter method had been eliminated by most states, but Gardner chose it as his way of making his final departure, believing it would buy him more time during the appeals process.

In 2004, Utah lawmakers abolished the firing squad but it wasn't retroactive, which meant that anyone who had previously made that choice would still have it honored.

Gardner's appeals continued until this day in 2010. Around midnight, he was strapped into a chair in the execution room where a target was pinned over his heart. The prisoner was offered two-minutes to offer up any final words but replied that he had none.

Five police shooters set up about 25 feet from the chair with their .30-caliber Winchester rifles pointing through slots in a wall. The executioners' identities were kept anonymous with one of their rifles loaded with a blank round so nobody knew which officer killed the inmate.

Ronnie Lee Gardner was declared dead two minutes after he was shot. He was the last person killed by a firing squad in the United States, which should have been the conclusion to the story but there was one last ironic twist.

In 2015, Utah governor Gary Herbert signed a bill bringing back the former method of execution. It returned as the backup option in part due to a shortage of lethal injection drugs.

Utah is now the only state in the nation that authorizes execution by firing squad.

JUNE 19

HIGH GEAR DIPLOMACY

President Richard Nixon and Soviet premier Leonid Brezhnev met for three summits while each was in office, totaling over one hundred hours in May 1972, June 1973, and June/July 1974. These meetings led to the arms negotiation treaty known as SALT II.

But it's what took place behind the scenes during those meetings in June 1973 that caused a diplomatic stir. It is customary for visiting heads of state to stay at Blair House, a simple walk across the street from the White House. But instead, Nixon made arrangements for Brezhnev to stay at the presidential retreat at Camp David (Maryland).

The Soviet leader was also an avid collector of fine automobiles. So Nixon presented him with a brand new Lincoln Continental. Brezhnev's eyes lit up when he saw it. He took the wheel, motioned Nixon into the passenger seat, and sped off at 60 mph, careening down the narrow, winding roads, to the horror of the Secret Service.

The Soviet leader blew through a stop sign, lurched into traffic, and onto a nearby highway. "That was something," said a trembling Nixon, who later wrote that "Diplomacy is not always an easy art."

Within hours of their first meeting, Brezhnev announced that he had already invited the president to Moscow for another summit.

JUNE 20

THE WAR WITHIN THE WAR

Hermann Göring and Joseph Goebbels were two members of Hitler's inner circle. What most observers were not aware of was that, at one time, the Nazi duo nearly became victims of a mob hit.

Countess Dorothy Dendice Taylor di Frasso was one of the many girl-friends of the American mobster Benjamin "Bugsy" Siegel. In 1939, the Countess took Siegel on a European holiday to her Italian villa where he was discussing selling weapons to fascist dictator Benito Mussolini.

But the mob boss became enraged when he discovered that other guests at the villa included anti-Semites Göring and Goebbels. Siegel, a Jew, immediately hatched a plan to kill them both. It was only through the pleading of his mistress that he agreed to spare the members of the German hierarchy.

Goebbels eventually committed suicide in 1945 followed by Göring the next year. In a stroke of mob irony, it was on this day in 1947 that Bugsy Siegel was killed in a mob hit in Los Angeles.

JUNE 21

THE GENERAL AND THE KID

Winfield Scott had trained as a lawyer but enlisted in the army in 1808. It was the beginning of a career that saw him play major roles in such conflicts as the War of 1812, the Black Hawk War, and the Second Seminole War.

In 1846, the United States and Mexico headed into battle. Scott planned an invasion of Anahuac (Mexico) while in New Orleans. A dedicated officer, the general wasn't an all-work-and-no-play type of person. A deterrent from the grind of battle was his passion for playing chess.

The game seemed like a natural hobby for a person like Scott who could use his tactical instincts without the fear of becoming a casualty of an actual conflict. He himself, along with those around him, fancied the officer to be a good player.

During the troops five-day December stay in the Crescent City, the 59-year-old commander asked an acquaintance at the local chess club to find him a worthy opponent. At eight o'clock that evening, the grizzled battlefield veteran found himself looking across the table at an eight-and-a-half-year-old local lad, clad in a lace shirt and velvet knickerbockers.

Scott believed he had been the victim of a prank and arose in disgust to exit the table, but the hometown players assured the general that the person chosen to play was uniquely qualified and that he was a serious opponent. It didn't take very long for the old soldier to find out that his challenger was authentic as he was checkmated by the youngster in ten moves! In the next game just moments later, the lad bettered his first performance halting the general in an amazing six moves.

Five decades his senior, Scott had been beaten twice in just sixteen moves by a child. It was the beginning of a southern legend that spread throughout the chess world.

That was their only match as the two players never saw each other again after the general's angry departure. In the future, things went better for Scott as in March 1847, US troops under his command invaded Mexico, successfully carrying out the first large-scale amphibious assault. They were able to claim total victory over the enemy a year later.

The boy who defeated him in that famous 1846 chess match also did pretty well for himself. His name was Paul Morphy and he was already a local celebrity when he was pitted against the general. He was blessed with an astounding memory and graduated from law school by age 20, a year earlier than he could be certified to practice in Louisiana.

On this day in 1858, he began a European tour where played multiple competitors from across the continent with great success.

In April 1859, a Paris banquet was held in his honor where he was proclaimed by the assembly as "the best chess player that ever lived." Later, in London, he sat for a private audience with Queen Victoria, who greatly enjoyed the game. At the end of the month, the one-time child prodigy returned home as a conquering hero.

However, fame was fleeting for Morphy who died of a stroke in 1884 at the age of 47.

JUNE 22

FLY ME TO THE MOON

In science classes, students are taught about the moons of the various planets. But the story of how Pluto's moon Charon was discovered is a story all its own.

On June 22, 1978, US astronomer James Christy was going to discard what he thought was a defective photographic plate of Pluto when his Star Scan machine broke down. While it was being repaired, he had time to study the plate again and discovered other pictures in the archives with the same "defect"—a bulge in the planet's image was actually a large moon.

At the time, Christy was working at the United States Naval Observatory in Washington, DC, which now serves as the official residence of the vice president.

JUNE 23

THE LONG GOOD-BYE

Vassar College in Poughkeepsie, New York, was one of the nation's first higher learning institutions for women. It was established in 1861 with a donation of $408,000 from its founder, beer brewer Matthew Vassar. In a gesture that lacked any notice of opulence, he chose to present the endowment to the Board of Trustees in a tin box.

On June 23, 1868, seven years after its founding, the 76-year-old businessman delivered his farewell address to the Board of Trustees. Little did he know that it would be his final words, as he died in the middle of a sentence while reciting from the eleventh page of the speech.

Some time after Vassar's departure, Emelyn Battersby Hartridge, Class of 1892, made fudge for the senior class auction. She credited the recipe to a classmate's cousin who resided in Baltimore. Her letter discussing the auction became the first documentation of the sweet treat in the United States. The former women's college went coed in 1969.

JUNE 24

THE MONEY FIELD

On this day in 1972, while fertilizing a soybean field, Lowell Elliott happened upon an American Airlines bag containing $500,000. The Peru, Indiana, farmer had heard that authorities were looking for a skyjacker who had parachuted out of a Boeing 727 the previous evening so he turned the money over to the FBI.

Airline officials got their money back shortly before the authorities nabbed the skyjacker. In gratitude to Farmer Elliott, American offered him and his wife a trip to Hawaii or whatever distant paradise piqued their fancy. Not interested in a Pacific getaway, the 61-year-old Elliott told American officials, "I'd like to get the cash reward."

The company's regional sales manager returned with a check for $10,000.

The hijacker, Martin McNally, was a 28-year-old unemployed military veteran. To get home from Peru after bailing from the aircraft, he had called a friend in Detroit, who drove southward and picked him up.

McNally was convicted in December 1972 on two counts of air piracy, even though his lawyers argued that jumping out of a 727 at 350 mph would have been impossible. However, a pilot and a flight attendant both identified him as the hijacker. He received two life sentences, with a chance for parole after nineteen years. But, because of an unsuccessful escape attempt in 1978, McNally wasn't released until January 27, 2010, at age 67. McNally's friend, who drove him home from Indiana, drew a ten-year sentence.

JUNE 25

ALMOST COLOR

In April 1951, CBS moved into New York City's Peace Theater, where it was soon determined that this would become their Field Sequential color studio.

It was a groundbreaking decision as all of the networks, during that period, were broadcasting in black and white.

Their debut show crossed the air waves on June 25, 1951, and was simply titled "Premiere." It was a variety program featuring many well-known acts and individuals.

Although there were 10.5 million monochrome (black and white) broadcasting sets in the United States, they were not equipped to receive a signal dispersed in color. Thus, no one could tell if the new technology was functioning properly.

The first Field Sequential (color) TV sets were made available to the public on September 28, 1951. They had a 12 1/2-inch screen and sold for $499.95 (nearly $5,400 in today's economy). However, less than a month later, production was ordered halted when the Korean War broke out.

By 1990, most stores had quit selling black-and-white sets.

JUNE 26

CAN YOU KEEP A SECRET?

There have been three presidents who have married after taking office. John Tyler (1844), Grover Cleveland (1886), and Woodrow Wilson (1915) each wed new brides while they were serving the nation as its chief executive. Tyler and Wilson were widowers while the 49-year-old robust Cleveland had been a lifetime bachelor.

Tyler had become president on April 6, 1841, following the unexpected death of William Henry Harrison. His wife, First Lady Letitia, suffered a paralytic stroke in 1839 that left her an invalid. She passed away in 1842 becoming the first First Lady to die while serving in the role, which was then filled by her daughter and namesake Letitia.

On January 20, 1842, Tyler was introduced to a 21-year-old New Yorker Julia Gardinier, the daughter of wealthy US senator David Gardinier. Following Letitia's death, the president, who was thirty-four years her senior, proposed to Julia for the first of several times in 1843, of which all were rejected. But a year later, she accepted although they chose to keep the engagement a secret.

It was many years before 24/7 news coverage with the roving paparazzi lurking about but, even in those days, there were journalists looking for a big story and, if it got out that the president of the United States was about to remarry, the couple would never have any privacy.

Tyler was especially concerned about stories pertaining to the couple's age difference. By the mid-1800s, the nation's capital was a rumor mill that included no shortage of reporters trying to make a name for themselves. Because of that, all of the wedding preparations were kept secret.

The first task was moving the ceremony out of Washington, DC. As opposed to the stately White House, it was decided that the beautiful Church of the Ascension on Fifth Avenue and West 10th Street in New York City would serve as the wedding site. It was also a short distance from the Gardinier family home. On this day in 1844, the secret ceremony was pulled off successfully, with only one newspaper, the *New York Morning Express,* reporting the nuptials. Julia became one of the nation's most popular First Ladies but was only in the position for little more than a year as her new husband was unable to retain the presidency during the 1844 election cycle.

Afterward, the couple moved to his Virginia plantation where they had seven kids—in addition to the eight Tyler had fathered with Letitia. The former commander in chief holds the record for most children sired by one who held the office, as his final offspring was born in 1860 when he was seventy. As of 2023, his grandson Harrison Ruffin Tyler was still living at the age of 94.

JUNE 27

THOSE FOUR WORDS

All US currency has the motto "In God We Trust" inscribed on it. But how did it get there?

The idea took form in November 1953 when Matt Rothert, the owner of the Camden Furniture Company in Arkansas, wrote a letter to secretary of the treasury George Humphrey and president Dwight D. Eisenhower.

Rothert, who was also a numismatist, pointed out that coins had "In God We Trust" embossed on them but the paper money did not carry the same words. He urged the government to take action by placing the saying on the nation's paper currency.

On May 17, 1955, the Banking Committee of the House of Representatives began discussions on the matter and eventually authored H.R. 619. Among the concerns was the constitutional question of the separation of church and state. However, on June 27, 1955, the Senate passed the bill with no objections which was followed two weeks later by President Eisenhower signing it into law.

Today, the motto that adorns all of the nation's paper currency remains in place, and it began with a letter from a small business owner in Arkansas.

JUNE 28

HOME IMPROVEMENT

In 1917, the United States entered the war in Europe bringing needed help to the Allied cause. On June 28, 1919, the Treaty of Versailles was signed at the Palace's Hall of Mirrors ending World War I.

In 1924, America came to the rescue once again as philanthropist John D. Rockefeller Jr., the son of the oil magnate, donated a gift of 100 million francs (equivalent to over $100 million today) to preserve the opulent Palace of Versailles where the treaty had been signed five years prior.

JUNE 29

ROLLIN' DOWN THE HIGHWAY

Former president Dwight D. Eisenhower wore a number of different hats during his lifetime. In addition to being the country's chief executive, he was also an outdoorsman, a military historian, a college football player and golfer, a West Point graduate (he was a member of the famous Class of 1915 which is considered the institution's greatest ever), a soldier, and the Supreme Allied Commander of the War in Europe.

In the summer of 1919, Lieutenant Colonel Eisenhower was assigned as an observer to a military experiment—the First Transcontinental Motor Convoy. The operation was a road test for military vehicles and was used to identify the challenges in moving troops from coast to coast using the existing infrastructure. The excursion covered 3,200 miles from Washington, DC, to San Francisco. It included 79 vehicles of all sizes and 297 personnel.

Ike was not a road engineer nor a vehicle mechanic but, during the expedition, he gained some useful insight in creating a network of connected roads and bridges. He reported on limited lane space which caused oncoming traffic to run off the pathways and then to encounter added difficulty when attempting to reenter the route.

Eisenhower singled out a western section of the Lincoln Highway, a transcontinental route that ran through Utah and Nevada, as being so poor that it warranted a thorough investigation before any further government money be expended. Contrastingly, he praised California for having excellent paved roads.

After World War II, the general hadn't forgotten what he learned decades earlier during the cross-country jaunt. After he was elected president, Eisenhower set about trying to improve the nation's road network. It all began on June 29, 1956, when he signed legislation funding the construction of the US Interstate Highway System.

On August 13, 1956, Missouri became the first state to begin work as crews in St. Charles County transformed the old US-40 into the new I-70.

On October 14, 1992, the Interstate Highway System was considered finished with the completion of I-70 through Glenwood Canyon in Colorado; it is considered to be an engineering marvel with a 12-mile span containing forty bridges and numerous tunnels.

When traveling the nation's most efficient roadway grid, drivers and passengers alike can thank an old soldier for getting them to their destination.

JUNE 30

WELCOME TO MY RIDE

On this day in 1953, the first production-ready Corvette from Chevrolet was built at an assembly plant in Flint, Michigan. It was dubbed as "America's first mass produced sports car of the post-war era."

JULY

If one morning I walked on top of the water across the Potomac River, the headline that afternoon would read: "President Can't Swim."

—Lyndon B. Johnson

JULY 1

THERE WAS ONCE A REAL ROCKET MAN

Among Sir Elton John's discography of his long array of hit songs was a 1972 work, "Rocket Man." It was about astronauts and the experience of space travel. What few realized was that, at one time, there was an actual rocket man.

Wernher von Braun worked for the US Army on an intermediate-range ballistic missile program, and helped develop the rockets that launched the United States' first space satellite, *Explorer I*, in 1958. In other words, he was a true rocket scientist.

von Braun's group of technologists was assimilated into NASA, where he became the center's first director on this day in 1960 and held that position until January 27, 1970. He was also involved in other projects such as the Apollo Moon-landing mission.

Before he became a world-renowned scientist, the native of Wirsitz, Germany, like millions of others, was forced to take part in Adolf Hitler's plan for a new world order. Von Braun's career began as a German aerospace engineer and space architect during the Nazi regime.

In the 1930s and 1940s, he worked in their rocket development program and was a leading figure in the development of the V-2 rocket (the world's first long-range guided ballistic missile) during World War II.

Following the war, he defected to the United States, along with about 1,600 other German scientists, engineers, and technicians, as part of a secret

American intelligence program. He worked against groups like the Nazis who were attempting to seize power through force.

In 1955, von Braun became a naturalized citizen of the United States. He and his family lived for a number of years in Huntsville, Alabama, prior to his death in 1977.

JULY 2

SMOKE 'EM IF YOU'VE GOT 'EM

On July 2, 1955, Senate majority leader and future president Lyndon B. Johnson suffered a near-fatal heart attack. A three-pack-a-day cigarette smoker, after his episode, he stopped the dangerous habit and did not resume it until after he left office in 1969.

Johnson made light of his condition while hospitalized when an aide inquired if he should cancel LBJ's recent order to purchase two suits. He had requested a brown one along with a blue suit. He replied to the aide, "Let them go ahead with the blue one. We can use that no matter what happens."

A few weeks later, on September 24, 1955, president Dwight D. Eisenhower also had a heart attack during a visit to his in-laws in Denver. After years as a four-pack-a-day smoker, he had quit permanently in 1949.

Each man suffered at least one other heart attack before eventually dying of cardiac disease.

JULY 3

A TRAIN WRECK WAITING TO HAPPEN

The 1890s were a difficult economic period for the United States. So much so that, at one point, industrialist J. P. Morgan came forward to loan his country 3.5 million ounces of gold to help bail it out of a financial mess.

While there were many ideas being floated about in 1896 about how to turn around the railroads, the most outlandish came from the Lone Star State where William George Crush, a passenger agent for the Missouri-Kansas-Texas Railroad Company, commonly referred to as the Katy line, decided to stage a train wreck. Crush was a friend of the famous showman P. T. Barnum (see *July 5*) and realized the value of publicity. When his madcap scheme gained approval from his bosses, it became the feature article of most newspapers—not just in Texas but nationally.

Crush's plan, he was born on this day in 1865, was to take two obsolete locomotives and put them on a track facing each other a couple of miles apart and give them a running start. The opportunity to see a head-on collision featuring two massive iron horses was just too good to be passed up by the public.

On September 15, 1896, two 35-ton locomotives built in the 1870s began their steam-powered showdown like two giant iron goats ready to butt heads. One had been painted a brilliant shamrock green while the other was glossed a bright red. Each engine would be followed by six boxcars in tow to create an even larger effect.

The area, with its sloping hills, provided spectator seating in the configuration of a natural amphitheater. Crush expected a crowd of around 25,000 but was even more pleased when the total surpassed 40,000 curious onlookers. There was no admission charged.

The churning beasts sped toward one another at more than 45 mph when they suddenly collided, touching off an explosion that spewed flaming hot materials throughout the suddenly terrified crowd. Three people died in the mishap and several others were injured. Many were treated by doctors seated among the audience who had attended to view the bizarre occurrence.

Crush was summarily fired a few hours later but when the stunt had its desired effect with improved business, he was quickly brought back to the company where he worked for fifty-seven years until his retirement. Despite the tragedy of the stunt, staged train wrecks continued to be held at various locations, drawing large crowds for many years.

JULY 4

INDEPENDENCE DAY

Americans annually celebrate the nation's independence on July 4th, but there were some other notable events linked to fireworks day. John Adams (the 2nd president) along with his friend, and sometimes enemy, Thomas Jefferson (the 3rd president), both died just a few hours apart on July 4, 1826. Former Revolutionary War soldier James Monroe (the 5th president) passed away exactly five years later to the day.

But the Fourth wasn't just a day for ex-presidents to meet Saint Peter, Calvin Coolidge (the 30th president) was born on Independence Day in 1872.

JULY 5

UNDER THE BIG TOP

Happy Birthday to P. T. Barnum who was born on this day in 1810. He was known as a master showman and one the founders behind the Barnum & Bailey Circus.

However, there was also a political side to the entertainment promoter as in 1875, he was elected to a one-year term as the mayor of Bridgeport, Connecticut. That was sandwiched between two stints as a member of the Connecticut State House of Representatives in 1865–1866 and again in 1877–1879.

In 1867, the impresario ran for a seat in the US House of Representatives but was defeated by his third cousin, William H. Barnum.

JULY 6

LOST THE HOUSE

Sometimes, a person needs to taste the agony of defeat before enjoying the sweet smell of victory. In 1978, Republican oilman George W. Bush, who was born on this day in 1946, had never sought political office and decided to make a run at the US House seat of Texas' 19th congressional district. He lost decisively to state senator Kent Hance—53.24% to 46.76%.

Bush went on to have better days as a candidate when he became governor of Texas (1995) and president of the United States (2001). However, he wasn't alone when it came to getting stung by the voters.

In 2000, Democrat Barack Obama was a little-known candidate for the seat in Illinois 1st congressional district but was soundly beaten by former Black Panther Party member Bobby Rush in the primary—61% to 30%. It was the first and only time that either future president attempted to get elected to the US House of Representatives and lost.

JULY 7

WHY IS THAT BUS YELLOW?

In the never ending quest for knowledge, inquiring minds have sought an answer to the query, "Why are school buses yellow?"

The man behind this disclosure was Dr. Frank W. Cyr, a former professor of rural education at Columbia University's Teachers College who was known as the "Father of the Yellow School Bus." He was born on this day in 1900 in Franklin, Nebraska.

In April 1939, Cyr organized a conference at Teachers College that drew transportation officials from each of the then forty-eight states, as well as specialists from school bus manufacturers and paint companies. It was there that the participants established forty-four national school bus construction standards, including the color yellow for buses.

The hue was selected because it was determined that the vehicle's black lettering on the bright body color was easiest to see in the semidarkness of early mornings and late afternoons.

Until the 1939 conference, there were no standards for the construction of school buses. In 1937, Cyr began a study of school transportation and found that children were riding to their campuses in all kinds of vehicles, including trucks and buses of various colors.

The conference met for seven days in New York City creating the measures that included specifications regarding body length, ceiling height, and aisle width. While many of those regulations have changed, the selected color of yellow has remained the same.

In April 1989, Cyr was honored at Teachers College marking the fiftieth anniversary of the original conference. He died on August 1, 1995, in Stamford, New York, at the age of 95.

JULY 8

THE HOMECOMING

Most presidents travel thousands of miles during their time in office. Because of the availability of top-of-the-line aircraft, the commander in chief is able to visit several countries in brief periods. But what if there were no planes?

That was the dilemma that faced US president Woodrow Wilson when it came time to negotiate the treaty for World War I. The peace talks were being held in Paris in an era where there was no *Air Force One* which meant that most of the travel would have to be done by ship and train. He departed the United States on December 4, 1918, less than a month after the fighting had concluded.

The journey made Wilson the first US president to visit Europe, where he addressed the troops, met with foreign heads of state, and participated in the negotiations of the Versailles Treaty.

Unimaginable by later standards, the 62-year-old Wilson and his entourage didn't return to the United States until this day in 1919 after being away from the White House for seven months!

JULY 9

RUN TO THE ATM

While the cost of some items remains constant, one thing is guaranteed—the expense of running for president increases with every campaign.

On several occasions in 2016, Donald Trump stated that he wasn't a politician but a businessman. He also said that he ran a self-funded campaign, but that statement was only partially true.

It is estimated that Trump spent $66 million from his own pocket, although many citizens also donated to his effort. Included in his campaign war chest was nearly $647 million raised by the candidate and the GOP. Amazingly, he spent just $285.5 million of those funds.

However, the former New York builder wasn't the first to dig deep into his own pockets. In 1992, fellow businessman Ross Perot spent $64 million of his personal funds to make an unsuccessful run as an independent. The Texas billionaire died on this day in 2019.

By comparison in 2020, the incumbent and his Democratic challenger Joe Biden, as well as outside groups supporting them during the general election, spent a combined $2.74 billion! Biden and his allies controlled about 61% of this sum ($1.68 billion), while the Trump campaign took in about 39% ($1.06 billion).

All of these funds were raised to try to get a job that pays a much smaller amount by comparison—$400,000 a year.

JULY 10

SPACE PICTURES

The *Telstar 1* satellite became the world's first active communications spacecraft as it was launched on this day in 1962 from Florida's Cape Canaveral. Two days later it made history by transmitting the first global television signal from the Andover Earth Station in Maine to the Pleumeur-Bodou Telecom Center in Brittany, France.

The first images beamed to Earth during that broadcast included views of the Statue of Liberty, the Eiffel Tower, remarks from president John F. Kennedy, clips from a baseball game between the Philadelphia Phillies and the Chicago Cubs, shots of the American flag waving in the breeze, and images of French singer/actor Yves Montand.

However, the ongoing space craze wasn't restricted to the United States. In December 1962, six months after the satellite's launch, the British rock band

The Tornadoes released an instrumental record entitled *Telstar* which was named after the spacecraft. The track reached number 1 on the US Billboard Hot 100 in December 1962.

JULY 11

IT DIDN'T HAVE TO HAPPEN

The most famous duel in American history took place on this day in 1804 when the sitting vice president Aaron Burr shot and killed the former secretary of the treasury Alexander Hamilton. Twenty-eight years earlier, the combatants were on the same side in George Washington's Continental Army and were among the throng that made the momentous crossing of the Delaware River on Christmas night, 1776.

But in the ensuing years, political differences made enemies of the former freedom fighters. In 1801, Hamilton's 19-year-old son Philip was killed at the Weehawken Dueling Grounds near present-day Jersey City defending his father's name. Hamilton advised his devoted offspring to salvage his honor without the risk of killing his opponent by "throwing away his shot," meaning to shoot first into the air with the hope that his adversary would reconsider the consequences. Initially Philip delayed raising his gun and when he did, his opponent, George Eacker, mortally wounded him.

Three years later, his father also faced down an opponent at the same location using the exact pistols from his son's fateful duel. Such actions were illegal in both New York and New Jersey but officials were more lenient in the Garden State. Weehawken was located on a secluded ledge overlooking the Hudson River.

The two war veterans were beyond their prime for a young man's display of resolution. Burr was forty-seven years old while Hamilton was either forty-six or forty-eight (there are no official records although it is known that he was born on the island of Nevis in the British West Indies). However, neither man was going to back down, even though they hadn't fired a weapon on a battlefield at another human being in more than a quarter of a century.

At 7:00 a.m., Hamilton and Burr took their positions after arriving at the site and then stepped off ten paces but, before firing, Hamilton asked for a delay. "Stop," he said. "In certain states of the light, one requires glasses." Burr patiently acquiesced.

It was one last opportunity for the conflict to conclude without another death in the Hamilton family but that wasn't to be. The former cabinet member fired his .56-caliber pistol but several witnesses later claimed that he deliberately missed his target. Burr then discharged his weapon hitting his one-time ally in the abdomen area above the right hip which fractured a rib, tore through the diaphragm and liver, before finally lodging in his spine. Thirty-one hours later, Alexander Hamilton, like his son Philip, was dead from being shot in a duel that could have been stopped.

JULY 12

WELCOME TO JURASSIC PARK

In the summer of 1979, exploration crews from Shell Oil were preparing to detonate seismic blasts in north-central Montana. However, three days prior to the scheduled man-made temblor, a team of Princeton University and nearby area paleontologists discovered the first whole dinosaur eggs ever unearthed in North America.

The search team was led by John Horner, a Princeton paleontologist, and Robert Makela, a Montana high school science teacher, whose discovery provided the first strong evidence that dinosaurs, unlike reptiles, but like birds and mammals, had cared for their young.

After the first egg was discovered on this day in 1979, the researchers were able to persuade Shell to move their seismic lines out of the area, and within a few weeks the team found forty more eggs in thirty different nests along with numerous bone fragments. The eggs were about six inches long and four inches wide and had black, pebbled shells.

The fossils were found less than 10 feet under the surface of sedimentary rock, mostly limestone and mudstone, a geologic area formed 80 million years ago.

The previous summer, the team discovered a nest of fifteen duck-billed herbivores, also known as Maiasaura, in the same area. In 1978, local paleontologist Laurie Trexler had found a full Maiasaura skull.

While Horner wasn't a household name outside his chosen field, many moviegoers are familiar with his other job. He served as a technical adviser to Steven Spielberg for the *Jurassic Park* film series.

JULY 13

FOUR YEARS LATER

Among the activities that take place every four years at the political conventions are the addresses given by the keynote speakers. In 1992, Zell Miller, the colorful Democratic governor from Georgia, delivered the first of two convention keynote addresses at Madison Square Garden in New York City.

He urged the faithful and the national television audience to vote for Bill Clinton as their next president which they did and he won.

In 2000, Miller was elected to the US Senate but had become disenchanted with some of the actions within his party—so much so that in 2004 he found himself once again on stage at Madison Square Garden as one of the convention's keynote speakers. But this time, the lifelong Democrat wasn't addressing the members of his party. He was speaking to the Republicans at their gathering on behalf of president George W. Bush.

Miller asked everyone to reelect the president over fellow senator and Democratic challenger John Kerry . . . which they did!

JULY 14

HAVE YOU HEARD THE ONE ABOUT THE PREACHER, THE PIANO PLAYER, AND THE PRESIDENTS?

No matter what the field of endeavor, it always seems that there has to be a standard bearer. Whether it's sports, politics, or television ratings, it always seems that there can only be room for one at the top.

That would be a difficult statement to doubt when it comes to modern-day ministers because there was one who was recognized by throngs throughout the world.

Billy Graham was born in North Carolina in 1918 and began his career in 1941 as pastor of the United Gospel Tabernacle in Wheaton, Illinois. It was the start of a ministry that concluded sixty-four years later on June 26, 2005, with its final crusade in New York City.

In between, Reverend Graham led 417 such gatherings, preaching in person to more than 210 million people around the world. In 1973, he addressed more than one million followers who crowded into Yoido Plaza in Seoul, South Korea—the largest live audience of his crusades.

As Graham was spreading the word of Jesus Christ, a young lad from Texas was making news as an American piano prodigy. Van Cliburn, who stood 6 foot 4 inches and physically resembled a basketball player, was quickly establishing himself as a world class classical musician.

While tense feelings festered between the United States and the Soviet Union at the height of the Cold War in 1958, the 23-year-old Cliburn won the first International Tchaikovsky Competition in Moscow, a contest designed to demonstrate Soviet cultural superiority on the heels of the country's launch of the first satellite, *Sputnik*.

When it was time to announce a winner, the judges asked permission of Soviet leader Nikita Khrushchev to award first prize to an American. "Is he the best?" Khrushchev asked. "Then give him the prize!" Cliburn returned home to a ticker-tape parade in New York City, the only time the honor has been bestowed on a musician of any genre.

While both men were accomplished, the two were quite different in terms of backgrounds, lifestyles, and habits. But there was one unique element where history repeated with each of them.

On July 14, 1950, Reverend Graham along with three of his friends met briefly with president Harry Truman at the White House. They spent 20 minutes speaking with the chief executive. At the end of their time together, the minister asked if they could pray with him, and he accepted.

Following his audience with the man who had given the order to drop the atomic bombs five years earlier, Billy Graham went on to meet with every US president who served in the office during his lifetime before passing away in 2018.

Cliburn followed in the steps of the minister, performing for every president since Truman until his death in 2013. Both men were also awarded the Presidential Medal of Freedom during separate ceremonies held at the White House.

JULY 15

THE "RIGHT" HANDED GUN

On the afternoon of July 15, 1881, the body of the infamous gunfighter Billy the Kid (birth name William Henry McCarty Jr.) was placed in a hastily constructed wooden casket and interred at the Fort Sumner military cemetery in the New Mexico Territory. He had been killed the previous evening by Lincoln County sheriff Pat Garrett who was seeking to collect a $500 reward which had been posted by the governor.

There are many stories about the notorious outlaw being left-handed. Hollywood was among those that bought into the tale by producing a film about McCarty in 1958 titled, *The Left Handed Gun.*

But not many in Tinseltown knew about tintypes, an early form of photography that used metal plates. They resulted in reverse images, and the famous Billy the Kid tintype that appears in most books has led to the mistaken belief that the outlaw was a pistol packin' southpaw while, in reality, he was actually a right-hander.

In the summer of 2011, that much-seen tintype was sold at an auction in Denver to private collector William Koch for $2.3 million.

JULY 16

BLAST OFF!

Alabama became the nation's twenty-second state on December 14, 1819. It is located on the Gulf of Mexico and was the starting point to the Moon.

On this day in 1969, astronauts Neil Armstrong, Buzz Aldrin, and Michael Collins blasted off in their Apollo 11 spacecraft from the Kennedy Space Center in Florida. Five days later, pilots Armstrong and Aldrin became the first human beings to walk on the lunar surface. They spent a total of 21 1/2 hours trekking the celestial body.

But few knew as they watched the star voyagers on television that Alabama played an important role in the historic mission. The rocket that launched Apollo 11 into space was known as the *Saturn V*. It was built at the Marshall Space Flight Center in Huntsville, Alabama.

The *Saturn V* was used by the national space agency, also known as NASA, for six years (1967–1973) with great success. The rocket helped launch six more missions to the Moon along with its final task of sending the *Skylab* space station into orbit. To this day, no country other than the United States has ever sent astronauts to the Moon.

While many know about the famous space centers in Florida and Texas, Alabama has also played an important part of traveling into the great beyond.

JULY 17

THE SWAMP KINGDOM

The original Disneyland theme park opened on this day in 1955. But where did Walt Disney come up with the idea for the world's most spectacular attraction? His father, Elias, was a professional carpenter by trade who, among other things, worked on the construction site of the 1893 Chicago World's Fair. He told his son about his experiences at the exposition and Walt never forgot those stories.

The youngster dreamed of one day building his own amusement park that could be open all year. Disneyland was the culmination of that dream.

Shortly after Disney opened his first theme park in Anaheim, California, he turned his attention to Florida. It would be bigger, more expansive, and known as Disney World. A study conducted in the late 1950s indicated that less than 5 percent of Disneyland's visitors were from the eastern half of the United States while 75 percent of the population resided there. Those numbers told the visionary all he needed to know but there was just one problem, he didn't own any land east of the Mississippi.

By the fall of 1964, rumors began to circulate about tracts being bought up in southwestern Orange and adjacent Osceola Counties. The early purchases came cheap at about $80 an acre but as the word spread, prices climbed. Through the process, Disney kept his identity a secret, hiding behind his shell companies. But by the spring of 1965, stories rumbled through the Sunshine State that Mickey Mouse's creator was the driving force behind the land grab.

In the 1960s, Orlando was far from the bustling hub that it is today. In fact, it was surrounded by a massive swamp where alligators roamed freely among the overgrown territory. Historically, the area had served as an encampment for soldiers during the Seminole Indian Wars of the 1830s.

By the time that the official press conference was held on November 15, 1965, Disney, through his dummy corporations, had purchased some 30,000 acres. As prices skyrocketed amid the rumors, the company was forced to pay a premium for the final few parcels, spending as much as $80,000 an acre.

The massive project proceeded and Disney World opened on October 1, 1971, but its namesake was not among the masses who attended the gathering. Walt Disney, the driving force behind the fantasy, died five years before the opening.

JULY 18

WELCOME TO THE CLUB

During the 2016 presidential debates, much was made by the Democratic nominee Hillary Rodham Clinton about Donald Trump's business practices and his history of bankruptcies. In true political form, her opponent attempted to explain the shortcomings as he proudly stated during interviews, "What I've done is I've used, brilliantly, the laws of the country . . . And if you look at people like myself that are at the highest levels of business, they use— many of them have done it, many times."

It began on this day in 1991 when the Trump Organization filed the first of six separate bankruptcies on its casino properties in Atlantic City. While the former president's losses came on the business side of his life, several of his predecessors suffered through some tough financial times on a personal basis.

Among the familiar names of that group were Thomas Jefferson, James Monroe, William Henry Harrison, Abraham Lincoln, Ulysses S. Grant, William McKinley, and Harry Truman who each dealt with significant money woes at some point in their lives.

While the words between the candidates were heated in 2016, it wasn't always that way. In January 2005, Trump married fashion model and businesswoman Melania Knauss. Among the guests at their wedding was Hillary Rodham Clinton.

JULY 19

MORE HOT AIR

Even though they may not agree, the French don't have a monopoly on the subject of hot-air ballooning. That's because Maryland can also claim some unique history when it comes to riding an inflatable across the sky.

In June 1784, Peter Carnes, a Bladensburg lawyer, innkeeper, and thrill seeker built a hot-air balloon from the original concept launched by France's Montgolfier brothers a year earlier. It was 35 feet in diameter, 30 feet tall, and carried just one passenger, 13-year-old Edward Warren.

The boy had volunteered to ride in the tethered apparatus over Baltimore's Howard Park. Surrounded by spectators and much hoopla, Warren became the first American to travel via hot-air balloon.

On this day in 1784, Carnes, who also ran the Indian Queen Tavern in Bladensburg, wanted to take his own ride in order to demonstrate his own flier and decided to make Philadelphia's Walnut Street Prison yard his takeoff point. He charged admission to view the event as the high walls prevented spectators from getting a free look.

The balloon rose to about 20 feet over the correctional facility before the tethers snapped sending the 230-pound pilot back to the ground, shaken but uninjured. Carnes landed in the prison yard as the balloon went adrift, eventually catching fire with its remaining pieces falling back to Earth. The demonstration brought an end to Carnes' ballooning career.

He moved to Georgia where he bought more than 1,100 acres in the town of Franklin. In 1791, Carnes was one of the privileged few who rode out on the Savannah Road to meet and welcome president George Washington to Augusta.

In 1794, the first American balloon maker died at the age of 45.

JULY 20

A ROCKY ROAD

On this day in 1969, astronauts Neil Armstrong and Buzz Aldrin, scoured the surface of the Moon collecting soil samples. Since these specimens had never been in the presence of earthlings, they were commonly referred to as "Moon rocks."

When the *Apollo* crew accomplished history's initial lunar landing, geologists were excited about seeing the first rocks following their return from the space frontier. The samples turned out to be similar to those known on earth as gabbros and anorthosites which were comparable to findings in Duluth, Minnesota, and breccias from the celestial impacts at Meteor Crater, Arizona.

Detailed study of the "Moon rocks" did find a new mineral that was named armalcolite. The moniker was derived from the first letters of the names of the *Apollo 11* astronauts (Armstrong, Aldrin, and Collins). The mineral had never been found on Earth although it is easy to overlook.

But, not long after its discovery among the Moon rocks, armalcolite was found in several "Earth rocks." It turned up in igneous dikes at Smoky Butte in Garfield County, Montana.

Although this find will not produce gorgeous specimens for the collector, it is important in that it shows that the same chemical and physical processes that formed the rocks of the Moon and meteorites are the same ones we see on Earth.

JULY 21

CHEATING THE REAPER

It is said that a cat has nine lives. However, could a man have five? Ernest Hemingway ranks among the greatest authors of all time; he was awarded the Nobel Prize in Literature (1954) and the Pulitzer Prize for Fiction (1953). Among his masterpieces of must reads are *The Sun Also Rises* (1926); *A Farewell to Arms* (1929); *To Have and Have Not* (1937); *For Whom the Bell Tolls* (1940); and *The Old Man and the Sea* (1952).

However, there were five occasions where it appeared that the adventurous writer had penned his final page, as he found himself in near-death situations. Here's how the novelist cheated the Grim Reaper:

1. During World War I, Hemingway served on the Italian front lines as an ambulance driver with the Red Cross. On July 8, 1918, his vehicle was struck by an Austrian mortar shell. The 18-year-old emerged with 237 bits of shrapnel (by his own count), an aluminum kneecap, and two Italian decorations.

   His experiences provided the background for his first best-selling novel, *A Farewell to Arms.*

2. A lover of deep-sea fishing, In April 1935, Hemingway accidentally shot himself in the calves of both legs while wrangling a shark. The incident took place while he was attempting to gaff the sea creature during a fishing trip off Key West.

3. In 1942 and 1943 during World War II, Hemingway spent less time writing and more time pursuing the Hun. He stayed busy scouring the Atlantic for German U-boats aboard his 38-foot wooden fishing craft, armed with a variety of explosives. Luckily, there were no confrontations.

   Hemingway became a war correspondent for *Collier's* magazine in 1944 and landed on Omaha Beach in the seventh wave of D-Day.

   In June 1947, at the US embassy in Cuba, the celebrated author was awarded a Bronze Star for his service as a war correspondent for having circulated "freely under fire in combat areas in order to obtain an accurate picture of conditions."

4. On January 23, 1954, a single-engine Cessna carrying Hemingway and his wife crashed near Africa's Murchison Falls when the pilot attempted an emergency landing to avoid hitting a flock of ibises. The trio was forced to spend the night in the jungle surrounded by elephants. The couple had been visiting on safari.

5. The following day, the Hemingways were transported to Butiaba where they boarded another small plane which crashed at the end of the runway upon takeoff and caught fire. Both were seriously injured but, along with the pilot, were able to get to safety. The writer walked out of the jungle saying, "My luck, she is running very good."

Ernest Hemingway was born on this day in 1899.

JULY 22

KEEPING THE BEAT

Millions of people around the world wear a device known as a "pacemaker" in order to regulate their heartbeat. What most of them don't know is that the contraption which is keeping them alive was created by fluke.

In 1956, Wilson Greatbatch was an assistant professor of electrical engineering at the University of Buffalo. While building a heart rhythm recording device for the city's Chronic Disease Research Institute, he reached into a box of parts for a resistor to complete the circuitry. The one he pulled out was the wrong size and when he installed it, the circuit it produced emitted intermittent electrical pulses.

Two years later, Greatbatch used his error to design the first practical implantable pacemaker in his barn in Clarence, New York. When he died in 2011 at age 92, the inventor had become a billionaire with nearly 350 patents. But on this day in 1960, Wilson Greatbatch filed his copyright application for the human cardiac pacemaker.

JULY 23

THE IMPOSSIBLE DREAM

On this day in 1958, the first nuclear-powered submarine the USS *Nautilus* departed Pearl Harbor, Hawaii, under top secret orders to conduct *Operation Sunshine*, the first crossing of the North Pole by a ship.

At 11:15 p.m. on August 3, 1958, *Nautilaus'* second commanding officer, William R. Anderson, announced to his crew, "For the world, our country, and the Navy—the North Pole." With 116 men aboard, the underwater vessel accomplished the "impossible" by reaching the geographic North Pole—90 degrees north.

JULY 24

LOW TECH IN SPACE

Each year, millions of dollars are spent on America's space program. Some of the best and brightest are employed to make sure that things run smoothly whenever the United States journeys into the great beyond. However, sometimes all of that accumulated knowledge can't replace a simple household object when it comes to solving a problem.

It is not unusual for a circuit breaker to go off at a house, casting everything into darkness. Fortunately, all that is needed is to flip a switch and everything returns to normal. But in July 1969, when the lights went out while *Apollo 11* was on the Moon, it could have been a disaster. One of the astronauts knocked loose the circuit breaker responsible for igniting the engine that was needed to propel them back to the orbiting command module, which was their only ride home.

In a very non-high-tech maneuver, copilot Buzz Aldrin used a felt-tip pen to push the breaker back into place. On this occasion, the astronaut found that his doctor of science degree from the Massachusetts Institute of Technology (MIT) wasn't necessary in resolving the situation.

Because of Aldrin's problem-solving skill, *Apollo 11* safely splashed down in the Pacific Ocean on planet Earth on this day in 1969.

JULY 25

RUNNING MATES

At the thirty-first Democratic National Convention in Chicago, the party nominated senator John J. Sparkman of Alabama on this day in 1952 for vice president on the ticket headed by governor Adlai E. Stevenson of Illinois. But that wasn't the only news surrounding the possibilities for the second spot.

Two women—India Edwards, the vice chairperson of the Democratic National Committee, and Sarah Hughes, Texas' first female district court judge, were each suggested as potential VP candidates but both withdrew their names before the balloting began.

However, on November 22, 1963, Judge Hughes once again found herself as part of a presidential storyline as she delivered the oath of office to fellow Texan Lyndon B. Johnson just two hours (2:38 p.m. CST) after President Kennedy's assassination.

JULY 26

THE FRENCH CONNECTION

In the greatest real estate deal in the young nation's history, the United States bought the Louisiana Territory from France and their cash-strapped emperor Napoleon Bonaparte for $15 million. Following his final defeat at Waterloo in 1815, the Frenchman was exiled to the desolate island of St. Helena where he lived for six years before succumbing to the ravages of cancer. During his banishment, there was no shortage of plots by various individuals and groups to secure his escape although none ever took place.

However, there was a family member who did make it to freedom. His older brother Joseph-Napoleon Bonaparte lived for a time in the United States. He initially resided in New York City and then Philadelphia but later moved to Bordentown, New Jersey, near the Delaware River. Joseph was the former King of Spain who was said to have brought along a fortune with him.

Another Bonaparte brother, Lucien, attempted to flee to America in 1810 but was captured at sea by the British and incarcerated in England.

Napoleon I wasn't the only family member to leave his mark on United States history. His grandnephew Charles Bonaparte became attorney general and, on this day in 1906, he founded the FBI.

JULY 27

THE WRIGHT STUFF

On this day in 1909, Orville Wright set a world record for staying aloft in an airplane—1 hour, 12 minutes, and 40 seconds. This was just six years after he and his brother Wilbur flew the world's first successful motor-operated aircraft. That flight lasted only 12 seconds.

JULY 28

IT FEELS LIKE HOME

Richard Nixon resigned the presidency in 1974 and returned home to Casa Pacifica, his beach estate in San Clemente, California. But five years later, the former commander in chief was seeking to move back to New York City where he had resided from 1963 to 1969. On July 28, 1979, the New York Times reported that the ex-president had put down a deposit on a $750,000, nine-room penthouse at 72nd Street and Madison Avenue. (In 2022, the property was estimated to be worth between $10–$11 million.)

The seven-member committee had informally approved the sale but that was before the building's co-op board began getting an earful. At the time, Nixon was still smarting from the Watergate scandal and when the shareholders found out that their new tenants would bring notoriety to the exclusive high-rise, along with distractions from a Secret Service detail, they quickly balked at the agreement. One week later, the one-time First Family agreed to break their deal. For those who felt betrayed by Nixon's White House actions, it was their method of enacting a semblance of revenge.

From there, the Nixons purchased a townhouse on East 65th Street, where they lived for less than three years. In 1981, they bought a million-dollar country home on four acres in Saddle River, New Jersey. They sold the estate in 1990 for $2.4 million. After moving to another residence in New Jersey, the former chief executive died in 1994.

JULY 29

THE SPY WHO FOUND HER WAY

Isabella "Belle" Boyd was born in 1844 in Martinsburg, Virginia. As a teenager during the Civil War, she was one of the Confederacy's top spies providing information on the enemy to some of the South's most prominent generals such as Thomas "Stonewall" Jackson.

She was finally captured by Union officials on July 29, 1862, and exchanged a month later. In March 1864, Boyd attempted to travel to England but was intercepted by a Union blockade and banished to Canada where she met and married a Union naval officer.

In 1866, following the war, the mismatched couple finally made it to Europe where her husband died shortly afterward. Boyd became a celebrity in the British theater where she told stories of her wartime exploits. Yearning for home, she and her daughter returned to the United States in 1869.

That same year, the one-time Rebel spy married John Swainston Hammond, an Englishman who, like her first husband, had also fought for the Union Army. Unfortunately, her life from that point was filled with difficulties resulting in a divorce and financial hardship.

When she died destitute in 1900 at the age of 56, it was Union veterans, her former enemies, who paid for Belle's funeral where six of them served as her pallbearers.

JULY 30

VOTE FOR FORD

Happy Birthday to Henry Ford who was born on this day in 1863 in Springwells Township, Michigan.

He was best known for his creation of the Model T automobile and the advancements with the assembly line. However there was another side to the inventor as in 1916, he threw his support behind incumbent president Woodrow Wilson, hoping he would maintain his promise to keep the country out of the war in Europe.

That wasn't to be as the United States was eventually part of World War I, although Ford didn't get hurt by the conflict, in fact far from it. By 1918, his net worth was $100 million ($1.2 billion in today's money).

JULY 31

DREAMING BIG

On July 31, 1971, astronaut Jim Irwin became the eighth human being to walk on the surface of the Moon. During his time on the lunar surface, he conducted experiments and collected samples along with his fellow space travelers David Scott and Al Worden. Each was a member of the US Air Force.

Irwin retired from the space program the following year but his quest for new adventures was not done.

In 1973, fueled by his creationist beliefs, the one-time air force colonel found himself on Mount Ararat, hunting for the legendary Noah's Ark on the first of several missions to eastern Turkey. Irwin nearly lost his life on the treacherous mountain terrain after being badly injured by falling rocks in 1982. He was carried to safety by a donkey.

In all, Irwin was involved in six expeditions during his unsuccessful quest for remnants of the biblical vessel. He went on to become a minister before passing away at the age of 61 in 1991 due to heart complications.

AUGUST

It is not often that nations learn from the past, even rarer that they draw the correct conclusions from it.

—Dr. Henry Kissinger, US Secretary of State (1973–1977)

AUGUST 1

SADDLE UP

On this day in 1876, Colorado became the nation's thirty-eighth state. It is also the home of the first rodeo.

On the 4th of July in 1869, the inaugural organized event where cowboys won prizes for displaying their skills took place in the town of Deer Creek. It was not called a rodeo at that time but was referred to as a "bronco busting contest."

However, even though it was held on Independence Day, the champion of that first competition was not an American. He was an Englishman with the sophisticated name of Emilnie Gardenshire, who was a cowboy for the Mill Iron Ranch. He rode a wild bronco named Montana Blizzard to win the championship. His prize was a new set of clothes.

While many people enjoy skiing and watching Broncos football, rodeo is still a major event in Colorado. Every January, the state's capital city of Denver hosts the National Western Stock Show that features the world's top riders and animals.

AUGUST 2

I DO NOT CHOOSE TO RUN

In the twenty-first century, there never seems to be a shortage of presidential candidates, as fundraising seasons get longer with each election cycle. On August 2, 1927, during a vacation at the "Summer White House" in the Black Hills of South Dakota, president Calvin Coolidge stepped outside to address a gaggle of reporters and clearly stated, "I do not choose to run for president in nineteen-twenty-eight. There will be nothing more from this office today."

And there wasn't. He didn't discuss it with the press corps and took no questions. At 11:30 a.m., the man known as Silent Cal simply turned around and walked back inside his house, beginning his return to private citizenship and leaving the media to figure it all out under the warm South Dakota sun. Later that day, his wife was informed of his decision by a visiting senator.

AUGUST 3

GATHER AROUND THE LANTERN

John Coolidge was not a man for his times. He was born in 1845 and grew up in an era before there was electricity in homes when people got to where they were going on foot, by wagon, or on horseback. He was raised on a farm in Plymouth Notch, Vermont, away from the growing eastern cities like New York and Boston and the new technologies of the twentieth century. During the Civil War, young John had risen to the rank of captain in the Vermont militia.

Coolidge was a man who knew both sides of work. He had done hard labor as a blacksmith and woodcutter in addition to white-collar duties as a banker and insurance broker. The native-born Republican had also served terms in Vermont's House of Representatives and State Senate. Coolidge was a commissioned aide-de-camp on the staff of Vermont governor William W. Stickney with the rank of colonel, and he was usually addressed as such by others.

The colonel had turned his back on the modern conveniences of the 1920s, as the home that his family had occupied since 1876 had no telephone or electricity. But on Friday August 3, 1923, the twentieth century arrived at his doorstep in the form of a messenger who had ended up there due to a series of events that began on the other side of the continent.

At around 8:00 p.m. eastern standard time, presidential secretary (today's equivalent to the chief of staff) George Christian, who was traveling with the chief executive in San Francisco, dispatched a message to vice president Calvin Coolidge, who was vacationing at his father's homestead. The notification stated that president Warren Harding had died from an unknown illness during his cross-country tour. The telegram reached the only Western Union office still open near Plymouth Notch—at White River Junction, Vermont—at 10:30 p.m. The White River operator did not know about the lone telephone in Plymouth Notch, so he called the message into the telephone exchange at Bridgewater, ten miles from the Coolidges' tiny village.

Bridgewater's telephone operator, scribbled down the information, cranked up his Model T Ford, and then headed out over the unpaved River Road to personally deliver Christian's important wire. Once it arrived, Colonel Coolidge awoke his son, addressing him as "Mr. President," then handed him the telegram. He and his wife Grace dressed and proceeded downstairs as a small crowd of witnesses and reporters began to arrive.

The vice president then turned to his friend, congressman Porter Dale, and asked, "Do you think my father, as Notary Public, has the authority to administer the oath to me?" It was an interesting request, as no previous president had ever been sworn in by a family member.

The soon-to-be commander in chief of the nation went across the road to the general store to use the nearest telephone and discuss the matter via long distance with secretary of state Charles Evans Hughes, a former presidential candidate, who was in Washington, DC. He stated, "It should be taken before a notary," and then approved the vice president's choice of the senior Coolidge. It was Hughes who dictated the oath of office to Coolidge's secretary.

Prior to the swearing in, the vice president sat at the desk where, as a boy, he completed his homework but in the early hours of August 3, he penned a note of condolence to Mrs. Harding. His father, who was a justice of the peace as well as a Windsor County notary, then administered the oath of office to his 51-year-old son in front of a kerosene lamp, making him the thirtieth president of the United States. His mother had died when he was just twelve, but he used her Bible for the ceremony. It was 2:47 a.m.

A short while later, the Coolidges returned upstairs to bed while a telephone lineman arrived to install a communications device with a line running through the kitchen window. Hours afterward, the new president and First Lady departed for Washington. Once his son had left the premises, the senior Coolidge ordered the telephone removed. Soon afterward, the press, the officials, and spectators were also gone and the old colonel comfortably returned to his nineteenth-century lifestyle.

Years after the event, the family patriarch was asked why he presumed to have the authority to administer the oath to his son to which he replied, "Nobody told me I couldn't."

AUGUST 4

THE IRON CROSS

There is no shortage of examples of the evils carried out by German dictator Adolf Hitler. His victims numbered in the millions of men, women, children, and the elderly. He ruled using fear and intimidating measures.

If there was one area where Hitler proved to be effective, it was on the battlefield during World War I. After being rejected by his home country of Austria, the young man who had originally yearned to be an artist enlisted in the German army. He was immediately accepted, as the authorities of Deutschland were desperate for anyone who could tolerate the horrible battle-field conditions and tote a rifle.

He not only proved to be an adequate soldier but an exceptional one when, in December 1914, Hitler received one of Germany's highest military hon-ors—the Iron Cross, second class, for bravery. In a letter to a friend, he wrote: "It was the happiest day of my life."

In April 1918, half of Hitler's regiment was wounded or killed during attacks, but he survived. Displaying his combat prowess, on this day of that year, the lance corporal received his second decoration of the Iron Cross (this time first class). A double honoree of the award was a rare achievement in German military annals.

The person who recommended Hitler for the second medal was his supe-rior officer, lieutenant Hugo Gutmann. Over the years, the recipient continued to proudly wear the decoration when he became the chancellor of Germany and throughout World War II.

Gutmann, who praised the Austrian reject, was a Jew who, like so many of his culture, was arrested by Hitler's Gestapo in 1938 but was released the fol-lowing year. In 1940, he and his family left Germany to escape the country's rampant anti-Semitism and emigrated to the land of one of his World War I enemies—the United States.

AUGUST 5

SPACE JUNK

Happy Birthday to Neil Armstrong, the first human being to walk on the Moon, who was born on this day in 1930. After becoming the most famous space traveler of all time, he died in 2012. It was announced in 2015 that the astronaut's widow Carol discovered several artifacts from her husband's lone lunar journey in a closet in their Cincinnati home. The items that were located in a white stowage bag included a camera that was mounted in the window of the Eagle lunar module, used to record the landing, along with two waist tethers.

During the journey, Armstrong described the objects to fellow Apollo 11 astronaut Michael Collins as "just a bunch of trash that we want to take back—LM parts, odds and ends." The items were donated to the Smithsonian Institute's National Air and Space Museum.

AUGUST 6

NO ONE WILL EVER BUY BOTTLED WATER!

In 2020, bottled water accounted for roughly 24 percent of total beverage consumption in the United States, making it the most-favorite type of beverage that year. To say that bottled water in the United States is a real money-maker would be accurate.

But even so, the natural swill of the Earth has been available for sale for quite some time. On August 6, 1767, an article in an issue of the *Massachusetts Gazette* of Jackson (MA) first specified the rates for enjoying the planet's natural elixir: one copper for "the Use of the Water" and then another copper for "every Quart Bottle to carry away."

That was long before the days of flavorings and recyclable plastic bottles. Today, water remains the world's most-favorite bottled beverage.

AUGUST 7

FACE THE MUSIC

Presidential campaigns are known for using music to inspire their crowds. George Washington was the first to utilize the strategy with the tune, *God Save Great Washington* which was a play on the British standard, *God Save the King*. Apparently the Father of the Country believed that if you defeat a nation in battle, then you can use their music when running for office.

Still the One is a song that was cowritten by the husband and wife team of John and Johanna Hall and was recorded by the group Orleans. On this day in 1976, it reached No. 5 on the Billboard Hot 100.

In late October 2004, George W. Bush was using the tune without permission during stops on his reelection campaign. John Hall, an ardent Democrat, disapproved of the action and sent the president a cease-and-desist notice, which remedied the matter. The songwriter eventually became part of his own campaign as he was elected to the US House of Representatives from New York's nineteenth district in 2006.

In 2008, Hall expressed similar displeasure toward Republican John McCain's campaign, which was also using the song without permission. They later dropped it from their playlist but that wasn't the end of the candidate's music problems.

That same year, the campaign became the target of recording artist Jackson Browne when it was discovered that the GOP nominee had been using his 1977 hit, "Running on Empty," at rallies. The singer/songwriter, a well-known liberal activist, filed suit against the McCain campaign and won an undisclosed settlement along with a public apology from the candidate.

There was also Bon Jovi, who issued a disapproving statement about McCain's camp for the unapproved use of the song, *Who Says You Can't Go Home*, although no legal action was taken and usage continued unabated.

AUGUST 8

GO BIG BLUE!!!

The University of Michigan has produced its fair share of notable individuals such as actor James Earl Jones, playwright Arthur Miller, and former president Gerald Ford along with a large ensemble of scholars and professional athletes. But it has also sent a respectable contingent of its graduates and attendees to a place where few have journeyed—outer space.

There has been no shortage of Wolverine alumni who have traveled to the great beyond and, in a couple of cases, they made up the entire flight crew.

The first came in June 1965 when Jim McDivitt, Class of 1959 (who graduated first in his class), and Ed White, also Class of 1959 (who earned an MS degree), made up the two-man team for *Gemini IV*. They tested the effects of space travel during their four days in orbit. White also accomplished the first US spacewalk. Tragically, he was one of the three astronauts killed (along with Gus Grissom and Roger Chaffee) in a fire during a test of the *Apollo 1* spacecraft in 1967.

The next all-Michigan lineup was aboard *Apollo 15* in the summer of 1971. It was the fourth mission to the Moon and had its share of firsts, including the initial walk into deep space, the introduction of a lunar rover to explore the Moon's surface, and the original satellite deployment by a crewed spacecraft.

The three-man unit of David Scott, who attended University of Michigan (UM) in 1949–1950; James Irwin (also see *July 31*), Class of 1957 (MS degree); and Alfred Worden, who attended UM in 1950–1951, spent 66 hours and 55 minutes conducting a series of experiments and collecting samples from the lunar surface. There were two more missions to the Moon after *Apollo 15*.

On this day in 1971, the crew members departed the recovery ship the USS *Okinawa* and were flown to Hickam Air Force Base in Hawaii to begin their post-flight assignments.

It was traditional that on each of the six Moon landings (*Apollo 13* was unable to land), an American flag was planted on the lunar surface. However, for years, there were stories that the crew of *Apollo 15* had made a switch and instead stationed a University of Michigan flag in its place. The rumor was untrue.

AUGUST 9

THE HIGHEST OFFICE

On this day in 1974, former president Richard Nixon and his wife Pat boarded the official presidential helicopter *Marine One* for the short flight from the White House to Andrews Air Force Base where they were soon bound for their home in southern California. In a seven-month period, Nixon and former vice president Spiro Agnew had both been expelled from the two highest positions in the federal government.

AUGUST 10

THE OTHER SIDE OF THE STORY

Happy Birthday to Herbert Hoover who was born on this day in 1874 and went down in history as one of America's most ineffective presidents. Whether that criticism was warranted is debatable, being that he was in office during the Great Depression, his tenure was a clear example of being in the wrong place at the wrong time.

The fact that often gets lost in the Hoover story is that he and his wife Lou were benevolent philanthropists. An example of that came in 1900 in China during the Boxer Rebellion.

While working as the lead engineer in China for Bewick, Moreing & Co., a private London-based mining firm, the Hoovers found themselves in the middle of the uprising which besieged 800 westerners in the city of Tianjin (formerly known as Tientsin). While under heavy fire, the Stanford graduate directed the creation of barricades, risked his life to save innocent Chinese children who were caught in the crossfire, and organized relief efforts for trapped foreigners. Meanwhile the future First Lady spent time assisting at local hospitals.

Hoover's humanitarian efforts continued in 1914 while he was in London when Germany declared war on France, which marked the initial steps toward World War I. The American consul general asked the future president to aid in the effort to bring stranded American tourists home. Hoover and his team successfully returned 120,000 Americans to the United States.

In 1920, the assistant secretary of the Navy wrote this about Herbert Hoover, "He is certainly a wonder, and I wish we could make him President of the United States. There could not be a better one."

Hoover was elected to the office in 1928, but he was defeated after just one term. The candidate who beat him was the same person who had written those glowing words—Franklin D. Roosevelt.

AUGUST 11

DR. WALKER—PLEASE REPORT

On this date in 1864, Dr. Mary Walker was serving her final full day as a prisoner of war. She had been held since April 10, 1864, in Richmond, Virginia.

In 1855, she earned her medical degree at Syracuse Medical College in upstate New York, becoming the nation's second female physician. Dr. Walker attempted to join the Union Army at the outbreak of the Civil War but was denied. She served as a surgeon at a temporary hospital in Washington, DC, before being hired by federal forces and assigned to the Army of the Cumberland and later the 52nd Ohio Infantry, becoming the first female surgeon in the US Army.

The New York native treated wounded soldiers at the First Battle of Bull Run in Virginia, as well as at the conflicts at Fredericksburg, Chickamauga, Richmond, and Atlanta. Dr. Walker became the first and only woman to receive the Medal of Honor and only one of eight civilians to receive the award.

Walker was exchanged for a Confederate surgeon from Tennessee on August 12, 1864.

AUGUST 12

THE OTHER NO-FLY LIST

Whenever travelers are flying to a destination, there are certain protocols that are carried out as part of the required safety measures. Those practices include having passengers and baggage scanned in addition to requiring the use of seat belts and other preventive equipment.

Even with all of the precautions, there is one famous family that has had more than its fair share of bad luck in the friendly skies. The Kennedys are best known as a power in politics, along with being one of the nation's wealthiest bloodlines.

However, if one should ever find themselves aboard the same flight as one of the well-known family members, it might be advisable to check into a refund for that ticket. That's because the old clan out of Boston has had many instances of bad luck when it comes to air travel.

* It began on August 12, 1944, during World War II when President Kennedy's older brother Joe Jr., who served in the military, was killed during a bombing run over England. It was scheduled to be his final mission before returning home.

* Three years later on May 13, 1948, JFK's sister Kathleen Kennedy Cavendish, who was known as "Kick," was killed in a plane crash over France. Her husband, the Marquess of Hartington, died at the hands of a German sniper four years prior during World War II.

* Robert Kennedy's in-laws, Ann and George Skakel, were killed in a private plane crash near Union City, Oklahoma, on October 3, 1955. Kennedy was assassinated by a gunman while running for president in 1968.

* On June 19, 1964, JFK's younger brother US senator Ted Kennedy was almost killed in a private plane crash near Southampton, Massachusetts. He spent five months in the hospital being treated for internal injuries.

* On July 16, 1999, John F. Kennedy Jr., his wife Carolyn, and sister-in-law Lauren Bessette were killed in a private plane being piloted by the former president's son. The investigation determined that he was not cleared for instrument flying, as the party was traveling at night from New York City to Hyannis Port.

While luck had its back to them, the odds were actually on the side of the Kennedy family members, as the chances of being involved in a plane crash are one in 11 million and the chances of becoming president and the odds of being related to a US president are one in 132 million.

AUGUST 13

DNA DOESN'T LIE

The private lives of many of America's presidents have made for some interesting reading over the years. Beginning with George Washington and up to the twenty-first century, there has been no shortage of stories—some true, some not—about the romantic adventures of the nation's commanders in chief.

Perhaps no president has been more scrutinized when it comes to relationships than Warren Harding who was in office for just two years, 1921–1923. Of his many female conquests, the one that drew the most notoriety was Nan Britton, a secretary who was thirty-one years his junior.

Following Harding's untimely death in 1923, Britton penned her 1927 autobiography *The President's Daughter.* In it, she detailed her six-year relationship with the married chief executive that she claimed produced a daughter, Elizabeth. Harding never saw the child but made generous child support payments that were hand-delivered by the Secret Service.

Britton's story made her the target of public ridicule and denials by the president's family members and friends. She died in 1991 at the age of 94 and Elizabeth passed in 2005 at age 86.

It took many decades, but on this day in 2015, the women were vindicated as DNA testing confirmed that president Warren Harding was Elizabeth's father. It was proven by using testing samples from descendants of Harding's brother and Britton's grandchildren.

AUGUST 14

A FAVORITE SON CANDIDATE

A US senator represents the individual state from which they were elected. However, that definition doesn't tell the story of former senator James Shields. He not only represented his state . . . he represented his states. Shields still holds a senatorial record that might never be broken.

After serving in the Mexican-American War, on this day in 1848, he was nominated by president James K. Polk, and confirmed by the US Senate to serve as governor of the Oregon Territory that was created on the same day. However, he declined the position in order to run for the Senate seat from Illinois.

His election was voided by the Senate on the grounds that he had not been a US citizen for the nine years, which was constitutionally required. In 1826, 16-year-old Shields had immigrated to the United States from Ireland. But he had been naturalized on October 21, 1840, and returned to Illinois where he campaigned for reelection. Shields won the special election to replace himself and was then seated.

In 1855, he was defeated for reelection in Illinois, so he moved to Minnesota. The vagabond politician was then elected as one of the first two senators from that state, but his term was only from 1858 to 1859, and, once again, he was not reelected.

In 1863, Shields relocated to Mexico where he operated mines before moving on to Wisconsin. However, in 1866, he landed in Missouri where he served as a member of the State House of Representatives and as railroad commissioner. In 1879, Shields was elected to fill the seat left vacant by the death of senator Lewis V. Bogy. He served only three months and declined to run for reelection.

Shields passed away just three months after leaving office, but Missouri wasn't his final move as he died in Ottumwa, Iowa. To this day, and probably forever, James Shields is the only person to serve as a US senator from three different states.

AUGUST 15

THE MAN FROM OKLAHOMA

In the 1930s, humorist/actor Will Rogers was one of the most recognized people on Earth and a favorite among Depression-worn Americans. He was so beloved that in 1932, the Oklahoma (Indian Territory) native spoke at both the Democratic and Republican National Conventions. He was also an aviation enthusiast and a strong supporter of air travel.

Rogers believed in the future advances of air travel but never lived to see it. On August 15, 1935, along with record-setting pilot and good friend Wiley Post, the celebrity pundit was killed in a plane crash near Point Barrow, Alaska. The pair were held in such high regard that president Franklin Roosevelt dispatched famed aviator Charles Lindbergh to the northern frontier to supervise the recovery of their bodies.

Today, each man has an airport named in his honor in Oklahoma City. Rogers' last film, *In Old Kentucky*, was released three months after his death.

AUGUST 16

NOW, OPEN WIDE

Clay Allison was a hard-drinking gunman during the days of the Old West who was known to have killed at least four people. But perhaps the most unlikely event took place during an encounter where no weapons were fired.

On August 16, 1874, Allison arrived in the town of Cheyenne in the Wyoming Territory. He had a painful toothache and soon made his way to the local dentist who immediately pulled the problem chomper. Unfortunately, it was the wrong tooth at which point Allison went about to even the score.

Grabbing a pair of forceps, the gunman proceeded to pull several of the dentist's teeth. It was definitely a bad day to be a tooth doctor in Cheyenne.

AUGUST 17

ON THE MOVE

On December 24, 1865, the Ku Klux Klan was founded by a group of Confederate veterans in Pulaski, Tennessee. It was created as an opposition group to the federal government's Reconstruction policies. Originally, most of the Klan's activities were limited to regions in the southern states.

However, by the 1920s, the group had spread its message of segregation into other areas as far away as New England. One such rally took place on August 17, 1923, where an estimated 1,000 white men and women participated in a KKK initiation ceremony just outside of Warwick, New York. Beginning at 9:00 p.m. the previous evening, the large crowd arrived for the function at an open field near the highway where they heard speeches against interracial marriage and viewed the burning of a cross more than 20 feet tall. The meeting lasted until the early hours of the morning.

Two years later, the Klan staged a massive demonstration down Pennsylvania Avenue in Washington, DC, where participant estimates numbered as high as 50,000. But by 2021, the group's messages of division had become old and tiresome and with that, their overall numbers shrank to about 3,000.

AUGUST 18

THE SOUND OF MUSIC

Among the events that New York is known for, it is also the home of the largest and most famous rock concert in American history. The Woodstock Music and Art Fair was held on a sprawling dairy farm in the tiny upstate town of Bethel. The enormous production, attended by an estimated 400,000 spectators, took place on August 15–18, 1969.

Some of the biggest names of the era in rock music appeared at Woodstock, including Jimi Hendrix, the Grateful Dead, The Who, Janis Joplin, and Jefferson Airplane. In all, thirty-two acts took the stage in an event that featured peaceful protests about the United States' involvement in the Vietnam War.

For that weekend of the festival, Bethel became the third largest city in New York State, as its regular population of just over 2,700 swelled to nearly a half-million. Those conditions coupled with a constant rainstorm forced one group of onlookers to forward a petition to declare a state of emergency in Sullivan County to governor Nelson Rockefeller.

The National Guard and Civil Defense Department helicoptered food and water to the attendees. Fifty doctors were airlifted to the grounds and established a quasi-MASH unit. They treated 5,000 cases of which more than 400 were drug related. There were two deaths, one from a drug overdose, the other was an individual who was accidentally run over while sleeping under a tractor. There were four miscarriages but also reports that as many as three healthy babies were born.

A 1970 documentary film of the event grossed $50 million in the United States from a production budget of $600,000. It also won the Academy Award for Best Documentary Feature. Several recorded albums have been released since the concert with the original *Woodstock* movie soundtrack sitting atop the Billboard charts for four weeks (July–August 1970) and selling two million copies.

While the musical lineup was impressive, the list of those who chose not to attend was even more so. That contingent included The Rolling Stones (Mick Jagger was shooting a movie); Led Zeppelin (playing a concert in New Jersey); Bob Dylan (family commitments); The Doors; and The Beatles. At the time, John Lennon was having immigration problems with the Nixon administration.

One other invite went out but it wasn't to a rocker, it was to the famous cowboy movie star Roy Rogers. Promoters wanted him to close the concert by singing his well-known tune, "Happy Trails to You." The request was turned down.

AUGUST 19

BOMBS AWAY!

During World War II, the United States dropped tons of explosives, most of them on enemy targets . . . but not all!

On August 19, 1943, American planes released seven bombs on the northeastern Nebraska community of Tarnov, mistaking it for either the Stanton Bombing Range, which was located 25 miles to the northeast, or another practice site to the southwest, near Silver Creek.

The exercise put the tiny town (population circa 80) on the map while, ironically, almost destroying it! Tarnov, Nebraska, was named after Tarnov,

Poland, when settlers made their way to their new home in 1889. During the war, the European community had been targeted by the German Luftwaffe.

The bombing in Nebraska took place between 4:00 a.m. and 4:30 a.m. when explosives were dropped by B-17 bombers that took off from the Sioux City Army Air Base. During the off-target attack, the southern portion of Tarnov was hit with three bombs that fell on the business district. Another explosive dropped through the porch roof of a house, angled into the pantry and went through the floor, lodging itself in the dirt. Six people were inside the structure, including two small children who were sleeping in their bedroom, but they were unharmed.

By noon, six bombs had been located. Besides the device that struck the house, another had narrowly missed a second dwelling, one hit a sidewalk, another landed in a street, and two fell east of the school. Two days later, a young boy discovered a seventh bomb in a nearby potato patch.

The practice shells were filled with sand and a small explosive charge, but none detonated. Although the bombing was investigated by the US Army, Tarnov residents never received a formal explanation for the chaotic mistake.

AUGUST 20

THE HARRISON TREE

Happy birthday to Benjamin Harrison, the nation's twenty-third president who was born on this day in 1833.

His arrival at the White House in 1889 should have come as no surprise as his bloodline included his great-grandfather Benjamin Harrison V, a signer of the Declaration of Independence; his grandfather William Henry Harrison, the ninth president; and his father John Scott Harrison, a two-term US congressman from Ohio.

There were two others who were distant descendants from the Harrison Family Tree—president Abraham Lincoln and entertainer Elvis Presley.

AUGUST 21

LOOK HOW YOU'VE GROWN

Hawaii became the fiftieth and final state on August 21, 1959. It is located in the Pacific Ocean and is made up of eight major islands. In fact, it is the only state that consists entirely of islands.

While Alaska is the country's largest state and California is its most populated, there is only one that is increasing in geographic size. Some might say that's impossible, but it's going on annually because Hawaii's geography is still growing in size.

It's the Big Island of Hawaii that is actually expanding. It is over 500,000 years old and has about 1 1/2 million visitors each year. The area has five volcanoes that overlap one another. Three of them are dormant but the two others, Mauna Loa and Kilauea are still active. When the lava flows from them, it hardens after cooling and adds to the state's landmass. From 1983 to 2002, the Big Island grew by 543 acres.

So while states like Texas and Florida continue to increase in population over the years, Hawaii just continues to get bigger in the true sense of the word.

AUGUST 22

MADAME EDITOR

Ann (Smith) Franklin became the sole editor and publisher of the *Newport Mercury* on this day in 1762, making her the first female editor in the United States. The publication dates back to 1758 and was one of the oldest newspapers still operating in the country. It closed in 2018.

Ann was the sister-in-law of another well-known newsman, Benjamin Franklin. In addition to being the country's first female editor, she was also the first woman to write an almanac, and the first to be inducted into the University of Rhode Island's Journalism Hall of Fame.

AUGUST 23

SMILE

When the history of the twenty-first century is written in its finality, many readers will come away sharing one common observation, which is that a great deal of the populace enjoyed having their pictures taken. The popularity of the camera-phone became a major player in America's newest national pastime.

Many of these photos are referred to as "selfies," which are images of the photographer taken by that individual. Each day, millions of these likenesses are created.

Throughout history, there have been a number of famous photos such as "V-J Day in Times Square" by Alfred Eisenstaedt (1945); Eddie Adams' "Saigon Execution" (1968); and Yousuf Karsh's iconic portrait of "Winston Churchill" (1941).

However, on this day in 1966, two of the most famous pictures in history were taken. They came from the spacecraft *Lunar Orbiter 1*, which took the first photograph of Earth from orbit around the Moon.

The unmanned NASA vehicle was primarily launched to photograph smooth areas of the lunar surface for selection and verification of safe landing sites for the future *Surveyor* and *Apollo* missions. The photos were transmitted back to Earth from August 18 through August 29, 1966, during its 80-day mission.

More than 2,000 high- and medium-resolution frames were taken, covering more than 1.9 million square miles of the Moon's surface. However, the two famous photos of the Earth from the distance of the Moon had not been preplanned.

The spacecraft was tracked until it impacted the lunar surface on October 29, 1966, during its 577th orbit. During its run, the *Orbiter* returned images of 99 percent of the Moon's exterior.

For the record, the first permanent photo ever taken was by inventor Joseph Nicéphore Niépce. It was a window scene from a camera set up at his studio in France in 1826. The single image had an unimaginable 8-hour exposure!

AUGUST 24

LIGHT MY FIRE

After defeating the Americans at the Battle of Bladensburg during the War of 1812, a British force led by major general Robert Ross marched on Washington, DC, on August 24, 1814. Inspired by the American destruction of Port Dover between May 14–16 earlier that year, the retaliatory attack saw the first and only time since the American Revolutionary War that a foreign power captured and occupied the capital of the United States.

It forced the government to flee, establishing the "Capitol for a Day" at Brookeville, Maryland. After setting the nation's capitol building ablaze, the British turned their attention northwest on Pennsylvania Avenue toward the White House (then known as the Presidential Mansion).

Urged by her husband to be prepared to evacuate, First Lady Dolley Madison had organized the household staff to save important treasures from the residence, including most famously the Lansdowne portrait of George Washington valued today at over $20 million. The following day, a heavy thunderstorm accompanied by a tornado passed through the city putting out the raging infernos. Nevertheless, only the exterior walls of the original property remained, requiring demolition during subsequent reconstruction, beginning in 1815, due to critical damage sustained during the event.

There may have also been another reason for torching the executive mansion. One year prior on April 30, 1813, the Canadian Parliament Buildings of York were set on fire by American troops. It was an act, that many believe, led to the retaliatory burning of Washington, DC, a year later.

AUGUST 25

JUST A COMMON FELLOW

If there is a road to riches, it is paved through 1600 Pennsylvania Avenue in Washington, DC. Today, former presidents are able to cash in following their time in office by writing books and giving speeches. In the twenty-first century, no one would ever dream of an ex-chief executive dying broke, but that wasn't always the case.

On August 25, Congress passed the Former Presidents Act of 1958, with respect to pension and other benefits payable to former US presidents. But prior to that, several ex-presidents, some among the most famous, made the dreaded journey from the White House to the poor house. It was a trend that saw the nation's former top office holder reduced to less than a middle class citizen.

That unenviable contingent includes: Thomas Jefferson (3rd president), James Madison (4th), James Monroe (5th), Andrew Jackson (7th), William Henry Harrison (9th), Abraham Lincoln (16th), Ulysses S. Grant (18th), William McKinley (25th), and Harry S. Truman (33rd).

AUGUST 26

THE LEGEND OF BLOODY ISLAND

In 1804, the Lewis and Clark expedition journeyed west from St. Louis. A century later, the city played host to the III Olympiad aka the Summer Olympics.

However, there is a place on the other side of the Mississippi River from the Gateway City that is known as Bloody Island. It was actually a sandbar that became a popular location for those wishing to settle disputes by dueling, since it was not under the jurisdiction of either Missouri or Illinois.

There were at least five duels that took place there involving lawyers, politicians, and businessmen. The last major showdown was on August 26, 1856 between Benjamin Gratz Brown and Thomas C. Reynolds. It became known as the Duel of the Governors.

Brown was the abolitionist editor of the *St. Louis Democrat*, and Reynolds worked as a pro-slavery district attorney of St. Louis. When the combatants fired their weapons, the newspaperman was shot in the leg and limped for the rest of his life while his adversary was unscathed.

Their poor aim resulted in a career in politics for each. Brown became governor of Missouri (1871–1873) while Reynolds eventually became a Confederate governor of the state (1862–1865).

AUGUST 27

THAT SONG WILL BE A HIT!

Happy birthday to former vice president Charles Dawes who was born on this day in 1865. Like so many others who had also held the office, Dawes was relatively inconspicuous during his tenure although he had other talents outside of politics.

Dawes was an accomplished musician who in 1911, composed a wordless tune, "Melody in A Major." In 1951, the same year that the former VP died, songwriter Carl Sigman added lyrics to the music and changed the title to *It's All in the Game.*

Seven years later, it was a #1 hit in the United States and Great Britain for singer Tommy Edwards. Since then, the song has sold millions of copies and been recorded by numerous artists. It is the only #1 single to have been cowritten by a US vice president or a Nobel Peace Prize laureate (Dawes was both).

AUGUST 28

BETTER LATE THAN NEVER?

On August 28, 1965, president Lyndon Johnson signed Public Law 89–141, enacting 18 U.S.C. 1751, which "prohibited the killing, kidnapping, conspiracy, assaults or attempt to kill or kidnap the President or Vice President of the United States of America." It made all of those acts federal crimes.

Unfortunately, the lawmakers were a bit late in getting around to mandating the new edict as four American Presidents (Abraham Lincoln, James Garfield, William McKinley, and John F. Kennedy) had already been assassinated years earlier.

AUGUST 29

A HARD DAY'S NIGHT

The Beatles were the phenomenon of the sixties who made musical history. But their live performances were few as the famous musical group gave their last commercial concert at San Francisco's Candlestick Park on August 29, 1966. They played for just 33 minutes as high winds swirled through the cavernous baseball stadium. Of the 45,744 seats that were available that evening, only about 25,000 were filled.

Even though the famous band was British, their last stadium appearance was in the United States.

AUGUST 30

FINDING A WAY

Businessman Donald Trump once said, "Sometimes by losing a battle you find a new way to win the war." His reference was to the strategies used in the business world, but he could have easily been speaking of one of the key moments of the American Revolution.

In March 1776, George Washington's troops were coming off a successful takeover of Boston, forcing the British to evacuate the city by sea. But there was little time to celebrate as the Americans needed to prepare for action at the next location. After studying the possible battle sites, the commander deduced that the redcoats would be moving southward and he must move his men into New York City. By mid-April, upon Washington's orders, 19,000 members of the Continental Army marched into Lower Manhattan.

Once they were settled, the Americans erected forts in northern Manhattan and on Brooklyn Heights across the East River on Long Island. Meanwhile, in July, the British established their own stronghold on Staten Island. They were led by general William Howe and his older brother vice admiral Richard Howe, commanding 32,000 redcoat soldiers. William proceeded with plans to take New York, which included utilizing his brother's fleet of 400 ships to control the waterways surrounding the city.

At one juncture, General Howe offered a pardon to the enemy army, to which Washington boldly replied, "Those who have committed no fault want no pardon."

On the night of August 26, Howe's troops, which consisted of a large throng of Hessians, advanced through Jamaica Pass forcing an American retreat toward the fortifications on Brooklyn Heights. The next day, the

British began digging trenches to pin the Americans in on one side while using the East River as a natural barrier on the back. It was at that point during the afternoon that the general made a critical decision, which may have cost the British a momentous opportunity to win the war, when he elected to delay the advancement of their position against the colonists.

Washington, who was with his troops in Brooklyn Heights, realized that there was no time to spare before his men would be completely surrounded with no available escape route.

On the evening of August 29, he ordered his 9,500 soldiers to gather their equipment and prepare to evacuate Long Island. It was a high-risk maneuver for, if they were discovered escaping by the redcoats, they would become easy targets and trapped on the water with nowhere to go.

They left a few campfires burning to serve as decoys for the British guards. Meanwhile, under the cover of darkness, American soldiers manned their boats and made the short-distance row toward freedom in Manhattan.

At 7:00 a.m. on August 30, commanding general George Washington accompanied the final contingent to safety. No troops had been lost in the crossing. But the defeat at Long Island was costly with 312 Americans killed, 1,407 wounded, and 1,186 captured.

However, had Washington not been able to evacuate the army from Brooklyn Heights, the cost would have been much greater, including the possibility that America might have remained a part of the British Empire.

AUGUST 31

CHECKMATE

When it comes to the White House, there are several traditions, most of which are connected to the holidays, such as the First Lady's selection of a theme for the Christmas decorating. There is also the famous Easter Egg Roll that began in 1814, along with the annual presidential pardon of a turkey at Thanksgiving which started in 1863 with Abraham Lincoln doing the honors to appease his 10-year-old son Tad.

Another established practice got its start on August 30, 1865, when president Andrew Johnson, who had escaped an assassination attempt just four months prior, welcomed the Brooklyn Atlantics and Washington Nationals amateur baseball clubs to the White House. It was the first time that athletic teams were recognized for their achievements by the chief executive at the historic mansion.

But the list of visitors has not been restricted to sports teams. Others, such as war heroes, astronauts, and entertainers, have accepted invitations to the

White House to meet the president. But in 1972, a national hero who had captured his country's imagination was spurned by the commander in chief.

At the time, the Cold War remained in full swing and the Soviet Union was the dominant power in the game of chess. They used their success as a propaganda tool denoting the superior intelligence of their players. In 1972, the USSR's Boris Spassky was in his fourth year as world champion in competition where the Soviets had held the title since 1948.

However, the individual who was grabbing the attention of the chess world wasn't part of the stable of great Communist players but surprisingly was an American. Bobby Fischer was a 29-year-old superstar who was well known by those who followed the world's top competitors.

He became a National Master at the age of 12 and won America's Junior Chess Championship at the age of 13, making him the youngest Junior Champ in history.

Two years later, on the cusp of his fifteenth birthday, Fischer won the US Chess Championship, giving him the title of International Master. Later that same year, he broke Spassky's record to become the youngest World Chess Federation Grandmaster. The two prodigies first played each other in 1960 when Fischer lost during a tournament in Argentina. There were more matches but he would not beat the Soviet for twelve years.

At sixteen, Fischer dropped out of high school to earn a living playing the board game that brought him worldwide notoriety. By 1962, he was considered the best non-Soviet chess player in the world.

The decade of the seventies proved to be the time when Bobby Fischer evolved into a household name. Through 1971, the Chicago native had won twenty straight games in international tournament play, which was the second-longest winning streak in the history of the game. He had earned the right to challenge Spassky, a player he had never beaten, for the world title.

By 1972, the chess world was clamoring for a Spassky-Fischer rematch. Officials in Washington, DC, also saw such a match as an opportunity to gain some positive public relations on the world stage, which was greatly needed due to the growing negativity toward the war in Vietnam.

The American was far from being a flag-waving patriot but declared that the match would pit "the free world against the lying, cheating hypocritical Russians!" He then stoked the fire by declaring himself the greatest chess player in the world.

Due to Fischer's difficult nature, negotiations weren't going well—to the point that it appeared that there wouldn't be a match. When president Richard Nixon got word that the contest might not take place, he dispatched national security adviser Dr. Henry Kissinger to coax the American challenger onto the world stage. Nixon didn't play chess, but eEven with Vietnam occupying most of his time, Kissinger phoned Fischer in New York to urge him to do his patriotic duty. The chess prodigy acquiesced and the long-awaited event was finally set for Reykjavík, Iceland.

The showdown ran for twenty-one games from July 11 to August 31, 1972. No other chess match had ever drawn so much attention from either the public or the media but it wasn't because there was suddenly a clamoring from so many people who wanted to learn the game. The truth was that it was another Cold War battle between the Americans and the Soviets which, no matter the event, was always good for high ratings and newsprint sales. Meanwhile, during the final week of August, the rivals were squaring off in multiple events in Munich, West Germany, as the XX Summer Olympics got underway.

The match went forward and on this day, Fischer sealed his title run with a final score of 12.5 to 8.5, making him the eleventh world champion and the first from the United States. Spassky won three games (including a forfeit in game 2), Fischer won seven, and there were eleven draws.

While chess fans outside the USSR hailed the American's accomplishment, when he returned home, the 39-year-old became an afterthought. He was passed over for the Presidential Medal of Freedom and never received an expected invitation to visit the White House. His frustration led to forfeiture of his world title in 1975 and he never played for the championship again. Fischer went into seclusion for twenty years before his death in 2008.

The eccentric champion is buried in the place where he became a symbol of the Cold War and enjoyed his biggest victory—Reykjavík, Iceland.

SEPTEMBER

I learned a long time ago that if you're going to be in politics, you can't murder and kill everybody who's against you. You've got to take it smiling.

—Jack Walton, governor of Oklahoma, 1923

SEPTEMBER 1

QUICK ON THE TRIGGER

Since the end of World War II, the relationship between the United States and Russia (aka the Soviet Union) has always been tense. The following two incidents might explain the distrust between the two countries.

On September 1, 1983, Korean Air Lines Flight 007 was traveling from New York City to Seoul when it was shot down by a Soviet fighter aircraft near Moneron Island over the Sea of Japan. All 269 passengers and crew aboard were killed. Among the 61 Americans who died was congressman Larry McDonald (R-GA). The aircraft was destroyed because it flew through Soviet prohibited airspace.

History was repeated as a Buk surface-to-air missile shot down Malaysian Airlines Flight MH 17 over Ukraine on July 17, 2014. It was Russian-made and fired from an area controlled by the country's backed separatists. All 298 on board were killed including 23 Americans.

SEPTEMBER 2

LABOR DAY NIGHTMARE

A massive hurricane struck the Florida Keys on this day in 1935. It was the strongest storm to make landfall in the United States, based on barometric pressure and one of the ten deadliest storms in American history.

At least 423 people (164 residents and 259 veterans employed on a road project) were killed by the hurricane. Bodies were recovered as far away as the southwest tip of the Florida mainland. In a stroke of good fortune, about 350 of the 718 veterans living in the Keys work camps were in Miami to attend a Labor Day baseball game when the storm hit. If not for that gathering, many more of the men, many of whom were World War I veterans, might have been killed by the storm.

SEPTEMBER 3

THE DELIVERY BOY

As a young man, John F. Kennedy served in the military during World War II. However, in 1939, 22-year-old JFK traveled to Europe, where he met with Alexander C. Kirk, the American Embassy chargé d'affaires in Berlin.

Rather than risk using a member of his staff who could be detected by Nazi spies, Kirk gave the Harvard University student a secret message about Hitler's impending attack on Poland. John returned to London and passed the message on to his father, the US ambassador to the United Kingdom, who in turn warned President Roosevelt. On this day in 1939, two days after Hitler's attack on the defenseless country, Great Britain declared war against Germany.

SEPTEMBER 4

IT WAS THE E-DAY INVASION

There have been many successful companies but not every product that a business produces is considered to be great.

Ford Motor Company has experienced its fair share of winners. Among its best-selling vehicles of all-time are the F-150 Pick Up Truck; the Model T; the classic Thunderbird, and the sporty Mustang. At the end of the 2021 fiscal year, Ford held total assets in the amount of $257 billion.

On this day in 1957, the company produced the most spectacular sales production in history. It was the rollout for the next Ford automobile that management hoped would join their line of elite success stories. It was named after the company's founder's son and known as the Edsel.

September 4 was "E Day" and featured the beginning of a public relations blitz that employed all forms of media. The advertising strategy included a never-before-seen one-hour television special that revolved around the new car. The broadcast that was shown October 13 on CBS included some of the biggest stars of the day such as Bing Crosby, Frank Sinatra, Rosemary Clooney, Louis Armstrong, and Bob Hope.

While the commercialism was spectacular, such could not be said of the product. Consumers complained that it was ugly, overpriced, of poor quality, and simply didn't live up to the hype. After just a few years, the Edsel joined the group of short-term business failures and was relegated to the automotive graveyard. The loss to the company on its futuristic-appearing project was estimated at $250 million, a staggering amount for the times.

However, the Edsel wasn't a total bust; in fact, it has become a rarity. Relatively few of them were built between 1958 and 1960 (when production ended), creating a demand and making them collector's items. At a 2022 auction in Scottsdale, Arizona, a 1958 Edsel Pacer convertible sold for more than $60,000. It is estimated that fewer than 10,000 units of the model remain.

SEPTEMBER 5

A DAY WELL EARNED

On this day in 1882, American workers celebrated Labor Day for the first time. It began as a proposal to the upstart Central Labor Union in New York City that a day be set aside as a "general holiday for the laboring classes." Over the years, it has been a time of celebration filled with picnics and parades.

While New York receives much of the credit, the idea of making it a national holiday came from the other coast. In 1887, Oregon became the first state to recognize Labor Day as an official public holiday.

SEPTEMBER 6

DO YOUR JOB

Theodore Roosevelt had never planned to be vice president and, like others, didn't want the job. However, he understood the way the political game was played, which means often doing something for the good of the party in hopes of gaining an eventual personal advantage.

All of Roosevelt's plans changed on the afternoon of September 6, 1901. While president William McKinley was greeting visitors in a reception line at the Pan-American Exposition in Buffalo, his VP was at Isle La Motte, an islet on Lake Champlain, where he was scheduled to address the annual meeting of the Vermont Fish and Game League. Just prior to delivering his speech, Roosevelt was pulled aside and told the terrible news by phone that the president had been shot.

At that juncture, with an uncertain prognosis, Roosevelt departed the island by rowboat, followed by yacht, and then by train in an effort to get to Buffalo as quickly as possible.

On Monday, September 9, having seen the nation's leader for himself as he convalesced just a short distance from the shooting, Roosevelt was optimistic after conversing with the doctors. He stated, "Everything is going on most satisfactorily with the president. I feel assured not only that he will recover, but that his recovery will be so speedy that in a very short time he will be able to resume his duties."

At the end of the week, with McKinley on the road to recuperation, Roosevelt traveled 260 miles to upper New York to hike Mount Marcy, the state's highest peak. But on Friday the thirteenth, a courier caught up with the energetic war hero and handed him a yellow envelope which contained a telegram that read: " The President's condition has changed for the worse." At the time, Roosevelt was ten miles from the nearest telephone as he began his descent.

McKinley died while his second in command was en route to his bedside, traveling by buckboard wagon and train. At 3:30 p.m., Theodore Roosevelt took the Oath of Office at the home of his friend Ansley Wilcox, who lived just a few blocks away from where the president had passed. Because of the suddenness of transpiring events, the new commander in chief had to borrow a change of clothes for the occasion.

With McKinley gone, Roosevelt was on his own as he had just become the youngest president (age 42) in the country's history.

SEPTEMBER 7

THE LEGEND OF LOST GOLD

Brothers Frank and Jesse James were two of the most notorious outlaws in the history of the Old West. It didn't matter if it was trains or banks, they were adept at collecting the cash and making a clean getaway.

In 1875, the James gang ambushed a Mexican pack-train near the border town of Calera, Mexico, and made off with $2 million in gold bars. They moved their haul using eighteen burros through the southwest territory's Wichita Mountains near Fort Sill, part of modern-day Oklahoma, where they stashed the precious metal in a ravine.

From there, the gang's luck changed on September 7, 1876, in Northfield, Minnesota. Eight members of the outfit botched a bank robbery, resulting in two of them being killed and all others suffering wounds, including Frank and Jesse.

Things didn't improve as in 1882, Jesse was shot and killed by fellow outlaw Robert Ford inside his own house after the men had shared breakfast together. Frank returned to the Wichitas in 1907 and bought a ranch near Fletcher. He began searching for the gold but couldn't remember where it was hidden. He also searched for $88,000 that they had left near Sand Springs and for another $110,000 that was stashed at Robbers Canyon, a short distance from Pryor. Both are Oklahoma towns.

Frank died in 1915 having never found any of the loot that he and his gang had left long ago along the trail in Oklahoma.

SEPTEMBER 8

THE FALL OF THE KINGFISH

On Sunday, September 8, 1935, at 9:22 p.m., the flamboyant US senator and former Louisiana governor Huey Long was mortally wounded while walking through the state capitol complex in Baton Rouge. Long was one of the most well-known and influential politicians of the Depression era. At the time of the shooting, he was planning a presidential run in 1936 against the incumbent and fellow Democrat Franklin D. Roosevelt.

But not everyone was a fan. There had been an impeachment and other assassination attempts in his history to the point that he kept his own security detail.

In August 1935, a month prior to his death, the "Kingfish," claimed to have uncovered a murder plot against him, the details of which had been discussed in a meeting at New Orleans' De Soto Hotel. According to Long, three well-known politicians, New Orleans mayor T. Semmes Walmsley along with former governors John M. Parker and Jared Sanders, had been present. He read what he claimed was a transcript of a recording of this meeting into the Congressional Record from the floor of the US Senate.

On September 8, 1935, the flamboyant lawmaker was struck once or twice by shots from a weapon fired by 28-year-old medical doctor Carl A. Weiss. He was immediately felled by some sixty-one rounds from Long's bodyguards along with police officers who were on the scene.

Shortly after being shot, the senator reportedly asked, "I wonder why he shot me?" Long died two days later of internal bleeding.

SEPTEMBER 9

THE OIL CRISIS

On March 15, 1910, 2,200 feet below the earth's surface, an oil well erupted in a densely populated area between the towns of Taft and Maricopa in Kern County, California. It became known as the Lakeview Gusher, which lost over four million barrels of "black gold." During its 544-day duration, it was estimated that some 9.4 million barrels of oil poured out, creating a creek of crude that ran downhill from the well site.

Finally, on this day in 1911, thousands of feet below the surface, the well caved in and sealed itself, bringing the worst accidental oil spill to that point in history to a conclusion. About half of the leakage was salvageable and able to be processed.

Exactly one century later, a British Petroleum oil rig exploded in the Gulf of Mexico, causing the latest, largest oil spill in history. The initial oil rig explosion killed eleven people and injured seventeen others as more than 200 million gallons of crude oil was pumped into the Gulf of Mexico over 87 days.

SEPTEMBER 10

GETTING THERE FIRST

The advent of the internet created a whole new language along with computer technology. As an example, prior to 1990, a server was a term to describe someone who brought dinner to a customer's table in a restaurant.

However, on this day in that year, the Archie server was created. It was the first internet search engine developed by Alan Emtage, Bill Heelan and Peter Deutsch at McGill University in Montreal (Canada). The student trio had put it together as a class project.

Archie comes from the word "archive." However, as a curiosity, it has often been associated with the Archie comic book characters created in 1939 in New York.

SEPTEMBER 11

SKY HIGH

On Memorial Day in 1983, eighteen years prior to the 9/11 attacks, a high-rise firefighting and rescue advocate Dan Goodwin successfully climbed several horizontal beams located outside of the World Trade Center's North Tower.

His stunt was meant to call attention to the inability to rescue people potentially trapped in the upper floors of skyscrapers.

Goodwin's concerns became reality almost two decades later when more than 1,300 people were unable to escape from the upper stories during the terrorist air assault on the WTC.

At the conclusion of his climb, Goodwin was arrested but later released.

SEPTEMBER 12

UNDER THE SEA

William Lewis Herndon was a sea captain who had explored previously unknown areas of the Amazon region. He was also the captain of the SS Central America which transported large amounts of gold from the California mines to the east coast.

On September 12, 1857, the ship was carrying 15 tons of precious metal, 474 passengers, and 101 crew when it was mortally damaged off the coast of Cape Hatteras during a hurricane. The captain evacuated as many of the passengers and crew as possible before going down with his ship. Two years after his death, in 1859, his daughter Ellen married Chester Arthur who eventually became the twenty-first president of the United States.

For more than a century, the ship's treasure rested on the seafloor of the Atlantic Ocean. But that changed in 1987 when the remains of the steamer was located about 160 miles off the coast of South Carolina. Significant amounts of gold and other artifacts were recovered. As items were being gathered, a group of thirty-nine insurance companies filed suit, claiming that they had already paid damages for the lost riches and thus had the right to it. The team (the Columbus-America Discovery Group) that found it argued that the gold had been abandoned.

After years of legal wrangling, 92 percent of the treasure was awarded to the discovery team in 1996. The total value of the recovered items was estimated at $400 million. In 2001, a single gold brick from the haul weighing 80 pounds sold for a record $8 million and was recognized as the most valuable piece of currency in the world at that time.

SEPTEMBER 13

O SAY CAN YOU BID

Two documented fragments from "The Star Spangled Banner"—the very flag that flew over Fort McHenry in Baltimore, Maryland, on this day in

1814 and inspired Francis Scott Key to pen the words to America's national anthem—sold for $65,725 as part of an auction that was held on June 25, 2011, in Dallas, Texas.

Most of the flag is on display at the Smithsonian's Natural Museum of American History in Washington, DC.

SEPTEMBER 14

ONE DECISION AFTER ANOTHER

Happy Birthday to Supreme Court associate justice Ketanji Brown Jackson who was born on this day in 1970. She was confirmed by the US Senate on April 7, 2022, by a vote of 53–47.

Three Republicans joined the majority who voted for Brown. One of those was 2012 presidential candidate Mitt Romney (R-UT).

Some observers found that unusual because on June 14, 2021, less than a year earlier, the Senate confirmed Jackson to the US Court of Appeals by a 53–44 margin. Curiously, in that decision, Romney voted against Brown's move to the federal bench.

SEPTEMBER 15

HOLY COW!

Happy Birthday to the twenty-seventh president, William Howard Taft, the only chief executive to tip the scales at more than 300 pounds. Among the residents of the White House grounds during his term (1909–1913) was one that grew into a national celebrity in her own right. She was a Holstein cow named Pauline Wayne.

The animal was a gift to the First Family from senator Isaac Stephenson of Wisconsin, a dairy farm owner in his home state. Her Capital City arrival on November 4, 1910, drew a great deal of attention making the front pages of many newspapers around the country. Several members of the White House staff greeted the 1,500 pound black-and-white grass-muncher at the DC train station and then escorted her to the stables of the nearby Navy Building.

Pauline produced about eight gallons of milk a day. She also gave birth to a calf who was named Big Bill after President Taft; Big Bill was later sent to live on a farm in Maryland.

The presidential bovine was so famous that she would appear at stock shows where small bottles of her milk were sold for 50 cents to her adoring fans. While on her way to the International Dairymen's Exposition in

Milwaukee in 1911, she "narrowly escaped death" in a slaughterhouse, according to several newspaper accounts from October 1911.

Pauline was being shipped in a private car that was attached to an entire train of cattle carriers bound for the Chicago stockyards. Somehow the president's cow went missing for 48 hours. The White House and the dairy show frantically "telegraph[ed] everywhere in search of her whereabouts," reported *The New York Times*.

So what was behind the cow's disappearance? According to the *Milwaukee Sentinel*, a train switch crew had mistakenly transferred Pauline's boxcar.

Some attendants found Pauline Wayne and soon convinced stockyard officials that this was indeed the president's missing cow, thus saving her "from the bludgeon of the slaughterer," reported the *Times*.

SEPTEMBER 16

WHEN WILL IT END?

The 1974 contest for the United States Senate from New Hampshire began on November 5, 1974. It became noteworthy as the longest contested election for the US Congress in the nation's history.

The political marathon started when the incumbent, Republican Norris Cotton, announced that he would not seek reelection. That pitted Democrat John A. Durkin against the GOP's Louis C. Wyman, who was a five-term member of the US House of Representatives. As Wyman was the more experienced office seeker, he was predicted by many to win easily. A *Boston Globe* newspaper poll was released just three days prior to the election on November 3 that showed Wyman with a commanding 50%–34% advantage.

When the tabulation took place, the Republican won the initial count but only by a slim margin of just 355 votes. As expected, Durkin immediately demanded a recount. The revised tally, which was completed on November 27, 1974, declared that the Democrat was the winner by a margin of ten votes.

Wyman wasted little time in appealing the recount to the New Hampshire State Ballot Law Commission. They conducted their own partial recount and announced on December 24, 1974, that the Republican had won by just two votes (110,926 to 110,924). At that point, many believed that the election was over except for Durkin who petitioned the Senate, which had a 60-vote Democratic majority, to review the case, based on the constitutional provision that each house of Congress is the final arbiter of elections to that specific body.

One week later, the page on the calendar flipped over to 1975, but there was still no resolution. On January 13, the day before the new Congress convened, the Senate Rules Committee tried unsuccessfully to resolve the matter.

That summer, Wyman contacted Durkin urging him to support a new, special election. He initially refused, but the next day reversed his position and announced he would support a new voting day.

The special election was held 10 1/2 months after the original effort on this day in 1975. Widespread attention in the media resulted in a record-breaking turnout (262,572), which gave the election to Durkin by a 27,000-vote margin.

SEPTEMBER 17

IT'S BEN . . . AGAIN!

The signing of the United States Constitution occurred on this day in 1787 at Independence Hall in Philadelphia. Some of America's most famous individuals scrawled their names on the parchment that became the law of the land.

In that group is Benjamin Franklin, who achieved a great deal in his lifetime. Among his accomplishments, he stands alone as the only person to have signed all four of the documents which helped create the United States: the Declaration of Independence (1776); the Treaty of Alliance with France (1778); the Treaty of Paris (1783); and the US Constitution (1787).

SEPTEMBER 18

CHARG-IT

The average American has around $6,000 of credit card debt. The individual who got the ball rolling for the buy now/pay later enthusiasts was John C. Biggins, a banker who worked for the Flatbush National Bank in Brooklyn, New York.

In 1946, he invented the forerunner of the major credit cards, which he called Charg-It. Issued by Flatbush National, it allowed people in a two-square-block radius to charge purchases to the bank. The area was limited by necessity—merchants had to leave sales slips with the bank—but promised ease for locals who could use the card at multiple businesses. In 1951, just five years after Biggins' invention, another New York institution, the Franklin National Bank, created the first bank credit card.

At the time of his death, on this day in 1971, Biggins was chairman of the Franklin Bank of Paterson, New Jersey.

SEPTEMBER 19

THE OTHER PILOTS

When it came to aviation in the early 1930s, most of the headlines belonged to Oklahoma City's record-setting pilot Wiley Post. His impressive list of accomplishments included the first solo flight around the world.

Although on September 19, 1932, two young African American aviators from the Sooner State set out to be the first of their race to make the transcontinental journey by air when they started a flight from Los Angeles to New York in an airplane that had been put together from scrap parts.

The trip required 41 hours and 27 minutes flying time which was spread over 21 days because the pilots, Thomas C. Allen of Oklahoma City and El Reno's J. Herman Banning, made twenty-five stops along the way to raise money during the 3,300-mile trek. They became known as the Flying Hoboes and were seeking a $1,000 prize that they had heard was being offered to the first Black pilot to make the trip.

The Great Depression was in full swing and money was scarce, so the pair began searching junkyards for usable parts and, by the summer of 1932, they had pieced together an aircraft for the competition. When Banning and Allen took off for the first leg of their journey, they had just $25 in travel cash.

"We'd get downtown, and we'd tell them we're the first Black pilots trying to fly across the country," recalled Allen. "Then they'd take us into some Negro restaurant, and they'd always take up a collection of a few dollars and help us on the way."

On October 9, 1932, at 9:30 a.m., the travelers arrived at Curtiss Airfield in New York. The city's media savvy mayor Jimmy Walker presented the key to the city to the Oklahomans and that evening they were the toast of audiences at several of the famous nightclubs in Harlem.

Unfortunately, the prize that had inspired the flight had turned out to be a ruse as there was no sponsor. Because of that, the duo had to barnstorm their way back home, participating in air shows.

But for a brief time in 1932, two guys named Thomas Allen and J. Herman Banning replaced Wiley Post as the most-talked-about pilots from Oklahoma.

SEPTEMBER 20

THE MOTOWN SAVIOR

Since the inception of the automobile, Detroit had flourished as the car capital of the United States. The industry provided an economic base that most other cities could only admire from afar.

But that changed in the 1970s with skyrocketing gas prices and foreign competitors making their way into the US auto market. America's "Big Three" vehicle producers (General Motors, Ford, and Chrysler) were scrambling to keep their bottom lines above water.

On this day in 1979, Chrysler Corporation hired 54-year-old Lee Iacocca and members of his team away from one of their chief rivals, Ford. He brought a record of success with him as the man behind one of the company's best-known vehicles, the Mustang.

It was in 1983 that he saved Chrysler from bankruptcy with the introduction of the company's first minivan. The vehicle not only rescued the business from going under but became Iacocca's automotive legacy.

SEPTEMBER 21

A ONE-DAY WONDER

Tennessee became the nation's sixteenth state in 1796. It's original capital city was Knoxville but there were a few other stops along the trail. One of those places was Kingston.

It began with the leaders of the Cherokee tribe and a treaty where they promised that they would cede their land if it became the site of Tennessee's capital. On this day in 1807, state leaders moved the capital to the area for a single day, technically fulfilling the requirements of the agreement.

The following day, the lawmakers returned to Knoxville. As a result, the Cherokee lost the land and Tennessee acquired the parcel around the US garrison at Southwest Point, now known as Kingston.

The city is one of four to serve as official capitals in Tennessee's history: Knoxville was the original in 1796; Kingston had its one day in 1807; it returned to Knoxville until 1812; it was relocated to Nashville from 1812–1817; then it went to Murfreesboro from 1818–1826; and it finally came back to Nashville where it has been since 1826.

SEPTEMBER 22

ANGRY WOMEN

By January 1975, Gerald Ford's approval rating had dropped to 37 percent. Even with his numbers going south, on July 8, 1975, Ford officially announced that he would seek the Republican nomination for the presidency in 1976 stating, "In order to finish the job I have begun."

On September 22 in San Francisco, California, Sara Jane Moore fired a revolver at Ford from 40 feet away. A bystander grabbed her arm and the shot missed its target. Moore was sentenced to life in prison but was paroled on December 31, 2007, after serving more than thirty years.

However, she wasn't the first to attempt to take down the sitting chief executive. It appeared that the president might not get an opportunity to finish the job after just over a year in office when the first attempt was made on his life.

On September 5, 1975, in Sacramento, California (just 75 miles from San Francisco), Lynette "Squeaky" Fromme, a follower of the murderous cult leader Charles Manson, drew a Colt .45-caliber pistol on Ford while he was shaking hands in a crowd. There were four cartridges in the weapon's magazine, but the firing chamber was empty and she was soon restrained by a Secret Service agent. For her unsuccessful attempt, Fromme was sentenced to life in a federal prison.

Ford is the only president with two assassination attempts that were carried out against him by women.

SEPTEMBER 23

DELAY OF GAME

On this day in 1976, America got a dose of the potential mishaps that can occur on live television. With only 8 minutes to go in the first presidential debate of that year, a technical glitch knocked out the sound, rendering the audio feed silent.

For 27 minutes, as repairmen worked frantically to make the necessary repairs, candidates Gerald Ford (R-MI) and Jimmy Carter (D-GA) waited on stage, "almost like robots," Carter later said. "We didn't move around, we didn't walk over and shake hands with each other. We just stood there."

Ford added, "I suspect both of us would have liked to sit down and relax while the technicians were fixing the system, but I think both of us were hesitant to make any gesture that might look like we weren't physically or mentally able to handle a problem like this."

Ford had been a football star at the University of Michigan in the 1930s and that evening received a true experience of a delay of game. In November, Carter won the election.

Years later, after both men had left office for the last time, they became close friends for the remainder of their lives. In January 2007, former President Carter delivered the eulogy for Gerald Ford at his funeral.

SEPTEMBER 24

TALE OF TWO PRESIDENTS

On this day in 1789, president George Washington nominated the first six justices to the United States Supreme Court. Each was confirmed by the Senate two days later. In the beginning, six was the total number of members on the court.

During his two terms, the Father of Our Country put forward fourteen names for Congressional approval, with twelve making it to the nation's highest court. Each of those continues to stand as the record for those categories.

However, not every chief executive's nominees have had smooth sailing like Washington's. President John Tyler had a particularly difficult time filling vacancies because he could not get the Senate to work with him. During Tyler's presidency, which was less than one term, the Senate rejected nine separate Supreme Court nominations! That is also a record.

SEPTEMBER 25

FOR THE COMPUTER, THERE'S NO PLACE
LIKE HOME

Happy birthday to Mary Allen Wilkes who was born on this day in 1937. She is one of the world's first programmers and was a logic designer known for her work with the LINC computer.

Wilkes designed the interactive operating system LAP6 for the LINC, one of the earliest such systems for a personal computer. She is also the first person to use a personal computer in the home. The Chicago native worked as an educator before becoming a lawyer in 1975. Her undergraduate degree is from Wellesley College and she is also a graduate of Harvard Law School.

SEPTEMBER 26

THE WAR OF WORDS

There was a great deal of talking taking place on September 26, 1960. That evening, the first-ever televised presidential debate took place between candidates John F. Kennedy (D-MA) and Richard Nixon (R-CA). The nominees were engaged in the question-and-answer session for one hour.

But the longest dialogue took place earlier in the day at the United Nations as Cuban dictator Fidel Castro addressed the General Assembly. His speech which lasted 4 hours, 29 minutes, was the longest in the organization's history, as noted in the *Guinness World Records*. However that was just a warm up as on February 5, 1986, the bearded island ruler outdid himself as he spoke for 7 hours and 10 minutes at the III Communist Party Congress in Havana.

SEPTEMBER 27

LUCK OF THE DRAW

State capital cities come in all shapes and sizes. Almost every state has moved its state capital at least once. Only Massachusetts, Nevada, North Dakota, Vermont, Washington, and Wyoming have had a single capital city since their inception as either colonies, territories, or states.

There are a fair share of towns and cities in history-rich Pennsylvania that can boast of their own contributions to the building of the nation. However, one of those is little known.

It took place on this day in 1777 when a two-year-old town hosted the Second Continental Congress, turning it into the US capital for 24 hours before the leaders headed west to York.

Washington, DC, has served as the capital city for more than two centuries, although there was little continuity in the seat of government during the nation's infancy. In its pre-DC days, the nation's hub was equated to the location of where Congress gathered. Eight cities served that designation between the signing of the Declaration of Independence in 1776 and 1785.

The final congressional action in Lancaster was to adjourn and agree to meet in York on September 30, 1777. The relocation was for defensive purposes, allowing leaders to put the Susquehanna River between themselves and the invading British forces.

SEPTEMBER 28

THE UNEXPECTED ALLY

On September 28, 1781, general George Washington and his force of 17,000 French and Continental troops began the final push that led to the defeat of the British and brought independence to the fledgling United States. The red-coat army was down to just 9,000 soldiers when their last-ditch effort began in an attempt to keep hope alive against their upstart adversary.

The British surrender finally came on October 17, 1781 at Yorktown, Virginia, after they'd been cut off by American ground forces with the help of the French navy. However, there was a third army that received little credit but did their share of damage to the enemy.

During the three-week standoff, a number of British troops encamped in the damp and humid Virginia countryside fell victim to deadly malaria carried by mosquitoes. Whatever remaining chance for victory they may have had quickly disappeared due to the attack by a small bug that carried a big bite. At one point, the British were considered the greatest military force on Earth, but that ended as they returned to their ships for the long trip home across the Atlantic.

In 1789, after years of debate by the politicians, the bald eagle was selected to represent the new country as its national symbol. However, if the job is ever available in the future, the patriotic mosquito may have a case as its replacement.

SEPTEMBER 29

BACK IN THE SADDLE AGAIN

Happy Birthday to Gene Autry who was born on this day in 1907 near the town of Tioga in north Texas. During the 1930s, 1940s, and 1950s, the singer/actor became one of the biggest names in entertainment as he experienced immense popularity from his movies, records, and television appearances. In each venue, he portrayed a western cowboy, which came naturally since he had worked on his father's homestead in Ravia, Oklahoma, as a young man.

While the nation was in the throes of the Great Depression, Gene Autry's singing and acting career was taking steps from early struggles to major stardom. From 1937 to 1942, he was voted the #1 Western Star by the *Motion Picture Herald* Exhibitors Poll.

Autry sold more than 100 million records, which included a dozen gold and platinum discs, along with the first record ever certified gold. His recording of

"Rudolph the Red-Nosed Reindeer" remains the second all-time best-selling Christmas single, with sales in excess of 30 million.

On July 26, 1942, during World War II, the "Singing Cowboy" publicly displayed his love for his country as he enlisted in the Army Air Force. However, Autry didn't just join the military at the height of his career, he was sworn in during a live broadcast of his popular weekly radio program *Melody Ranch*.

He served as a transport pilot aboard C-109s flying in southeast Asia and over the Himalayas from July 1942 to October 1945. He was honorably discharged from the service in 1946 having been awarded the American Campaign Medal, the Asiatic-Pacific Campaign Medal, and the World War II Victory Medal.

After the war, the western entertainer returned to performing and broke into the new medium of television with the same success that he enjoyed in his other ventures. He also expanded his business holdings into California's lucrative real estate market; he purchased and sold several major radio stations; and when Major League Baseball expanded its group of teams in 1961, Autry won the rights to become majority owner of the newly created Los Angeles Angels.

The decorated veteran passed away in 1998 from lymphoma three days before his ninety-first birthday. At the time of his death, his estate was estimated at more than $300 million.

In 2002, Autry's beloved Angels won baseball's biggest prize, the World Series. As the players celebrated on the field, the public address system played the Singing Cowboy's signature hit song, "Back in the Saddle Again."

SEPTEMBER 30

THE LONE EAGLE ON TOUR

When Charles Lindbergh took off in his plane, the *Spirit of St. Louis* from New York's Roosevelt Field at 7:52 a.m. on Friday May 20, 1927, he was nothing more than an obscure air-mail pilot. The San Diego resident was the latest idealistic flier seeking to capture the $25,000 Orteig Prize for being the first to solo the Atlantic from New York to Paris. Six men had already died trying to accomplish the feat but when the Detroit native safely landed some 33 1/2 hours later at Le Bourget Airport, he instantly became the most celebrated person on Earth.

With his nation clamoring to see him, Lindbergh embarked on a 95-day national tour just weeks after the historic flight. He visited 92 cities encompassing all 48 states, gave 147 speeches, and accumulated an additional 1,290 miles riding in parades. At each stop, he arrived behind the controls of his trans-Atlantic costar the Spirit of St. Louis.

On this day in 1927, the popular pilot flew his plane from Oklahoma City toward McIntyre Field in Tulsa. Along the way, he winged his way over the tiny town of Pawhuska but couldn't find a place to land because the community had no airport. Subsequently, the chamber of commerce had been given an approximate time for the flyover as the locals turned out in droves.

In the process, the aviator dropped a handwritten letter from the plane's window which read, " I, Charles Lindbergh, am happy to have been invited to fly over your City. I am sorry I am unable to land but do thank you for your hospitality."

The following day, Lindbergh made the short flight from Tulsa to Davis Field in Muskogee. Before landing, he flew over the School for the Blind so that its students could hear the engine of his historic aircraft.

OCTOBER

The president makes numerous appearances at various functions. There was the time that Calvin Coolidge was expected to attend a fair. A reporter asked if he would be saying anything to the crowd? He replied, "No. I am just going as an exhibit."

OCTOBER 1

TOUGH TIMES IN THE BIG EASY

New Orleans is a city with the reputation as a place where the good times roll and the party never stops. But there have been several occasions in its history where Mother Nature put the brakes on the celebration with a stark dose of reality. The coastal community has had no shortage of man-made and natural disasters throughout its time.

On October 1 and 2, 1893, the Cheniere Caminada hurricane (also known as the Grand Isle Hurricane), struck the Gulf Coast. The storm devastated some 500 miles of coastline from Timbalier Bay to Pensacola. Winds of 100 mph were estimated at Grand Isle and Pointe à la Hache. A tidal surge crashed the north end of Grand Isle, destroying everything in its path as the eye passed between 11:00 p.m. and midnight.

The storm surge was as high as 15 feet in the Louisiana bays. Two thousand people died with property losses estimated at around $5 million.

But not all of the news from the Big Easy was bad as in 2010, the hometown Saints won professional football's biggest prize, the Super Bowl.

OCTOBER 2

EVERYBODY IS READING THE GAZETTE!

Due to the growing numbers of readers using electronic media, many of today's major print outlets are having a difficult time turning a profit. However, on October 2, 1729, Benjamin Franklin bought a newspaper, the *Pennsylvania Gazette*. It eventually became the first publication in the colonies to become profitable.

In 1752, Franklin published a third-person account of his pioneering kite experiment in the *Gazette*, without ever mentioning himself in the article. It was also the first paper to publish a political cartoon.

One of the more popular aspects of the newspaper was a gossip column authored by the distinguished Founding Father.

Despite the fact that Ben died in 1790, the *Gazette* continued on for another twenty-five years before ceasing publication. However in 1821, it returned from the journalistic graveyard as the *Saturday Evening Post*, which today is published on a bimonthly basis.

OCTOBER 3

TIMING IS EVERYTHING

In 1990, Bill Clinton was seeking his fifth term as governor of Arkansas even though there were rumors that he was actually more interested in running for president. He stayed in his home state most of that summer and fall, trying to convince the voters that the governor's job was his top priority. The topic had become such an important issue that a question arose during a televised debate when he was asked, "If elected for a fifth time, would you promise to serve out the term and not run for president?"

"You bet," Clinton responded with his typical quick, eager-to-please self-assurance. "I told you when I announced for governor . . . and that's what I'm gonna do. I'm gonna serve four years. I made that decision when I decided to run."

The statement surprised his campaign staff, who had not been briefed, but it went over positively with the state's voters. The general election campaign that year contained its fair share of rumors and accusations but, in the end, Clinton cruised to a victory—57 percent to 43 percent.

Turn the clock to this day in 1991. Standing at the front doors of the Old State House Museum in Little Rock, governor Bill Clinton announced his intention to seek the 1992 Democratic Party's nomination for President of the United States.

While some residents of Razorback country felt that they had been double-crossed by their leader, the fact was that many of the Democrats' top candidates had decided not to run due to president George H. W. Bush's high approval ratings in 1991. According to Gallup polls, following the success of Operation Desert Storm, Bush enjoyed a peak approval rating of 89 percent in February 1991. From there, the incumbent's favorability slowly decreased, reaching the pre-crisis level of 61 percent in October 1991.

While those types of numbers would usually be good enough to win an election, fortunately for Clinton, he had a year to change the minds of the voters, which he did.

OCTOBER 4

DOG GONE

On October 4, 1777, American troops were engaged in battle against the British at the Battle of Germantown (PA) during the Revolutionary War. Amid the fighting, one of the Yankee soldiers found a little terrier running around who appeared to be lost. The soldier took the pooch to his commander who was a well-known devoted dog lover—general George Washington.

He checked the pooch and found a collar with the owner's name on it—general William Howe, the opposing leader of the British troops who the Americans were trying to defeat. Washington ordered that the dog be taken to his tent where he was fed and cleaned.

It would have been easy for the commander to keep his enemy's pet as a prisoner-of-war but the American general couldn't do that because he had such a great love for animals.

The two sides halted the fighting, known as a military cease fire, as an American messenger brought the little dog back to its owner along with a note from the American leader explaining how his soldiers had found the helpless animal and were returning him. Although they were in conflict, Howe expressed his thanks for finding his beloved pet and referenced General Washington's actions as an "honorable act."

Four years later, the American troops won the war.

OCTOBER 5

KEEP YOUR EYES ON THE PRIZE

On this day in 2009, president Barack Obama was nominated to be awarded the Nobel Peace Prize. The chairman of the committee was Thorbjørn Jagland, the former Norwegian prime minister who said, "We have not given the prize for what may happen in the future. We are awarding Obama for what he has done in the past year. And we are hoping this may contribute a little bit for what he is trying to do."

Apparently Jagland was not aware that over the previous year, Obama was busy getting elected to the presidency; going through the transition period; selecting a new Supreme Court justice; and vacationing in Hawaii. He was presented the award in December.

OCTOBER 6

YOU AIN'T HEARD NOTHIN' . . . YET!

The 1927 release of *The Jazz Singer* began the ascendance of the "talkies" and marked the beginning of the end of the silent film era. The star of the historic motion picture was Al Jolson.

But Jolson, a major entertainer of the 1920s, was not supposed to be in the notable film. The role was originally meant for George Jessel who had performed the part on Broadway in its theater version. However, when contract problems arose between Jessel and the film's producers, Warner Brothers, the change was made and Jolson was cast in the lead.

Jessel and Jolson were friends but did not speak to each other for some time afterward because of the casting change with *The Jazz Singer.*

The Warner Brothers (Albert, Harry, Jack, and Sam) were scheduled to be at the film's premiere in New York City on October 6, 1927. But on the day before the big event, 40-year-old Sam died in Los Angeles from a cerebral hemorrhage.

Ironically, it was Sam who was the driving force behind Vitaphone which allowed sound to be added to previously silent motion pictures. None of the Warner brothers were at the first showing of the film that transformed their studio into a major player in the movie industry.

OCTOBER 7

ROYAL GIFT

Before George Washington was America's first battlefield hero, he was a planter and Mount Vernon was the place where he raised an assortment of crops. So what does the leader of a European country give to the general who has recently defeated the most powerful military force on Earth?

What the commander wanted to celebrate his return home to Virginia was a mule. They were sturdier than horses, which would be ideal on such a massive estate. However, acquiring the kind of animal that Washington wanted was tricky since they were only bred in Spain.

Word made its way across the Atlantic to King Charles III on the Iberian Peninsula who shipped Washington a Spanish mule. It arrived on this day in 1785 and the future president named him Royal Gift.

OCTOBER 8

REAL LEADERS ALWAYS LEAD

US Army sergeant Alvin York was America's biggest hero of World War I. He was awarded the Medal of Honor for leading an attack on a German machine-gun nest, taking 32 of the weapons, killing 28 German soldiers and capturing 132 others near Chatel-Chehery, France. That action took place on this day in 1918.

Prior to being drafted into the military, York had been a hard drinker and prone to fighting in saloons. During a night of heavy boozing when he and a friend got into a fight with other barroom patrons, York's friend was killed. The event shook him so much that he quit drinking and became a Christian.

OCTOBER 9

PERSONAL FOUL

Most polls show that football is America's favorite spectator sport. That's an interesting fact, considering that it almost ended about the time that it started.

Originally played on college campuses, the game was extremely rough as it included slugging, gang tackling, and unsportsmanlike behavior. A number of players died (18 in just the year 1905, with 20 times fewer players participating than there are today!). For those reasons, interest in becoming a football player was on the decline.

President Theodore Roosevelt saw merit in the game. It built bodies and could build character, a sense of teamwork and never giving up. Ten of the Rough Riders, the soldiers who fought with him in Cuba, listed their occupations as football players when they enlisted in 1898.

On this day in 1905, Roosevelt summoned representatives of the Big Three (Harvard, Yale,and Princeton, the universities that first played the game under the rules of the day) to the White House. In his best table-thumping style, he convinced them that the game's guidelines needed to be changed to eliminate foul play and brutality.

As a result, the American Football Rules Committee was formed and, in 1906, plays designed to open up the game and make it less dangerous were introduced. Some of the changes included: the introduction of the forward pass; the distance to be gained for a first down increased from five to ten yards; and all mass formations along with gang tackling were banned.

Football became less dangerous to play, injuries and deaths decreased, and the game grew into the major attraction that it is today.

OCTOBER 10

KEY YOUR ENEMIES CLOSE

In Vermont, any person convicted of a felony still retains the right to vote in federal elections and can also run for office—even while they are incarcerated.

On October 10, 1798, congressman Matthew Lyon was found guilty of violating the Alien and Sedition Acts, which prohibited malicious writing against the American government or its officials. He was also the first person to be put on trial for violating the acts on charges of criticizing Federalist president John Adams in a Vermont newspaper.

The problem stemmed from Lyon's disagreement with Adams and a group of Federalists who were pushing to go to war against France. He was sentenced to four months in jail and ordered to pay a $1,000 fine plus court costs for openly conveying his thoughts.

In addition to being the first House member to have an ethics violation charge filed against him, Lyon also had the distinction of being the only person to be elected to Congress while in jail. Following his sentencing, he ran a successful campaign from behind bars in the fall of 1798.

In 1799, the representative's constituents took up a collection to pay his penalty and reelected him to Congress while he was residing in a Vergennes (VT) jail.

Following the presidential election of 1800, the congressman got a measure of revenge against Adams by casting the deciding vote for Thomas Jefferson after the contest went to the House because of an electoral tie.

OCTOBER 11

THE FORGOTTEN EXPLORER

Even though he never touched its soil, Christopher Columbus has received much of the credit and accolades for discovering the North American continent, while others accept that Leif Erikson was the first European to sail to the New World.

However, some experts believe that it was another Norseman, Bjarni Herjólfsson who was actually the first known European to discover the mainland of the Americas.

It is speculated that sometime around 985, Herjólfsson and his men sailed to Greenland to visit his father who was a member of Erikson's crew. But that summer, with no map or compass, they were blown off course by a storm. He saw a piece of land that was not Greenland. It was covered with trees and mountains but the Norseman refused to stop and look around.

Today, scholars of the early history of exploration believe that there were three lands seen by Bjarni. They were Newfoundland, Labrador, and Baffin Island.

After Herjólfsson made his report in Norway, Erikson bought the ship that Bjarni had used for the voyage. He hired a crew of thirty-five and set out to find the land. It was believed that it was that ship which was used for his historic journey to Vinland (coastal North America).

OCTOBER 12

DRIVING A FORD

On October 10, 1973, vice president Spiro Agnew's past caught up with him as he was forced to resign the office because of crimes that he had committed in the 1960s as governor of Maryland. Two days later (on this day), president Richard Nixon nominated longtime Michigan congressman Gerald Ford as Agnew's successor.

A popular member of Congress among members of both parties, the former University of Michigan football star was confirmed by the Senate, 92 to 3, in November and by the House, 387 to 35, a month later.

Less than a year afterward and under investigation due to the Watergate scandal, Nixon followed Agnew out of the White House doors, which elevated Ford to the nation's highest office on August 9, 1974. The resignations made Gerald Ford the only person to become president and vice president without winning a general election for either office.

In 1976, Ford made his only run for an office in the executive branch and lost.

OCTOBER 13

UP, UP AND AWAY

On this day in 1860, two years after the French photographer Gaspard-Félix Tournachon (aka Nadar) took images of Paris from a tethered balloon, James Wallace Black shot a photograph of Boston from a balloon hovering at 1,200 feet.

The image, which provides a clear picture of the downtown area including Boston Common, is believed to be the world's oldest surviving aerial photograph. Within months, Black's observation technique was used as aerial reconnaissance by Union and Confederate Armies during the Civil War.

Unfortunately, the other shots that were taken that day no longer exist. Much of the area pictured in that surviving photo was destroyed in the Great Boston Fire of 1872 and remains as important evidence of what the city looked like prior to the disaster.

OCTOBER 14

THE FIRST BOOM

On this day in 1947, US Air Force captain Chuck Yeager became the first pilot in history to fly faster than the speed of sound. The former World War II fighter ace broke Mach 1 (750 mph) in the Bell X-1 rocket plane jetting over California's Edwards Air Force Base. The historic effort triggered the first-ever "sonic boom."

While Yeager was rewriting the record book, most of the crew was not aware that the previous evening, he broke three ribs after falling from his horse but refused to tell anyone, fearing that he might be replaced, so the injury remained a secret between him and wife Glennis who the plane was named after (*Glamorous Glennis*).

OCTOBER 15

THE VALUE OF A DOLLAR

Daniel Parke Custis was born on this day in 1711. In 1735, his father deeded him 275 acres of land, along with 100 slaves, in Virginia's New Kent County on the Pamunkey River, where he had already been living as a wealthy bachelor. He came into his own as a vestryman of Saint Peter's Parish, an officer of the county militia, and a successful planter.

In 1748, the 37-year-old Custis began courting 16-year-old Martha Dandridge, daughter of a local planter and county clerk. He and Martha married on May 15, 1750, at Chestnut Grove, her New Kent County residence. They went on to have four children.

Daniel and his second son (Daniel Jr.) became ill on July 4, 1757. The boy survived, but Daniel Sr. died four days later, most likely from a virulent throat infection.

The business-savvy Martha became one of the wealthiest and most available young widows in Virginia and had no shortage of male suitors. Months later, she began seeing another local planter who lived more than 125 miles away and was a veteran of the French and Indian War. His name was George and after some visits in 1758, the couple began to plan their future together.

The 26-year-old had a large estate of his own located on the Potomac River where he raised livestock and crops. He had also inherited several holdings from his father's property years earlier.

On January 6, 1759, Martha married George, who then took over as manager of the Custis property for the benefit of the children. With the estates of the newlyweds combined, George Washington soon became the wealthiest businessman in Virginia and, until John F. Kennedy assumed office in 1961, the nation's richest president.

OCTOBER 16

THE GOOD NEWS IS . . . YOU WON THE ELECTION!

On this day in 2000, governor Mel Carnahan (D-MO) was running for the US Senate when the twin-engine Cessna, piloted by his son Randy, crashed during a campaign tour near Goldman, Missouri, a suburb of St. Louis. Both Carnahans, along with a campaign advisor, died in the crash.

However, never let a small matter like the death of a candidate stop an election. Even though deceased, Missouri law would not allow Mel Carnahan's name to be removed from the ballot. Three weeks later, the departed politician won the election, with his wife being selected to fill the seat for the next two years.

OCTOBER 17

YOU CAN BET ON IT

On May 28, 1830, president Andrew Jackson signed the Indian Removal Act, which ordered the relocation of American Indian communities in the eastern United States to territories west of the Mississippi River. The law set the stage for forced displacement of several tribes including those that were part of the infamous Trail of Tears.

However, on this day in 1988, Native Americans were on the winning side as Congress passed the Indian Gaming Regulatory Act (IGRA) that was signed by president Ronald Reagan. It allowed tribal sovereignty to create casino-like gaming as directed by the tribes, which has resulted in a multibillion dollar industry. Today, many Native Americans refuse to handle twenty dollar bills because they are adorned with Jackson's portrait.

OCTOBER 18

EVERYTHING IS OKAY!

Throughout the United States, there are a fair share of towns and cities that are known by their unconventional names. Among those are Coward, South Carolina; Uncertain, Texas; and Last Chance, Iowa.

One such community got its start around 1806, when a French trader named Joseph Bogy established a trading post in an area known as Three Forks.

A fire destroyed most of the business district in 1936, including two general stores, a church, the post office, and two vacant buildings. Only two businesses, a filling station, and a blacksmith shop survived the disaster.

Even with that, local residents are happy to greet visitors when they say, "Welcome to Okay, Oklahoma!" The catchy name for the town was adopted on this day in 1919.

OCTOBER 19

GENERAL, YOU MAY RETAIN YOUR SWORD

At the conclusion of the Revolutionary War, British general Charles Cornwallis was so mortified by his defeat that he dispatched his second in command, brigadier general Charles O'Hara, to surrender his forces.

When O'Hara offered Cornwallis' sword to George Washington, the American commander asked his second in command, major general Benjamin Lincoln, to accept it. It was a traditional gesture for the vanquished commander to offer his weapon to his conqueror during a surrender.

At the ceremony held on the afternoon of October 19, 1781, O'Hara was allowed to retain his officer's blade and then led a column of British troops out of Yorktown. As they departed, he directed the redcoats to lay down their weapons upon departure.

Eighty-four years later, in a repeat of history during the surrender ceremony of the Civil War, the victorious Union commander Ulysses S. Grant allowed Confederate general Robert E. Lee to retain his sword.

As opposed to Cornwallis, Lee was present at the gathering and personally ordered his men to go home following the conclusion of the formalities. Grant allowed the Confederate soldiers to keep their weapons in order to hunt for food and provide for their families.

OCTOBER 20

THE CONSTITUIONAL TIGHTROPE

On this day in 1803, the Senate voted for ratification of the Louisiana Purchase by a 24–7 margin with the treaty signing taking place eleven days later. In the aftermath, some Federalists continued to view America's greatest real estate deal as unconstitutional, although it was never challenged in court. But what if it had been?

Such a move would have set the stage for a major judicial showdown featuring president Thomas Jefferson taking on his cousin and political rival, Supreme Court chief justice John Marshall.

OCTOBER 21

AT ONE TIME, THEY CALLED HIM AL

In August 1862, fifteen-year-old Al was standing outside the Mount Clemens (MI) train station where he worked. As usual, freight cars were being transferred to a side track. However, when one of the cars approached the station at high speed, the teenager saw the station master's two-year-old son, Jimmie, playing on the tracks in the locomotive's path.

Al reacted immediately by snatching the boy from his dangerous position and moving them both to safety. They received just minor wounds during the life-saving effort. Jimmie's grateful father expressed his gratitude by offering to teach his inquisitive employee how to use the station's telegraph machine, which was an ample reward for the boy with limited formal education.

Al was a nickname used by the young man's friends. As he became an adult, the story of his train station heroics as well as use of his nickname subsided, but his quest for knowledge, especially when it came to science, continued to grow.

By 1878, Al—now going by his birth name, Thomas—was working as a full-time scientist. On the night of October 21–22, he and his staff watched as they finally made a breakthrough on a project they'd worked on for more than a year, conducting over 1,200 experiments.

The culmination of their efforts came with a cotton-thread filament that burned for 14 1/2 hours—a major step toward the creation of the modern electric light. The person behind it all was Thomas Alva Edison who saved the life of a small boy before leaving his mark on history and science.

OCTOBER 22

SIMILAR BUT DIFFERENT

It became evident early on during the 2016 presidential campaign that the two frontrunners, Donald Trump and Hillary Clinton, didn't care for each other. Their comments cut hard and deep during their campaign rhetoric. That's not unusual, but that year was a war of words that had rarely been heard in election circles. During polling, each received high negative ratings from prospective voters.

But the pair did have some common bonds, such as, they were both transplants to their political parties. Trump had belonged to several groups and non-organizations over the decades leading to his White House residency. His long and winding road map to Washington, DC, began when he was originally a Democrat until 1987; then a Republican from 1987 to 1999; and a member of the Reform Party from 1999 to 2001. He returned to the Democratic Party from 2001 to 2009; switched back to the Republican Party again from 2009 to 2011; was an independent from 2011 to 2012; and finally settled with the Republicans in 2012.

This isn't the first time that a chief executive has pulled the old switcheroo, as Ronald Reagan changed from the Democratic Party to the Republican Party before Trump arrived on the scene.

In the early 1960s, Clinton, maiden name Rodham, was a Republican and a supporter of 1964 GOP nominee Barry Goldwater. She became a Democrat a few years later during her time as a student at Wellesley College.

On this day in 2016, the former Republican led the ex-Democrat by 3.5% in combined averages of the major polls. But just like the candidates who had changed parties, the poll numbers would also go a different way over the campaign's final two weeks.

OCTOBER 23

THE OUTLAW LIFE

In the late nineteenth century, a number of well-known criminals had been pursued by the law. Among those were John Wilkes Booth, John Wesley Hardin, and Jesse James.

Also on that list was Harry Tracy. In 1898, Tracy and three accomplices engaged in a gunfight at Brown's Park, Colorado, in which a posse man was killed. He and another member of his gang were captured but escaped in June 1898 from the jail in Aspen, Colorado. In late 1901, the outlaw was again apprehended, convicted, and incarcerated at the Oregon State Penitentiary.

On June 9, 1902, Tracy was involved in another escape. This time, he killed three corrections officers and three civilians before fleeing.

The fugitive evaded the dragnet for a month and then set up an ambush near Bothell, Washington, where he murdered two more lawmen. Tracy ran, took hostages, and got into a third shootout in which he killed two more posse members. On August 6, he was cornered and shot in the leg near Creston, Washington, before taking his own life rather than being arrested again.

A former member of the Wild Bunch with Butch Cassidy and the Sundance Kid, Tracy is considered the last great outlaw of the Wild West. Happy Birthday to Harry who was born on this day in 1875.

OCTOBER 24

TARGET IN SITE

David McCampbell of the United States Navy was the commander of Carrier Air Group 15 aboard the aircraft carrier USS *Essex* that attacked a force of sixty Japanese aircraft successfully shooting down nine of the enemy, a single-mission record for an American pilot during World War II. When he returned to his ship from the 95-minute battle, his Grumman F6F Hellcat fighter was almost out of ammunition and gas. His wingman for the sortie, ensign Roy Rushing, also shot down six Japanese aircraft.

The heroic action took place on this day in 1944, earning the Medal of Honor for the flight commander.

McCampbell was also the only US pilot to twice shoot down five or more enemy aircraft in one day. The Alabama native became the only carrier pilot to receive the Medal of Honor.

After a 31-year career in the Navy that began at the US Naval Academy, McCampbell retired as a captain in 1964 having commanded numerous units as well as ships. He died in 1996 and is buried at Arlington National Cemetery.

OCTOBER 25

VINDICATED!

In February 1868, Andrew Johnson was impeached but not removed from office as the Senate was unable to garner the necessary votes. His impeachment problems began when he attempted to remove Edwin Stanton as secretary of war. Congress believed that he had violated the Tenure of Office Act and the fight was on.

Even though Johnson survived the impeachment, Congress repealed the law in 1887, at the urging of president Grover Cleveland. For most, that fact vindicated Johnson.

However, on this day in 1926, the Supreme Court delivered the final word on the matter as it ruled, once and for all, in the case of *Myers v. United States* that the act was unconstitutional. Unfortunately for the seventeenth president, the verdict was a little late as it was made posthumously, exonerating Johnson who had died in 1875.

OCTOBER 26

HI-YO SILVER

Every day numerous boats and ships pass the Statue of Liberty. That was the case on the quiet, moonlit night of September 26, 1903, as a tugboat escorted the barge *Harold* out of what is today the South Street Seaport past the symbolic sculpture of freedom.

The *Harold's* load consisted of nearly 7,700 silver-and-lead bars, or "pigs," that were destined for the glowing Asarco Refinery blast furnaces of Perth Amboy, New Jersey. The silver, along with the smelters, belonged to the prominent Guggenheim family, which had made its fortune in global mining and smelting.

But the cargo never arrived, at least not in its entirety. Somewhere in the Arthur Kill tidal strait, aka the Staten Island Sound, the Harold capsized, sending most of the payload to the bottom of the strait.

In an interview with *The New York Times*, the salvage company's owner was quick to pass blame describing the barge's deckhands as the, "dumbest skunks I ever had to do with." A secret retrieval effort recovered about 85 percent of the lost "pigs," but that still left nearly 1,400 bars unaccounted. On today's market, they are estimated to be worth as much as $20 million and have attracted fortune hunters from throughout the world.

The famous family would be involved in another well-known mishap at sea. Nine years following the loss of their silver, Benjamin Guggenheim, the son of the family patriarch, was one of those who died aboard RMS *Titanic*. He had been born on this day in 1865.

OCTOBER 27

YOUTH WILL SERVE

Stevens Thomson Mason was born on this day in 1811. He was an American politician who served as the first governor of Michigan from 1835 to 1840.

Coming to political prominence at just 19 years of age, Mason was appointed his territory's acting secretary by President Andrew Jackson before becoming the acting territorial governor in 1834 at the age of 22.

As territorial governor, Mason was instrumental in guiding Michigan to statehood, which was secured in 1837. A member of the Democratic Party, he was elected as Michigan's first state governor at age 24.

Mason was and remains the youngest state governor in American history. He died of pneumonia on January 4, 1843, at just 31 years of age.

Due to political wrangling, the former territorial leader was buried four different times.

OCTOBER 28

WHAT'S IN A NAME?

On October 28, 1682, British social reformer William Penn led a contingent of like-minded followers who were seeking religious freedom. They landed in what is today Philadelphia, Pennsylvania. While the area once served as the new nation's temporary capital, it's not the original.

The first Philadelphia was located in the modern country of Turkey and established in 189 BCE by King Eumenes II of Pergamon. It is believed that Penn liked the name and borrowed it from the ancient city for his community in the New World.

OCTOBER 29

FORD TO NYC . . . DROP DEAD!

President Gerald Ford declared flatly on this day in 1975 that he would veto any bill calling for a federal bailout of revenue-strapped New York City and instead proposed legislation that would make it easier for America's largest municipality to go into bankruptcy.

"I can tell you now that I am prepared to veto any bill that has as its purpose a federal bailout of New York City to prevent a default," the president said.

However, the only victim of Ford's bailout rejection was the president himself. In the following year's election, one of the states he lost was New York with its 41 electoral votes. Had he won that additional state, Ford would have captured the election.

OCTOBER 30

MEET THE PRESS

If one is attempting to break into the music business, it doesn't hurt to be connected to important individuals, especially when your father is well known. Such was the case for Margaret Truman of Independence, Missouri.

She had been raised by piano-playing parents and sang as a child in the church choir back home. Her formal voice training began at sixteen and she yearned for a career singing opera. Even though Margaret's father didn't work in the music business, he was still a person of influence as the sitting President of the United States—Harry S. Truman.

The family name helped get her onto the national stage, which included tour appearances in Detroit, Pittsburgh, and Washington, DC, as well as the famous Hollywood Bowl. On this day in 1947, Margaret performed with the renowned St. Louis Symphony Orchestra.

In most cases, the media reviews were polite but it was evident that she was not on the same level as the great soprano of the era, Maria Callas. However, there was one performance that raised the ire of the Commander-in-Chief.

President Truman made headlines of his own following a concert in Washington, DC, that was held on December 5, 1950. Paul Hume, the *Washington Post*'s music critic, wrote that Margaret, "cannot sing very well. She is flat most of the time."

The angry dad and World War I veteran immediately responded with a letter to the journalist, warning that if they ever met, "You'll need a new nose, and plenty of beefsteak for black eyes, and perhaps a supporter below!"

The man from Missouri never carried out his threat and Hume sold the letter for more than $3,000 in 1951. It was auctioned in 2002 for $193,000.

After her father left office two years later, Margaret worked as a television and radio host, as well as authoring a biography of President Truman along with other books. She died in Chicago in 2008 at age 83.

OCTOBER 31

LIKE FATHER, LIKE SON

In 1927, sculptor Gutzon Borglum began work on the four presidential images (George Washington, Abraham Lincoln, Thomas Jefferson, and Theodore Roosevelt) on Mount Rushmore. The project was nearing completion when Borglum died on March 6, 1941, of coronary sclerosis. At that point, his son Lincoln took over the project and declared it completed on this day in 1941.

NOVEMBER

It's a very good historical book about history.

—Former vice president Dan Quayle

NOVEMBER 1

ONCE AND FOR ALL, GOOD-BYE!

Paul Tibbets, the American pilot of the *Enola Gay*, the plane that dropped the first nuclear bomb, didn't have a funeral or headstone. As he neared death, the general decided he didn't want a funeral service or a marker as he worried it would become a place for protesting nuclear armament.

Instead, when Tibbets passed away on this day in 2007, he was cremated and his ashes were scattered over the English Channel.

NOVEMBER 2

ABSENTEE BALLOT

If a US citizen is unable to make it to their polling place, they have the option of voting by absentee ballot.

On November 2, 2004, Leroy Chiao set a record by becoming the first NASA astronaut to vote from space in a presidential election. At the time, he was commanding *Expedition 10* aboard the International Space Station (ISS). The first astronaut to cast a vote of any type from space was NASA's David Wolf, who was aboard the Russian Space Station Mir during the mid-term election in 1997.

A special electronic absentee ballot mechanism makes it possible for astronauts to be able to vote from space.

NOVEMBER 3

A REAL AMERICAN?

Republican senator Barry Goldwater of Arizona was planning to run against John F. Kennedy in the 1964 presidential election. That potential matchup never took place as JFK was assassinated on November 22, 1963.

However, at one time, there was some question as to whether Goldwater could legally serve as president had he won. In 1964, the conservative lawmaker was the Republican Party's nominee but the Constitution required that the commander in chief be born in the United States. Goldwater was born in 1909 in Arizona, which had yet to become a state and did not do so until 1912.

Persons living in the Arizona Territory, which at one time was part of the New Mexico Territory, in 1848 and those residing in the area of the Gadsden Purchase were automatically granted US citizenship upon the admission of statehood.

Thus, it didn't matter in any sense as on this day in 1964, Goldwater lost to Lyndon Johnson in the general election by a 22.5% landslide.

NOVEMBER 4

AND THE WINNER IS . . .

In 1922, William Ross was elected governor of Wyoming by appealing to progressive voters of both parties. On October 2, 1924, Ross died from surgical complications following an appendectomy. The state's Democratic Party then surprised many voters by selecting his unnominated widow, Nellie, to run for as his successor in a special election the following month.

On this day in 1924, she won easily, 55% to 44%, becoming the first female governor in the history of the United States. That seemed totally appropriate as Wyoming had been the first state to allow women's suffrage. As governor, she continued her late husband's policies, which called for tax cuts, government assistance for poor farmers, banking reform, along with laws protecting children, women workers, and miners.

Ross ran for reelection in 1926 but was narrowly defeated. She refused to campaign for herself and supported Prohibition which many viewed as mistakes. The former governor remained active in the Democratic Party and in 1928, she received 31 votes from ten states for vice president on the first ballot.

NOVEMBER 5

TWO IS ENOUGH

On this day in 1940, Franklin D. Roosevelt was reelected president of the United States for an unprecedented third term, defeating Republican candidate Wendell Willkie. He repeated the historic moment with another victory four years later.

However, it didn't take Congress very long after FDR's death in 1945 to place term limits on occupancy of the Oval Office. On March 21, 1947, Congress passed the Twenty-Second Amendment—restricting presidents to two terms in office.

NOVEMBER 6

LANDING GEAR DOWN

On this day in 1945, just months after the end of World War II, the US Navy achieved the first landing on an aircraft carrier by a jet-powered aircraft when a Ryan FR-1 Fireball landed on the deck of the USS *Wake Island*. Ensign Jake C. West, USN, was at the controls of the aircraft as part of the US Navy's first jet combat squadron. The war ended before the first American Navy jet fighter could enter the conflict.

When Ensign West entered the pattern to land on the vessel, it would have been expected that the maneuver was specifically planned and carefully considered; however, it was not. In fact, the first jet landing on an aircraft carrier was the result of an in-flight emergency.

NOVEMBER 7

YOUR CHEATIN' HEART

On this day in 1962, President Kennedy's younger brother Edward was elected to his first of eight terms as a US senator from Massachusetts. It was the same seat that had previously been held by JFK (1953–1960).

Like his father and older brothers, "Ted" as he was known, attended Harvard University but, as opposed to his siblings, his road to a diploma was a bit of a rocky ride. In May 1951, Kennedy, a freshman, was expelled from the institution when he was caught having a friend take a Spanish test for him. He returned two years later.

Even with that indiscretion along with other incidents, he was able to keep his seat in the Senate for forty-seven years, although he never carried the stature of his older brothers. He was still in office when he died in 2009.

NOVEMBER 8

NEVER BUCK A HERO

The dictionary defines a phobia as an extreme or irrational fear of or an aversion to something. However, observing from afar, Bill Clinton did not appear to be afraid of much of anything in his path.

In 1992, he had been elected president with less than 50 percent of the popular vote (43%) while surviving attacks about his womanizing and his tactics to avoid military service during the Vietnam War. During his first two years in office, his job-approval rating had held consistently at around 50 percent and everything appeared to be going his way at the White House.

But the first inkling of public concern came with the midterm elections of 1994 as the Republicans took control of both houses of Congress for the first time since 1954. However, that didn't bother Clinton.

Speculation began to surface in 1994 as to who the Republicans would nominate to take on the incumbent in 1996. There was one potential prospect that had Clinton's campaign staff losing sleep. Colin Powell was a 58-year-old, African American, retired four-star general who was one of the top officers during Operation Desert Storm.

A Powell candidacy would have meant Clinton's worst nightmare becoming a reality. In September, a Gallup poll measured the favorability ratings for Powell to be higher than for any other potential candidate in the 1996 race. "Running as a Republican in a two-way race against Bill Clinton," the poll summarized, "Powell handily beats the sitting president, 54% to 39%."

The United States has a long line of winning generals who went on to the White House and Clinton didn't want to be evicted by America's newest hero. However, as the public waited for an announcement of some kind, there was nothing for Team Clinton to do but sit, wonder, and hope.

On this day in 1995, almost a year to the day before the next election, the Arkansan got his answer. At a press conference held in Alexandria, Virginia, the former battlefield commander announced that he would not be a candidate. One of the key reasons behind the decision was his wife's concern for his personal safety.

At that point, the election was essentially over, as Clinton coasted to an easy victory a year later. But his team's fear had not been without foundation as a *Voter News Service* poll released a surprising set of results the day after the 1996 election.

The survey included Powell as the Republican nominee, in place of senator Robert Dole (R-KS), and the results were astonishing. Using a sampling of 3,697 registered voters (that's about three times the norm), Powell won the election with 50%. Clinton was far behind at 38% and third party candidate Ross Perot had 9%. It proved that the president's apprehensions had been well grounded.

NOVEMBER 9

THE ANGRY ACTOR

On Friday April 14, 1865, president Abraham Lincoln was shot and killed by the actor John Wilkes Booth while watching a play at Ford's Theatre in Washington, DC. Ironically, it wasn't the first encounter between the men at that venue.

Months prior on November 9, 1863, Booth was performing at Ford's in the role of Raphael in the play, *The Marble Heart*. Among those in the audience that evening, seated in the Presidential Box, was the commander in chief himself, Abraham Lincoln.

At one point during the performance, Booth was said to have shaken his finger in Lincoln's direction as he delivered a line of dialogue. The president's sister-in-law, sitting with him in the same box turned and said, "Mr. Lincoln, he looks as if he meant that for you."

The surprised leader replied, "He does look pretty sharp at me, doesn't he?"

Lincoln notified the manager that he would like to meet the actor following the performance. The request was rejected by Booth, a hard-line Confederate supporter.

NOVEMBER 10

WE WANT ELVIS!

Elvis Presley was arguably the best-known performer in the history of rock-and-roll music. Although he was recognized throughout the world, his concert appearances outside the United States were limited to just a few selected locations.

During his career, Elvis played every major city, and many that weren't, in the United States. But in 1957, he did six concerts on foreign soil—the only time he ever did so. There were three appearances in Canada: Toronto (April 2), Ottawa (April 3), and Vancouver (August 31).

A few weeks after his Canadian performances, the musical sensation appeared in Hawaii doing three shows in two days, November 9 and 10. At the time, the islands had yet to become a state, although they were a territory, so the final performance of day two (November 10) was his last outside the United States.

However, for the next two years, Elvis spent a great deal of time away from home as he was drafted into the US Army. He was stationed for seventeen months in West Germany. Upon his discharge, he returned to making the "Three Ms"—music, movies, and money.

It was never confirmed, but it was suspected that his manager Tom Parker, who handled Elvis' schedule, didn't want his star touring abroad since he himself was a military deserter from his home country of the Netherlands, and it could have led to complications.

NOVEMBER 11

GOOD DAYS, BAD DAYS

Henry Gunther was an American private who was likely the last Allied soldier from any of the warring nations to be killed during World War I. He died on this day at 10:59 a.m., about one minute before the Armistice was to take effect at 11:00 a.m. local time in France.

Gunther had recently been demoted from sergeant for disobeying an order during battle and was seeking to regain his rank just before the war ended. In a complete about-face, the US Army posthumously restored his rank and also awarded him a Divisional Citation for Gallantry in Action along with the Distinguished Service Cross.

NOVEMBER 12

WELCOME TO VILLA HAYES

Many who studied about Rutherford B. Hayes for the first time probably knew little about him beforehand. That would not be the case for a student in Paraguay where the former US president is a national icon. From 1864 to 1870, the South American country was engaged in one of the bloodiest conflicts in the history of the Western Hemisphere—the War of the Triple Alliance.

Two-thirds of the nation's population died in the conflict. But even after the war ended, Argentina and Paraguay continued to battle over a final resolution. Diplomats from both countries traveled to Washington, DC, to allow President Hayes to arbitrate the dispute. On November 12, 1878, Hayes decided in favor of Paraguay—and he's been a hero of the country ever since.

Once every fifty years, the town of Villa Hayes (named in his honor) hosts a huge festival. The next one is scheduled for 2028.

NOVEMBER 13

RAIN MAKER

On this day in 1946, the first artificial snow from a natural cloud was produced. Vincent Joseph Schaefer of the General Electric Company flew in an airplane over Mt. Greylock in western Massachusetts dispensing small dry-ice pellets over a tract for about 3 miles from a height of about 14,000 feet.

Snow fell at around the 3,000 foot mark but because of the dry condition of the atmosphere, it evaporated before reaching the ground. Schaefer had previously produced icy flakes in a cold chamber on July 12, 1946.

The mechanism became so popular that by 1952, the first snowmaking system was in regular use at Grossinger's ski resort in New York's Catskill Mountains. Today, virtually every American ski area produces artificial snow as snowmaking has grown into a multimillion dollar global industry.

NOVEMBER 14

MADAME COMMISSIONER?

Condoleezza Rice was born on this day in 1954. Her resume of accomplishments is as impressive as anyone who has served in government over the past many years.

She grew up in racially torn Birmingham, Alabama, where, as an eight-year-old, she was exposed to a church bombing that killed four young Black girls on a quiet Sunday morning in 1963. One of those was her 11-year-old friend Denise McNair. It was eventually discovered that the murders were the work of the Ku Klux Klan.

But Ms. Rice didn't let hate detour her from making a difference. She graduated with BA and PhD degrees from the University of Denver along with her MA from the University of Notre Dame. In addition, she is a classically trained musician and concert pianist who has accompanied a wide range of musical greats like cellist Yo-Yo Ma and soul singer Aretha Franklin.

The multitalented Rice speaks, in addition to English, French, Russian, German, and Spanish. She also ice skates.

In 2001, she became the national security advisor for the George W. Bush administration. In 2005, Dr. Rice began a four-year tenure as the US secretary of state, the first African American woman to do so.

One might surmise that all of those experiences would professionally satisfy most individuals, but not so for Condoleezza Rice.

In 2002, in an interview with the *New York Times,* she admitted that her dream job was to become the commissioner of the National Football League. She stated, "I think it would be a very interesting job because I actually think football, with all due respect to baseball, is a kind of national pastime that brings people together across social lines, across racial lines. And I think it's an important American institution."

Although by 2023, she had yet to attain her ideal profession, for three years (2015–2017), Dr. Rice served as a member of the College Football Playoff Selection Committee. As usual, she was the first African American woman to do so.

NOVEMBER 15

THE PRICE OF FREEDOM

On this day in 1993, thirteen Cuban defectors stole an aging biplane and overcame heavy thunderstorms and broken navigational equipment to reach freedom in Florida.

Their landing at 5:45 a.m. at the Opa Locka Airport just north of Miami followed a week of preparations and four hours of flying a zigzag course to confuse Cuban radar. Less than six hours after touching down, they were granted political asylum and released, like the more than 3,000 other Cubans who made it across the Florida straits that year.

The Cuban defectors included the plane's mechanic, four married couples, and their children—two toddlers, a 7-year-old and a 9-year-old. The An-2 single-engine plane, built by Russia in the 1950s, had been used as a crop-duster.

NOVEMBER 16

FOLLOW THE YELLOW BRICK ROAD

Whenever an American is asked where most of the nation's gold is stored, the answer is often Kentucky's Fort Knox. Current holdings ring in at 147.3 million ounces. That's about half of the US treasury's stored gold (as well as valuables of other federal agencies).

But the grand prize goes to the New York Federal Reserve Bank (a.k.a. "The Fed") in Manhattan. Their holdings include the largest known monetary-gold reserve in the world, with about 6,190 short tons (5,620 metric tons) in storage as of 2019.

The Fed opened for business on this day in 1914. During those first hours of operation, it took in $100 million from 211 member banks. That is equal to $2.89 billion today.

NOVEMBER 17

HERE'S A FISH STORY

In November 1985, US president Ronald Reagan and Soviet general secretary Mikhail Gorbachev conducted their first summit meeting to discuss their countries' reduction of nuclear weapons. It was held in Geneva, Switzerland.

During the summit, the Reagans stayed at a chateau on loan from Prince Karim Aga Khan. The prince's young son left the president a note, asking him to take care of his pet goldfish while he was there. Unfortunately the next day, November 17, one of them died at which point, Reagan ordered Secret Service agents to locate and buy an identical replacement as soon as possible.

Agent Bill Henkel was summoned. "We've got to find another goldfish for that boy," said chief of staff Donald Regan. "Your job is on the line, Henkel!"

The quick-thinking commander in chief then stuck the dead fish in his pocket and forgot about it while meeting with Gorbachev. For the next few hours, the deceased water inhabitant was undercover as the two most powerful leaders discussed making the world a safer place.

Before returning to the United States, Reagan left a note for the prince's son explaining what happened. A Reagan aide joked, "And we'd come to Geneva thinking our toughest job would be to handle the Russians."

NOVEMBER 18

NO TRUER WORDS WERE EVER SPOKEN

The Gettysburg Address is arguably the greatest speech in American history. Although there were moments when it appeared that those famous words and passages might never be uttered by its author but rather remain as notes on paper. In 1863, seventeen acres of land at the battle site had been secured by the state of Pennsylvania to be dedicated as a permanent memorial and cemetery.

On this day in 1863, Lincoln departed Washington for the 85-mile train ride. During his northward journey, he began to feel weak and his face turned pale. The president conveyed to his private secretary John Hay, who was traveling with him, that he felt ill but continued on to his destination. He arrived in Gettysburg on this night in 1863 before the ceremony and stayed over at a local official's private home.

At the dedication the next day, Lincoln rose from his seat and delivered his historic 273 word address in less than two minutes but, because he was so brief, the crowd didn't react immediately when he had concluded. Only once he'd put on his famous stovepipe hat and begun to fold up his copy of the speech did the audience start applauding.

Lincoln's reaction to their response was that he had disappointed the attendees. That evening, on the return trip back to the nation's capital, his health continued to worsen. Over the following days, doctors downplayed his condition so as not to upset the public which was already caught up in the perils of war reports.

The nation's leader was limited in his activities for the next three weeks before being allowed to return to the job full time. However, William Johnson, Lincoln's most trusted servant, who had accompanied the family from Springfield, Illinois, and tended to the president during his recuperation, later developed smallpox and died weeks later in January 1864.

NOVEMBER 19

THE WATER WAR

For centuries, fights between individuals and countries have taken place for many reasons. Some are valid, others not so much.

Even though the United States has yet to celebrate its 300th birthday, that has not kept it from taking part in its own version of the water wars. In America, Ground Zero was the Colorado River which served as the dividing line between seven states that included California and Arizona.

As early as 1923, California planners had their eyes on a river project and began charting a course for an aqueduct to bring its water further west. With a few initial concrete blocks in 1934, the Bureau of Reclamation commenced construction of Parker Dam.

The move didn't sit well with many Arizonans including governor Benjamin Moeur who viewed California's aggressive seizure of Colorado River water as a violation of the law. On November 10, 1934, the angry official declared martial law and dispatched 100 National Guard troops to use ferryboats to inspect the dam's construction but ran into some bad luck as they got tangled in some cables and had to be rescued by enemy forces.

Although no shots were ever fired, the novelty of land-locked Arizona attempting to form a navy and the strange nature of the conflict attracted a great deal of media attention. As it turned out, the Parker Dam War was only the opening salvo in a long and bitter legal contest between the two states that lasted more than half a century.

Despite numerous setbacks during the construction of the reservoir, Parker Dam was finally completed and dedicated on this day in 1938.

NOVEMBER 20

1-2-3 . . . SMILE!

When a person plans to travel outside of their home country, they need all of the usual items such as a toothbrush, clothes, and very important—a passport. Each year, many of those who go to foreign lands put off getting the required little booklet until the last minute.

The Department of State has issued passports to American citizens traveling abroad since 1789, but it did not have sole authority to do so until 1856. Some have become collector's items, such as those issued by president George Washington, with his official signature, in 1796, less than three months before he left office. They were known as Mediterranean passports and he signed only a few before leaving office.

Passports were required from August 19, 1861, to March 17, 1862, during the Civil War. A major addition for the document book happened on this day in 1914 when the US State Department started requiring photographs for all passports.

Today, passports are accepted in various states as legal identification to vote, authorization for employment, proof of citizenship, or any situation that might otherwise require a birth certificate.

NOVEMBER 21

SOMETIMES YOU'RE THE WINDSHIELD . . .
SOMTIMES THE BUG

On November 19, 1963, two days before leaving for Texas, president John F. Kennedy and his longtime secretary Evelyn Lincoln had a discussion in the Oval Office. He told her, "You know, if I am reelected in '64, I am going to spend more and more time making government service an honorable career . . . To [do] this I will need as a running mate in '64, a man who believes as I do . . . it is too early to make an announcement about another running mate—that will perhaps wait until the convention."

"Who is your choice of a running mate?" Lincoln asked.

Without hesitation he replied, "At this time I am thinking about Governor Terry Sanford of North Carolina. But it will not be Lyndon" (a reference to the incumbent Lyndon Johnson).

For JFK, the decision was being made a year before the election would be final—Johnson was on his way out! The two officials had never gotten along, which was very apparent during their final trip together.

The disagreements between the president and LBJ continued in Fort Worth on November 21 regarding the seating arrangements for Friday's motorcade through downtown Dallas. One argument inside the Presidential Suite at the Hotel Texas became so intense that it was heard by Mrs. Kennedy, who was in the next room, and was also caught by the ears of members of the hotel's staff who were in the hallway.

It appeared that LBJ might be staring at the same fate that quashed fellow Texan John Nance Garner in 1940 during his reelection bid for vice president with Franklin Roosevelt. However, in less than 24 hours following a series of unexpected events, Johnson went from a tossed-aside vice president to the new Leader of the Free World!

NOVEMBER 22

START SPREADING THE NEWS

Two separate judges presiding over murder trials both came to the same conclusion that hearing about the assassination of a president might influence jurors' verdicts during their deliberations. Due to those circumstances, one judge in Long Island, New York, and another in Blountville, Tennessee, ordered their jurors sequestered.

With no phone calls and everyone who interacted with the jurors instructed not to mention the major historic event, those twenty-four jurors all made it through the weekend, never realizing their president had been murdered. No doubt, they may have been among the very few people in America that day who didn't hear the tragic news of President Kennedy's assassination on November 22, 1963.

NOVEMBER 23

THE ONE THAT GOT AWAY

The Lincoln assassination was part of a conspiracy where most of the participants met death as the price for their part in the crime. Four of them were hanged and one was shot. However, there was one of them who got away.

Conspirator Mary Surratt's son John was part of the original plot to kidnap the president and then exchange him for Confederate prisoners of war. That was to take place on March 17, 1865, as Lincoln's carriage departed for the White House, returning from Campbell General Hospital in Washington, DC, where he had been visiting the wounded. However, at the last moment, the chief executive changed his plans and remained in the city for a meeting.

The day after John Surratt's twenty-first birthday (April 14, 1865), actor John Wilkes Booth killed Lincoln. Surratt was questioned but denied any involvement in the assassination. On April 18, his mother was arrested but her son had already fled to Montreal, Canada, where he was given sanctuary by a Catholic priest. He remained there until his mother's execution on July 7, 1865.

The one-time postmaster then fled to Europe where he traveled to several locations. At one point, Surratt enlisted with the Pontifical Zouaves, a unit of the official army of the Papal States. He remained hidden in their army until he was exposed.

On this day in 1866, the fugitive was arrested in Alexandria, Egypt, and extradited back to the United States. Surratt was tried for his role in the kidnapping plot which ended in a mistrial. Unfortunately for the government's legal team, the statute of limitations ran out before he could be retried.

In 1872, John Surratt married Mary Hunter, a second cousin of Francis Scott Key, the composer of *The Star Spangled Banner*. The former conspirator resided in Maryland where he became a teacher and tobacco farmer and, in 1916, died at the age of 72.

NOVEMBER 24

LOOKING BETTER IN A SWEATER

On November 24, 1963, two days after the murder of president John F. Kennedy, accused assassin Lee Harvey Oswald was shot and killed by local nightclub owner Jack Ruby in the basement of the Dallas city jail. But it may have been the suspect's sweater that played a key role in his own demise.

Oswald was being escorted by authorities to an armored vehicle in the basement in order to be transferred to the county lockup located just down the block. At the last minute, he asked to be allowed to wear a darker sweater that would help him stand out in the glare of the television lights. This delayed the transfer another 5 or 10 minutes or until about 11:20 a.m. (CST). It was at that time that Ruby arrived at the location.

Oswald was shot at 11:21 a.m. and taken to Parkland Hospital, which had been JFK's final stop 48 hours earlier, where he died afterward. The killing of the suspect was the first major American historical event to be broadcast live as it happened. Among those that followed included:

July 20, 1969: US astronauts took the first walk on the moon.

January 28, 1986: Space Shuttle Challenger exploded 73 seconds after takeoff killing its entire crew.

September 11, 2001: United Airlines Flight 175 crashed into the South Tower of the World Trade Center after being taken over by terrorists. Another plane had already struck the North Tower.

NOVEMBER 25

BEFORE MACY'S

The famous Macy's department store first sponsored a Thanksgiving Day Parade in New York City in 1924. It is still around today, but they were not the first to host such an event.

Gimbels, a well-known retail outlet in Philadelphia, beat Macy's to the punch by four years with their own version of a Turkey Day procession that fittingly concluded at the store's massive toy department.

That parade took place on this day in 1920 on Philadelphia's streets with a modest showing that involved fifteen cars and fifty people. It was aimed at raising enthusiasm for the Christmas shopping season.

The event continued and grew with the support of numerous local sponsors. However, Gimbels remained in the news by making their name at the national level with a couple of other projects. On October 29, 1945, their New York store celebrated the debut of the first ballpoint pens that went on sale at a price of $12.59 each (a substantial amount in 1945!). The retailer sold out their allotment of 30,000 of the new writing utensils within the week.

Gimbels, the host of the nation's oldest Thanksgiving Day parade, ceased operations in 1986.

NOVEMBER 26

DINNER CONVERSATIONS

In 1992, governor Bill Clinton of Arkansas challenged the incumbent president George H. W. Bush in the election for the nation's highest office. As usual, the candidates had large campaign staffs to help them on the road to victory.

The lead strategist for Clinton was another southerner, 48-year-old James Carville of Louisiana. An intense planner, he was considered an expert at using the media in assisting his office seekers in getting their message to the voters.

Across the table from Carville was 39-year-old Mary Matalin. In 1992, she served as the deputy campaign manager for political operations of President Bush's reelection effort. At times, like in so many other elections, the contest became bitter and tense. However, in the end, Clinton was able to upend the sitting president.

What many who observed the campaign didn't realize was that the two officials, Carville and Matalin, were dating at the time. But it was obvious that their relationship had no effect on their jobs as each worked diligently for their respective side. About a year following the election, on this day in 1993, the Louisiana Democrat and the Illinois Republican set aside their political differences and were married. This date in 2023 will mark their thirtieth wedding anniversary.

NOVEMBER 27

THE NUMBERS GUY

Happy Birthday to Chaim Weizmann, the first president of Israel, who was born on this day in 1874. He was a biochemist who took office in 1949. When he died in November 1952, a large number of Israelis wanted Weizmann's successor to be the man he had referred to as, "the greatest Jew alive."

The person who many believed would be best suited for the job was also academically gifted and at the time was teaching math classes at Princeton University in New Jersey. On November 17, the embassy of Israel sent a letter to the 73-year-old professor officially offering him the presidency.

He responded in kind, "All my life I have dealt with objective matters, and hence I lack both the natural aptitude and the experience to deal properly with people and to exercise official function."

The person who turned down the presidency of the Jewish homeland was the Father of the Theory of Relativity, Albert Einstein, who died three years later.

NOVEMBER 28

A HERO ON AND OFF THE SCREEN

The events of November 28, 1942, changed the way that the nation's fire codes would be written forever because that was the night of the infamous Cocoanut Grove Nightclub fire in Boston. An array of flammable decorations coupled with a shortage of emergency exits were major contributors in the deaths of 491 victims.

The tragedy became the second deadliest single-building fire in the history of the country, ranking only behind Chicago's Iroquois Theatre blaze of 1903 which claimed 602 lives.

Among those lost at the nightclub was the popular cowboy movie star Buck Jones who had just finished filming *Dawn on the Great Divide*. Witnesses stated that the motion picture hero was among those helping patrons get to safety before succumbing to the intense smoke. He died later that evening in a Boston hospital.

His final film was released three months later.

NOVEMBER 29

LET'S GET NUKED

In the summer of 1945, the United States ended World War II when it dropped two atomic bombs on Japan. At that point, no one could have imagined that nuclear energy would soon be used as an everyday part of people's lives.

That was especially true for the populace of Arco, Idaho. In 1951, just six years following the war, the nearby Experimental Breeder Reactor No. 1 (EBR-I) became the world's first power plant to produce electricity using nuclear fission. This noteworthy piece of equipment was operational for twelve years before being shut down in December 1963.

During that time, on July 17, 1955, Arco made history by becoming the first town in the world to be powered by nuclear energy. On that day, the remote community of 1,200 residents received their power from the US Atomic Energy Commission for one hour before being reconnected to their regular provider, the Utah Power and Light Company.

However, the news from the EBR-I wasn't all positive as on November 29, 1955, the reactor suffered a partial meltdown during a coolant flow test. Nearly half of the core of the small reactor melted, reaching temperatures of more than 2,000°F. Repairs to the equipment were made and no casualties were reported.

In 1966, president Lyndon Johnson dedicated EBR-I as a National Historic Landmark.

NOVEMBER 30

SHE'S GONE!

Probably the most sought-after tickets in Washington, DC, are those that are distributed for the White House tours. The passes are free to the public but, because they are limited, it's a matter of getting in line earlier than the other tourists.

Visitors enjoy exploring the mansion but sometimes, the same is not true for the occupants, especially the teenagers who have resided there. Realistically, it's not much fun for a young person to live in a museum.

One such individual was Susan Ford, the daughter of the thirty-eighth president Gerald Ford who held the office from 1974–1977. On this day in 1976, the first daughter was a 17-year-old college freshman who was home for holiday break while her mother was away shopping. The gates were left open, as the First Lady was returning from her outing.

Susan saw the opportunity, she jumped into her shiny Ford Mustang and whizzed away unchaperoned. "When I got outside the gate, I was like, 'Oh my gosh, I'm alone. Is this really a smart thing to do?'"

Now on the run, Ms. Ford, who was a student at Mount Vernon College for Women (which today is a part of the George Washington University) in northwest Washington, DC, picked up a friend and the pair made their way to a Safeway supermarket parking lot, where they behaved like typical college students by sharing a six-pack of beer. Their two-person party was legal as the drinking age at the time was eighteen.

As it was the pre-cell era, she found a pay phone and called the White House security detail to tell them that she was all right. The president's daughter informed the Secret Service that she would return to the mansion by 7:00 p.m. The stop was necessary as she needed to pick up her tickets for that evening's concert by the pop duo Hall and Oates.

After some time on her own, Susan headed home and upon her arrival was told that her father wanted to see her in the Oval Office, where she received one of his "talks" before heading off to the concert, along with her own agent, which seemed totally appropriate considering the circumstances. That's because Hall and Oates biggest hit song during the 1970s was titled, *She's Gone*.

DECEMBER

I'll be sitting on top when the sky falls down, and It All Goes Wrong Again.

—Lyrics from "When It All Goes Wrong Again," by
Art Alexakis, singer-songwriter and guitarist

DECEMBER 1

HE SHOT . . . WHO?

The Supreme Court makes the ultimate verdict when it comes to legal cases. However, on August 16, 1889, one of its justices was arrested for murder!

Stephen J. Field had been on the Court for 26 years since being appointed by Abraham Lincoln in 1863. Four years prior, he replaced David Terry as chief justice of the California Supreme Court because Terry had killed one of the state's senators (David Broderick) in a duel. Terry later married Sarah Althea Hill, who was suing a silver millionaire, claiming he had been her first husband.

In 1888, Field heard the case in his capacity as judge on the Ninth Circuit and ruled against Mrs. Terry. The courtroom erupted into pandemonium with David Terry, at one point, brandishing a Bowie knife. Field ordered the couple jailed for contempt and they, in turn, publicly announced their intent to seek revenge on the justice.

About a year later, Field and his bodyguard, US marshal David Neagle, were traveling by train to San Francisco. They encountered the Terrys in the dining room of the station in Lathrop, California. David Terry approached Field while Sarah returned to the train. He slapped the Justice as Neagle identified himself as an officer, pulling his revolver and ordering him to stop.

Terry began to fumble with his jacket as if he might be carrying a weapon. Neagle took no chances and fatally shot him while Sarah came running up with a satchel holding a loaded gun. At that juncture, the local sheriff arrested Field and Neagle for murder.

The charges against Field were soon dropped but Mrs. Terry pushed for the case against Neagle. The matter eventually made its way to the Supreme Court where, with Justice Field recusing himself, it was decided in Neagle's favor.

Field served on the Court until he retired on this day in 1897. He wanted to break John Marshall's record of thirty-three years on the bench and did so by one year before his death in 1899.

DECEMBER 2

SEEING THE OTHER SIDE

Following the raid at Harpers Ferry, John Brown was put on trial at Charles Town, Virginia. One of his attorneys was a local lawyer named Lawson Botts. He was assigned to the case to defend the abolitionist even though he openly supported the Southern cause.

Brown was found guilty for inciting a rebellion and hanged on this day in 1859. Among those in the crowd who witnessed the execution was future presidential assassin John Wilkes Booth.

After the trial, Botts became captain of a Confederate volunteer company known as the Botts Grays. He was commissioned as a major in June 1861 and became a colonel a year later. The attorney-turned-soldier was praised for his conduct during several battles before he was mortally wounded in action at the Second Battle of Bull Run leading to his death on September 11, 1862.

He died defending the South's right to continue using slaves, even though it was three years after his former client John Brown was hanged as an abolitionist.

DECEMBER 3

TOO LATE FOR JUSTICE

On January 3, 1786, Elizabeth Wilson was hanged in Chester, Pennsylvania, for the murder of her infant twins. That was done in the name of justice but was she guilty?

The condemned woman denied killing her children and cast the blame on their unmarried father. A confession to that fact was signed by witnesses although when it came time to charge someone with the crime, the burden fell upon the young mother.

Elizabeth's trial took place in October 1785, but surprisingly she never refuted any of the charges against her. The jury, which had doubts about her guilt, deliberated for several hours before returning their verdict. Following the conviction, the judge had little choice but to sentence the woman to death by hanging with a date for her execution set for December 7, 1785.

Elizabeth's brother William vigorously undertook her case in an effort to secure a pardon for his sister at the hands of the Commonwealth's executive authority, the Supreme Executive Council which, at the time, was under the leadership of the famed Founding Father Benjamin Franklin, an avid voice against capital punishment. On December 3, William arrived at the jail to meet with his sibling and begin gathering information to help her case.

The Council's vice president Charles Biddle also believed in her innocence. On December 6, 1785, just one day prior to the scheduled administration of the sentence, William presented the confession signed by the witnesses to the Council. However, instead of an outright commutation, the panel granted a stay of execution which allowed the brother more time to investigate, but he did so to no avail except to delay the hanging until January 3.

On the eve of the enactment, William, who was ill, secured another stay from Biddle who specifically wrote on the order, "Do not execute (Elizabeth) Wilson until you hear further from Council."

The deadline-pressed William took the mandate from Biddle and hurried through a storm during the 15-mile ride from Philadelphia to Chester. At one juncture, he attempted to negotiate a waterway on horseback but the animal could not complete the crossing, at which point he threw himself into the freezing obstruction and swam across with the signed stay tightly gripped in his cold hand. After making it to the other side, he was able to locate another horse and continued his race against time to the jail.

But for all of his effort to save his sister, William arrived just minutes after the hanging had taken place. When the sheriff saw him with the order, he quickly cut the rope, hoping against hope, trying frantically to revive the fallen woman, but it was too late to save her.

Biddle later wrote, "For my own part, I firmly believed her innocent. . . . The next day when Council met, and we heard of the execution, it gave uneasiness to many of the members, all of whom were against her being executed."

Following his sister's death, William withdrew from society, wandering westward across southeastern Pennsylvania and ultimately living his final nineteen years in a cave near Hummelstown.

DECEMBER 4

I WILL SUPPORT AND DEFEND
THE CONSTITUTION

The United States has a long and storied history of immigrants who eventually became citizens who made major contributions. Among that group of transplanted Americans include Nobel Prize winner Albert Einstein (Germany); wardrobe creator Levi Strauss (Germany); former secretary of state Madeleine Albright (Czechoslovakia); and scientist Nikola Tesla (Austrian Empire, Croatia).

After the United States entered World War II, Congress acted to provide expedited naturalization of noncitizens serving honorably in the US Armed Forces.

The Second War Powers Act of 1942 exempted noncitizen service members from many naturalization requirements.

The Act also authorized the first overseas naturalizations in the nation's history. That took place on this day in 1942 when US Army soldier James A. Finnell Hoey became the first person to receive US citizenship abroad. The native of Belford, Ireland, took the oath at Camp Paraiso in the Panama Canal Zone.

DECEMBER 5

LOOKING UNDER ROCKS

Certain pursuits require training that usually necessitates a setting that is as close to the environment where the participants will be conducting their work. So how did the Apollo astronauts prepare for their lunar mission on the moon while on Earth?

One of the major aspects of the journeys would be to collect soil samples and return home with them. To rehearse that part of the job, astronauts from Apollo missions 13 through 17 trained on Hawaii's big island from December 5–12, 1970.

Because of the fact that the island's volcanic basalt terrain is similar to that on the Moon, locations like the dormant Mauna Kea volcano were ideal for astronaut training. A group of nineteen astronauts selected by NASA took part in the geology training course.

They practiced walking and doing their experiments on the hardened lava beds in order to prepare for their time on the lunar surface.

DECEMBER 6

THE DAY BEFORE THE DAY OF INFAMY

On the night of December 6, 1941, a message to a Japanese delegation in Washington, DC, was intercepted, broken, and distributed by the Signal Intelligence Service, or SIS. The telegraphed message, which would become known as the Fourteen Part Message, clearly spelled out the Japanese claims that America was trespassing in the Far East.

President Franklin Roosevelt, after reading the first thirteen parts at 9:30 p.m., commented that this meant war. Officers in the SIS agreed, and felt confident that American Armed Forces would be on full alert.

The fourteenth part of the letter began to arrive at 5:00 a.m. on December 7. It declared in a single sentence that Japan was breaking off relations with the United States and that the secretary of state should be notified at 1:00 p.m. (EST)—dawn in Hawaii. The president was informed immediately.

General George Marshall, chief of staff of the US Army, decided to alert the commanders of both the Hawaiian and Philippine departments that the potential for attack was high. However, because of the sensitivity of the message, it was sent by telegraph.

That meant that it wasn't delivered to the ground commander in Hawaii until the Japanese bombers were already flying through the morning fog over Pearl Harbor.

DECEMBER 7

JUST PEACHY

In almost every aspect of life, there are those who want to be first. However, only one can be first. In the growth of the nation, many are surprised as to the first state.

It was one of the smallest colonies that is located just south of New Jersey. The country's first state was Delaware. On December 7, 1787, the colony's thirty delegates gathered in the town of Dover to approve the US Constitution. When Delaware took that step, it became state number one.

Before it was recognized as the first state, the region was known for something else. In the 1500s, Spanish settlers brought peaches to Delaware. By the 1600s, the area was overrun with juicy citrus. They had so many that farmers used them to feed their livestock. In 1875, Delaware peach farmers produced a record 6 million baskets of the fruit.

Today, Delaware produces about 2 million pounds of peaches each year.

DECEMBER 8

HOME OF THE JETSONS

Most major cities have a focal point. In Seattle, Washington, that landmark can be seen for miles—it is the famous tower known as the Space Needle.

It was built for the 1962 World's Fair that drew over 2.3 million visitors. The Needle is an observation tower that includes a rotating restaurant. Located in the Lower Queen Anne neighborhood, it was completed on December 8, 1961, and was once the tallest structure west of the Mississippi River rising 605 feet above the city. It was built to withstand winds of up to 200 mph.

On April 19, 1999, the city's Landmarks Preservation Board designated the tower as a historic location.

However, the Space Needle is also the inspiration for the condominium complex that served as the home for the futuristic cartoon family *The Jetsons.* Like the Needle, the animated series also made its debut in 1962.

DECEMBER 9

TWO OF THE SAME? NOT!

For those who are trying to predict the presidential and vice presidential winners of the next election, one thing is for sure. The two people on the ticket won't come from the same state.

That's because the Constitution's Twelfth Amendment states, "The electors shall meet in their respective states and vote by ballot for President and Vice President, one of whom, at least, shall not be an inhabitant of the same state with themselves."

If the two candidates of a party's ticket were from the same state, that state would be eliminated from participating in the electoral college. The amendment was proposed by Congress on this day in 1803 and ratified by the requisite three-fourths of the state legislatures on June 15, 1804.

DECEMBER 10

A RECLUSIVE GENIUS

In the world of American poetry, there is perhaps no more-recognized name than that of Emily Dickinson who was born on this day in 1830.

Although the native of Amherst, Massachusetts, wrote almost 1,800 poems, she won no literary awards and only ten individual works were published during her lifetime. The first full volume of her work was not compiled and released until after her death.

Before the arrival of billionaire Howard Hughes during the next century, Dickinson was probably America's most famous recluse. She lived much of her life in isolation, never married, and most of her friendships were conducted by correspondence. Her homestead has since been converted into an Amherst museum.

Upon her death in 1886, Emily's younger sister Lavinia discovered hundreds of the poems. The younger Dickinson kept a promise that she had previously made to older sibling and burned most of the poet's correspondence. But no such instructions were left for the administration of the nearly forty notebooks and loose sheets that were stored in a locked chest, which Lavinia resolved must be published. The first of many volumes to come, Dickinson's *Poems* debuted in November 1890.

DECEMBER 11

ONE MISTAKE AFTER ANOTHER

As the year of 1777 was winding down, general George Washington and his troops had much to reflect on since their successful attack on the enemy at Trenton, New Jersey, 12 months earlier. From the beginning of the war, the Continental Army had been pounded by the British during most of their encounters but over the bygone year, they could proudly cite their wins at Princeton (NJ), Fort Stanwix (NY), and Saratoga (NY) as evidence that their commander's hit-and-run strategy was finally producing victories.

Although the time included several battles where the enemy had not been vanquished, including efforts that led to colonial losses at Fort Mifflin (PA), Brandywine (PA), and Germantown (PA). Additionally, there was the continuing problem of weary troops who were undernourished, underpaid, and exhausted. The British also continued to hold a major advantage in terms of troop numbers and supplies.

Washington clearly understood the dilemma and following the Battle of Matson's Ford (December 11, 1777), just outside of British-occupied Philadelphia, he ordered his men to relocate about 12 miles west to an area known as Valley Forge. Once there, they began constructing hundreds of log huts that would serve as the army's winter encampment. It is estimated that the American forces numbered more than 10,000.

However, over the following weeks, Washington's men struggled to survive in the frigid conditions and the ongoing problem of desertion continued to plague the commander. It would have been a perfect opportunity for the enemy to mount an offensive.

British general Sir William Howe had passed on two other important occasions to press the issue against the Continentals. Although Valley Forge was a strategically sound location for withstanding an attack, the battered and bruised condition of the American troops made them prime targets for a major British offensive. But once again, the enemy commander was concerned with other matters.

He had begun an ongoing romance with Elizabeth Betsey Loring, a colonial woman, that occupied much of his time.

When the spring thaw of 1778 arrived, about 2,000 American troops had either died from the elements or deserted of their own accord, but there had still not been an attempt by the British to mount an attack.

It was the third missed opportunity for the Mother country to end the war during the past sixteen months and the final straw for the beleaguered redcoat general as he was removed from his command in March 1778 in favor of Sir Henry Clinton. In the end, the bypassed chances proved too costly as the American forces gained more momentum each year, eventually securing their independence in 1781.

DECEMBER 12

THE JAY WAY

To be selected as a justice of the United States Supreme Court is very prestigious. It is a lifetime appointment which means that an individual can leave the office one of three ways: resignation, impeachment, or death. There are many judges who hope to someday be nominated by the president for one of the nine posts on the bench.

After a period of time, many choose to resign in order to spend their golden years with their families. In 1805, justice Samuel Chase was impeached but also acquitted and served on the Court until his death in 1811. Overall since 1789, 105 justices have died in office while 58 retired.

John Jay was one of America's Founding Fathers who was born on this day in 1745. In October 1789, the 43-year-old American-trained lawyer, was sworn in as the nation's first chief justice of the Supreme Court. He was appointed by George Washington.

Jay lived to the ripe old age of 83, which was rare for the era, but didn't remain on the Court for the long run. On June 29, 1795, after serving less than six years as chief justice, he resigned, not for family reasons but because he had been elected governor of his home state of New York.

The jurist had no time to campaign as he had spent several months in England with representatives of the United States and Great Britain to negotiate the details of Jay's Treaty, a document that the leaders hoped would settle any outstanding issues between the two former combatants which had been left unresolved since the conclusion of the American Revolutionary War.

Jay won the election while he was crossing the Atlantic on his return to the United States.

DECEMBER 13

A TOWN CALLED WASHINGTON

Everyone knows that the nation's capital was named after George Washington. But years earlier, on December 13, 1776, a tiny New Hampshire town was the first in the colonies to honor the name of the fledgling nation's first great statesman and general. The town called itself Washington and continues to do so.

DECEMBER 14

YOU ARE PARDONED

On December 14, 1863, more than a year into the War Between the States, president Abraham Lincoln announced a grant of amnesty. But this one differed from any pardon that the nation's leader would issue.

That's because the recipient was Emilie Todd Helm, his wife Mary Todd Lincoln's half-sister and the widow of a Confederate general. She was absolved as one of the first under the president's Proclamation of Amnesty and Reconstruction, which Lincoln had announced less than a week before.

The plan was the president's blueprint for the reintegration of the South into the Union. Part of the plan allowed for former Confederates to be granted amnesty if they took a loyalty oath to the United States. The option was open to all other than the highest officials of the Southern coalition.

DECEMBER 15

CAN I MAKE A CALL?

Happy birthday to J. Paul Getty who was born on this day in 1892 in Minneapolis. In the early years of the twentieth century, armed with a degree in economics and political science from Oxford, he made several successful strikes in the oil fields of northern Oklahoma. He had already become a millionaire by the age of 23.

In 1957, *Fortune* magazine named him the richest living American while in 1966, the *Guinness Book of Records* named him as the world's richest private citizen, worth an estimated $1.2 billion (equal to $ 10.8 billion in 2022). He was also the owner of one of the world's finest art collections.

In 1959, Getty bought Sutton Place, a historic manor about 30 miles southwest of London, and moved there. The spacious estate is spread over 775 acres. The tight-fisted businessman purchased it for about $840,000 from the Duke of Sutherland because he felt that the cost of living was getting too high to remain in the United States.

One of the first upgrades that Getty made to his 72-room mansion was to have a pay phone installed. It was in plain sight at the home's entryway with the clear understanding that if a visitor needed to make a call, the procedure was to grab their change and start dialing. The miserly American oilman lived the last seventeen years of his life in merry old England.

DECEMBER 16

THE OTHER TEA PARTIES

The Boston Tea Party is the most famous protest in the history of the United States. On the night of December 16, 1773, members of the Sons of Liberty tossed cases of British tea into Boston Harbor to protest the policy of taxation against the colonies. A total of 340 chests of British East India Company tea, weighing over 92,000 pounds (roughly 46 tons), were dumped overboard into the sea during the three-hour revolt.

However, Boston was just the beginning for this type of demonstration. Further protests involving shipments of tea took place within the following year in Charleston (SC); Philadelphia (PA); New York (NY); Princeton (NJ); Chestertown (MD); Annapolis (MD); York (ME); and Greenwich (NJ).

Additionally, history made another appearance in Boston on March 7, 1774, as protestors took over the store of a local merchant and made off with sixteen chests of tea which were promptly taken to the harbor and, just like before, broken open and deposited into the water. The uprising is known as the second Boston Tea Party.

DECEMBER 17

MORE FROM THE FLY GUYS

On this day in 1903, Orville Wright piloted the first powered flight 20 feet above Kitty Hawk, North Carolina. That historic journey lasted 12 seconds and covered 120 feet. Three more attempts were made that same day with his brother Wilbur setting the record with a flight lasting 59 seconds and covering 852 feet.

But the brothers were more than just the first pilots. Outside of their home in Dayton, Ohio, they turned an 84-acre pasture into the world's first airport known as the Huffman Prairie Flying Field. The term airport didn't evolve until 1919.

Huffman was also the site of the world's first permanent flight school. However, because the Wright Brothers' initial journey was so monumental, much of what they accomplished in the following years was often overlooked. Today, the Huffman Prairie Flying Field is located on the Wright-Patterson Air Force Base. It was designated a National Historic Landmark in 1990.

DECEMBER 18

"ONE-EYED" CHARLEY PARKER

Among those who voted in the presidential election of 1868 was the well-known stagecoach driver known as "One-Eyed" Charley Parker. The sharpshooter marked a ballot in an election in Soquel on California's north coast near Santa Cruz. It is believed that vote was cast for Ulysses S. Grant.

Parker died on this day in 1879, at which time it was discovered that the tough-talking, hard-drinking man was actually a woman! She was born in New England as Charlotte Darkey Parkhurst before being orphaned and had gone west to become one of the most reliable drivers of metal shipments during the gold rush. Her participation in the election, even though incognito, made her one of the first, if not the first, women to vote in a US presidential election.

DECEMBER 19

MISERY AT THE MINE

Nevada's Comstock Lode was one of the richest gold strikes in history, although it would not be known only for gold but rather for its immensely rich silver deposits. The silver ore had initially been discovered in 1857 by brothers Evan and Hosea Grosh but, as luck would have it, they died before they could record their claims.

In late summer of 1857, Hosea had an accident with a pick and died after his foot became badly infected. His brother also met a tragic ending when his feet were frozen as he and a friend were caught in a snowstorm trying to cross the Sierra Nevadas. He did not want his legs amputated and died on this day in 1857.

When miners rushed in after the discovery of gold, they were unable to remove their riches because of the heavy blue-gray clay that clung to their tools. Although when the sticky soil was analyzed, it was found to be loaded with silver particles of exceptional purity worth $2,000 a ton.

The discovery of the material was bad news for Henry Comstock who had become so disheartened that he sold his claim before finding out what was in it!

DECEMBER 20

UNLUCKY 13

Hoover Dam was a Depression era project that was completed in 1936. There were 112 deaths associated with its construction. On December 20, 1922, the first person on record to die in its building process was J. G. Tierney, a surveyor who drowned while looking for an ideal spot for the reservoir. Coincidentally, his son, Patrick W. Tierney, was the last man to die while working on the project, exactly thirteen years later to the day.

DECEMBER 21

THE SCORCHED EARTH

It was December 1864 and Sherman's March to the Sea was in its final days during the Civil War. Northern troops had cut a path through Georgia that kept the Confederacy on the defensive and the man who could see trouble on the horizon for his town was Richard Arnold, the mayor of Savannah.

Union general William T. Sherman assumed that he would have to invade the picturesque city and destroy it as he had so many others along the way. In the early morning hours of December 21, after Southern troops had evacuated Savannah, Mayor Arnold along with a group of alderman, hurried to their horses to meet up with Union general John W. Geary, as his troops were the nearest to the city and were preparing to invade. The officials pleaded with the Yankee officer to accept their offer for a peaceful surrender in order to avoid any destruction of property to which the general agreed.

Just before dawn and according to the appeasement, Geary and his soldiers entered the city unopposed. A few days later, the Union forces enjoyed Christmas as they had complete run of the community and lived like royalty until their departure on January 27, 1865. Sherman and Geary had kept their word and spared Savannah from a wartime destruction. Unfortunately, as the 62,000 Union troops marched into their next destination in South Carolina, those towns were not as lucky.

DECEMBER 22

A SECRET VISITOR FOR CHRISTMAS

On Sunday December 7, 1941, the Japanese launched the infamous surprise attack at Pearl Harbor, Hawaii, that pushed America into full-scale war. England and its strong-willed prime minister Winston Churchill had been battling Adolf Hitler's Third Reich since 1939. Meanwhile, behind the scenes, president Franklin Roosevelt was attempting to help the British, along with other European nations, without direct US involvement. Polls showed that US citizens did not want to be involved in another war, but the attack on America's naval fleet dashed any hopes of a peaceful resolution.

The day after Pearl Harbor, Churchill began putting together a plan to visit the United States and promptly issued his own invitation to call on the First Family. On this day in 1941, a visiting vessel docked in Norfolk, Virginia, carrying the prime minister and others.

Just hours before Churchill's arrival, the chief White House butler, Alonzo Fields, walked into an argument between the nation's high profile First Couple. The upcoming visit was so secretive that the president had kept it from his wife.

"You should have told me!" insisted Eleanor. FDR tried to placate the situation by telling her that Churchill was arriving that night to stay for what he termed "a few days."

When he descended upon the presidential palace, the leader of the British Conservative Party rewrote the book for White House protocol. He took up residence in the mansion's Blue Room, not just for a few days but for the next three weeks. It was common for foreign dignitaries to be housed by their embassies when visiting the nation's capital but Churchill's background was different than most of his fellow Brits since his mother Jennie was an American (born in Brooklyn, New York), a fact he strategically mentioned whenever he was giving speeches to US crowds.

The British Bulldog, as he was known, had at least two forebears who fought against the redcoats during the American War of Independence.

Churchill turned the White House's second-floor Rose Suite into a mini-headquarters for the British government, with messengers carrying documents to and from the embassy in red leather cases. The prime minister didn't travel to Washington alone. His entourage, some eighty-six members strong, included his 19-year-old daughter Mary, along with a contingent of military advisors, stenographers, valets, detectives, private secretaries, and a code clerk—who were lodged elsewhere.

Eleanor continually dropped exasperated hints about the men getting enough sleep. "It was astonishing to me that anyone could smoke so much and drink so much and keep perfectly well," she later wrote of her famous guest.

On the night of December 27, after watching a movie with Roosevelt and Canadian prime minister Mackenzie King, Churchill adjourned to his suite. Once inside, he attempted to open one of the bedroom windows when he was struck by a pain in his chest and arm. Sir Charles Wilson, his personal physician, diagnosed the episode as a "heart attack" but, not wanting to alarm his patient, he simply told him he'd been overtaxing himself.

The prime minister left for England on January 14, 1942, flying home via Bermuda. The three-week war conference, with its many meetings and late-night strategy sessions, pushed FDR and his staff to their limits.

However, in the end, the summit did exactly what was necessary. It joined the two old enemies together to prepare to take on their adversaries on opposite sides of the globe.

In addition to fighting the enemy during World War II, another lesson was learned from the Churchill visit, which was that the White House was built as a working sanctum and not a lodging stopover for visiting luminaries. To accommodate them, the State Department began renting Blair House in 1942, which is located directly across the street from the mansion on Pennsylvania Avenue. By the end of the year, and at the insistence of the First Lady, the government agreed to purchase the property for $150,000.

DECEMBER 23

IT'S BOURBON . . . NOT BOURBON

There are a number of well-known streets and highways throughout the United States. However, none more so than the one that is most associated with a good time, which is New Orleans' own Bourbon Street. Although historic, when tourists attempt to guess the origin of the roadway's name, they are quite often mistaken.

In 1720, Adrien De Pauger, a French engineer and cartographer, arrived at the settlement. He had been appointed by colonial administrator and New Orleans' founder Jean-Baptiste Le Moyne de Bienville to draw up the plans for the new city. De Pauger designed the streets of the Vieux Carre, today known as the French Quarter, and charted the original map of the city that eventually became known as The Big Easy. The nickname arrived in the 1960s.

It was on this day in 1721 that colony officials transferred their capital from Biloxi (MS) to New Orleans (LA).

Bourbon Street's moniker did not originate with the famous alcoholic beverage. At that juncture, the brown liquor had not even been invented when the street design was laid out on the map by De Pauger. During that time, the area that later became the state of Louisiana was part of the colony of New France, and named for the French royal House of Bourbon, for which bourbon, the drink, was ultimately named. Some claim that those spirits were first poured in 1783.

DECEMBER 24

WHO CLEANS THE HOUSE?

The Vanderbilt family has always been synonymous with great wealth. But who was the first president's namesake who built an estate larger than Mount Vernon?

In the late nineteenth century, George Washington Vanderbilt constructed the Biltmore Estate located just outside of Asheville, North Carolina, in the Blue Ridge Mountains. It is the largest private residence in the United States and took five years to erect the 250-room mansion.

Vanderbilt traveled through Europe purchasing paintings, porcelains, bronzes, carpets, and antiques to furnish his palace, which he opened to friends for the first time on Christmas Eve in 1895.

Today, it is a US National Historic Landmark which in 1956 was permanently opened to the public as a house museum and hotel where some rooms run more than $1,000 per night.

DECEMBER 25

MERRY CHRISTMAS

It was 1862 and marked the second Christmas of the war that continued to drag on between the states regarding their rights. On Christmas Eve, troops from both armies shivered in the open weather of Eastern Virginia's Rappahannock River, having been exposed to a wet snowstorm a half-mile below the town of Fredericksburg.

In a feeble attempt to stay warm, they laid on rubber blankets topped with woolen covers. The young men huddled as close as possible to steal warmth from their comrades.

On Christmas Day, members of each side patrolled the area until they noticed one another on the opposite banks of the river. However, instead of aiming their rifles, they began the unusual exercise of conversing with their enemy. During the exchange, the subject of trading goods was broached.

The Yankees used a "trading boat" which was similar to toy ships that children would play with at a park. They employed handkerchiefs for makeshift sails and began floating the small craft across the Rappahannock as the two sides began to barter across the near frozen water. The North sent over coffee, sugar, and pork, while the Rebels returned the favor with southern specialties like corn and tobacco.

Soldiers from both sides spent a festive Christmas together and, for a few hours, forgot about the weather, the war, and who they might be forced to shoot a few hours later. Before departing, shouts to the Confederate troops of "Merry Christmas, Johnny" were returned with the greeting, "Same to you, Yank"—even though it might become their duty to fire their rifles before evening.

DECEMBER 26

GERMANS AGAINST GERMANS

On Christmas night 1776, general George Washington led his army of 2,400 across the Delaware River. They were flanked by a 1,900-man diversionary force under colonel John Cadwalader and another 700 troops directed by general James Ewing.

The following morning, the Continental troops arrived in Trenton, New Jersey, to invade the encampment of 1,400 Hessian soldiers fighting on the side of the British. Hessians were German mercenary troops who were hired by the redcoats to fight against the Americans. Their biggest problem stemmed from the Christmas night celebration that left many of them in no condition to fight.

However, the British weren't the only ones purchasing the services of the Deutsche. The American colonists included large numbers of German immigrants, many of whom had initially settled in Pennsylvania. By 1775, at least

100,000 had entered the colonies, making up a third of the Keystone State's population.

During the Revolution, a number of battles featured Germans fighting each other while representing the two opposing sides. But just like their counterparts, the war provided paydays for all.

In total, as many as 5,000 Hessian soldiers who had been hired by Britain to fight in the war remained in America after the end of hostilities.

DECEMBER 27

MAKING A CHANGE

The vice presidency is one of those jobs that gets little attention even by those who are holding the office. Former second in command, under George H. W. Bush, Dan Quayle once said, "The job is just awkward, an awkward job."

Many who have been in the position would rather be doing something else. One of those was John C. Calhoun who knew when he had had enough.

On this day in 1832, Vice President Calhoun, citing policy differences with president Andrew Jackson, resigned sixteen days after having been elected to fill a vacant South Carolina Senate seat. He remained the sole vice president in US history to resign until October 10, 1973, when, following a federal investigation, Spiro Agnew resigned after being charged with income tax evasion.

Calhoun had advocated for states' rights and defended the slaveholders of the South against the Northern opposition. In 1824, he ran for president but partisan attacks by his rivals forced him out of the race and he settled for the vice presidency under John Quincy Adams.

In 1828, he was again elected vice president as voters chose Jackson to replace Adams. However, he found himself at odds with the newly elected Old Hickory over high tariffs. Upon his departure from his former job, Calhoun spent most of the following seventeen years in the Senate.

DECEMBER 28

WHICH IS THE REAL CAPITAL?

Bismarck is the capital of North Dakota, but there was originally some disagreement over which town would have that distinction. When North Dakota became a state in 1889, the city of Jamestown was set to take on capital status. But many Bismarck residents weren't happy about the decision since their city had served the prior role of capital of the larger Dakota Territory.

Some of the dissatisfied citizens of Bismarck headed east on horseback and stole the state records from Jamestown. Eventually, the state legislature was persuaded to comply with their demands and decided it would meet in Bismarck. However, they never formally voted on the town's capital status, though any debates about the matter essentially ended once the new North Dakota State Capitol Building was opened there in 1934.

Why a new building? On this day in 1930, the 47-year-old structure caught fire and needed to be replaced.

DECEMBER 29

BUILDING BLUES

Salem is the capital city of Oregon but, like other states such as the aforementioned North Dakota, the Beaver State hasn't had much luck with their own capitol buildings. On the evening of December 29, 1855, a fire destroyed the first statehouse and many of the territory's public records.

Oregon's second capitol structure stood until April 25, 1935, when it was also gutted by flames. Its third seat of government was dedicated on October 1, 1938. However, on March 25, 1993, an earthquake damaged the dome, requiring closure for repairs until September 1995.

DECEMBER 30

THE DANGER ZONE

Most political assassinations and attempts that have taken place in the United States were carried out using a firearm, like that of president William McKinley in 1901.

But that wasn't true for former Idaho governor Frank Steunenberg. When violence broke out during an 1899 miners' strike, Steunenberg declared martial law and asked McKinley to send federal troops to his state. Many of his union supporters felt betrayed. In 1901, the governor left office after completing his second term.

December 30, 1905, was a snowy day in Caldwell, Idaho, as Steunenberg was returning home from his office. He pulled a wooden slide that opened the gate which triggered a bomb that blew him ten feet into the air. Within an hour, he was dead.

The 1907 trial that followed in Boise was almost as sensational as the crime. Three prominent leaders of the radical Western Federation of Miners were acquitted in an alleged conspiracy to commit murder. Among the trio's team of defense attorneys was the prominent Clarence Darrow.

The only conviction for the crime was handed down to Harry Orchard, a mine worker who implicated himself and others in a 64-page confession. He was given a life sentence and died in 1954.

DECEMBER 31

TIMES SQUARE

The first rooftop celebration atop One Times Square, a fireworks display, took place in 1904 and was produced by the *New York Times* to inaugurate their new headquarters to celebrate the renaming of Longacre Square to Times Square.

The first ball-dropping celebration atop One Times Square was held on December 31, 1907.

In 1942 and 1943, the ball lowering was suspended due to the wartime dim out. The crowds who still gathered in Times Square celebrated with a minute of silence followed by chimes ringing out from an amplifier sitting aboard a truck parked at the Square.

The original New Year's Eve Ball weighed 700 pounds and was 5 feet in diameter. It was made of iron and wood and was decorated with one hundred 25-watt light bulbs.

In 2008, the ball grew to 12 feet in diameter and weighed 11,875 pounds. It is built to withstand high winds and fluctuating temperatures. Waterford Crystal introduces a different pattern for each New Year's celebration.

BIBLIOGRAPHY

BOOKS CONSULTED

Antonson, Rick. *Route 66 Still Kicks: Driving America's Main Street* (Skyhorse, 2012).

Crocker, Jack. *Okay: The Encyclopedia of Oklahoma History and Culture* (Oklahoma Historical Society, https://www.okhistory.org/publications/enc/entry?entry =OK002).

Dahlberg, Tim, Mary Ward, and Brenda Greene. *America's Girl: The Incredible Story of How Swimmer Gertrude Ederle Changed the Nation* (St. Martin's, 2009).

Dingell, John. *The Dean: The Best Seat in the House* (HarperCollins, 2018).

Gillett, Mary C. *Army Historical Series: The Army Medical Department, 1818–1865* (Center of Military History, United States Army, US Government Printing Office, 1987).

Holtz, Allan. *American Newspaper Comics: An Encyclopedic Reference Guide* (University of Michigan Press, 2012).

Kennedy, William Pierce. *Matthew Lyon Cast the Deciding Vote which Elected Thomas Jefferson President in 1801* (US Government Printing Office, 1942).

Middlekauff, Robert. *The Glorious Cause: The American Revolution, 1763–1789* (Oxford University Press, 2007).

Oshinsky, David M. *Polio: An American Story* (Oxford University Press, 2005).

Sterling, Bryan B., and Frances N. Sterling. *Will Rogers' World: America's Foremost Political Humorist Comments on the 20's and 30's and 80's and 90's* (M. Evans, 1993).

Trump, Donald J. *The Art of the Deal* (Random House, 1992).

Uschan, Michael V. *Joe Biden* (Lucent, 2010).

ARTICLES CONSULTED

Abbott, Karen. "A Chess Champion's Dominance—and Madness," *Smithsonian*, https://www.smithsonianmag.com/history/a-chess-champions-dominanceand -madness-4307709/ (December 12, 2011).

Alexander, Kathy. "Bill Cook—Leading the Cook Gang," Legends of America, https://www.legendsofamerica.com/we-billcook/ (December 2021).

Andrews, Evan. "6 Daring Train Robberies," HISTORY, https://www.history.com/news/6-daring-train-robberies (August 22, 2018).

Applebome, Peter. "Wrangling Over Where Rodeo Began," *New York Times* (June 18, 1989).

Arbeiter, M. "15 Things You Might Not Know About the Space Needle," Mental Floss, https://www.mentalfloss.com/article/66548/15-things-you-might-not-know-about-space-needle (March 24, 2016).

Beil, Gail K. "Wiley College: The Great Debaters," *East Texas Historical Journal* 46(1), https://scholarworks.sfasu.edu/ethj/vol46/iss1/8/ (February 2008).

Belmore, Ryan. "Today In Newport History: August 22, 1762—Ann Franklin Takes Over Newport Mercury, Becomes First Female Editor in U.S.," WUN: What's Up Newp, https://whatsupnewp.com/2022/08/today-in-newport-history-august-22-1762-ann-franklin-takes-over-newport-mercury-becomes-first-female-newspaper-editor-in-u-s/ (August 22, 2021).

Beschloss, Michael. "Harry Truman's Extreme Home Makeover," *New York Times*, https://www.nytimes.com/2015/05/10/upshot/harry-trumans-home-improvement.html (May 9, 2015).

Bohn, Kevin. "George H. W. Bush on Bonding with Bill Clinton," CNN, https://politicalticker.blogs.cnn.com/2013/03/05/george-h-w-bush-on-bonding-with-bill-clinton/ (March 5, 2013).

Bomboy, Scott. "Gerald Ford's Unique Role in American History," National Constitution Center, https://constitutioncenter.org/blog/gerald-fords-unique-role-in-american-history (July 14, 2021).

———. "The Man Who Delivered California to the U.S., and Was Fired for It," National Constitution Center, https://constitutioncenter.org/blog/the-man-who-delivered-california-to-the-u-s-and-was-fired-for-it (March 10, 2022).

Bonecutter, Hank. "Dodging the Roadkill: Bank Robbery," Clarksville Online, https://www.clarksvilleonline.com/2018/11/28/dodging-the-roadkill-bank-robbery/ (November 28, 2018).

Brady, Patricia. "Daniel Parke Custis (1711–1757)," *Encyclopedia Virginia*, Virginia Humanities, https://encyclopediavirginia.org/entries/custis-daniel-parke-1711-1757/ (retrieved December 22, 2021).

Brissette, Karen T. "DUI: How to Avoid a Drunk Driving Arrest and Conviction—Franklin Pierce," bloggy come lately, http://bloggycomelately.com/dui-how-to-avoid-a-drunk-driving-arrest-and-conviction/ (April 28, 2018).

Brown, Matthew. "Fact Check: It's True, U.S. Government Poisoned Some Alcohol During Prohibition," *USA Today*, https://www.usatoday.com/story/news/factcheck/2020/06/30/fact-check-u-s-government-poisoned-some-alcohol-during-prohibition/3283701001/ (June 30, 2020).

Brumfield, Ben, and Aparnaa Seshardi. "DNA Test Reveals President Warren Harding's Affair and Love Child," CNN, https://www.cnn.com/2015/08/14/us/president-harding-affair-dna-revelation/index.html (August 15, 2015).

Cahn, Lauren. "12 Strangest Gifts Ever Given to U.S. Presidents," *Reader's Digest*, https://www.rd.com/list/strangest-gifts-ever-given-to-u-s-presidents/ (October 25, 2021).

Calzonetti, Claire. "Ted Turner: 'You've got to be able to take disappointment in life,'" CNN World, Amanpour, https://www.cnn.com/2015/07/31/world/ted-turner -amanpour-interview/index.html (July 31, 2015).

Campanella, Richard. "1721, Pivotal Year for Early New Orleans," *Geographies of New Orleans* (March 28, 2021).

Carr, J. Revell. "George Washington: Mediterranean Ship's Passport Issued December 21, 1796," LSU Law, https://www.law.lsu.edu/maritimeart/washington1796/ (retrieved June 6, 2022).

Cavendish, Richard. "The Sinking of the Maine," *History Today* 48(2), https://www .historytoday.com/archive/sinking-maine (February 1998).

Cheng, Lisa. "Nine Secrets of Mount Rushmore," *Travel and Leisure*, https://www .travelandleisure.com/attractions/landmarks-monuments/mount-rushmore-unique -facts-history (updated September 27, 2022).

Clines, Francis X. "The Powell Decision: The Announcement; Powell Rules Out '96 Race; Cites Concerns for Family and His Lack of 'A Calling,'" *New York Times*, https://www.nytimes.com/1995/11/09/us/powell-decision-announcement-powell -rules-96-race-cites-concerns-for-family-his.html (November 9, 1995).

Conradt, Stacy. "5 Foods Thomas Jefferson Introduced or Made Popular in America," Mental Floss, https://www.mentalfloss.com/article/62565/5-foods -thomas-jefferson-introduced-or-made-popular-america (March 9, 2016).

Crook, Jason. "Feb. 13 in History: VP Strikes Multiple Fans with Drives," NBC Sports, Golf Channel, https://www.golfchannel.com/news/date-golf-history -february-13-vice-president-spiro-agnew-struck-gallery-members-errant-shots (February 13, 2013).

Crow, David. "Hamilton: The Real History of the Burr-Hamilton Duel," Den of Geek, https://www.denofgeek.com/movies/aaron-burr-alexander-hamilton-duel -real-history/ (July 3, 2020).

Cutolo, Morgan. "Can You Guess Which U.S. State Produced the Most Presidents?," *Reader's Digest*, https://www.rd.com/article/most-presidents-born/ (May 21, 2021).

Deffree, Suzanne. "Lunar Orbiter 1 Takes 1st Photo of Earth from Moon Orbit, August 23, 1966," https://www.edn.com/lunar-orbiter-1-takes-1st-photo-of-earth -from-moon-orbit-august-23-1966/ (August 23, 2019).

DeFrange, Ann. "No Sour Grapes Remain in Sallisaw; Festival Scheduled," *Oklahoman*, https://www.oklahoman.com/story/news/1990/10/12/no-sour-grapes -remain-in-sallisaw-festival-scheduled/62549491007/ (October 12, 1990).

Dibble, Lauren. "History of the Sport of Polo: The 19th Century," Complete Guide to Polo, https://completeguidepolo.wordpress.com/2015/03/09/history-of-the-sport -of-polo-the-19th-century/ (March 9, 2015).

Dijkhuizen, Susan. "The History of the Conveyor Belt," https://blog.habasit.com/us/ ?s=history+of+the+conveyor+belt (retrieved December 25, 2021).

Druckman, Bella. "The United Nations Headquarters in Long Island's Lake Success," Untapped New York, https://untappedcities.com/2021/05/19/united-nations-lake-success/ (retrieved March 24, 2022).

Ellerbee, Bobby. "America's First Color Broadcasts Begin On CBS," Eyes Of A Generation . . . Television's Living History, https://eyesofageneration.com/june-25-1951-americas-first-color-broadcasts-begin-on-cbs-let-me-start-wit/ (retrieved February 16, 2022).

Engle, Grant. "Bales, Robb Discuss Unique Life of Being Commander-in-Chief's Daughter," *Chautauquan Daily*, https://chqdaily.wordpress.com/2012/08/22/bales-robb-discuss-unique-life-of-being-commander-in-chiefs-daughter/ (August 22, 2012).

Evans, Mike. "On This Day in 1945: The Ballpoint Pen, a Revolution in Writing, Rocked New York," MacFilos, https://www.macfilos.com/2020/10/29/the-ballpoint-pen-a-revolution-in-writing/ (October 29, 2020).

Fabry, Merrill. "Now You Know: What Was the First Credit Card?," *TIME*, https://time.com/4512375/first-credit-card/ (October 19, 2016).

Fischer, John. "Hawaii, the Big Island—Hawaii's Island of Adventure," About.com (retrieved October 13, 2014).

Fraga, Kaleena. "How Nikola Tesla's Death Brought A Tragic End To The Iconic Inventor's Groundbreaking Career," ATI, https://allthatsinteresting.com/nikola-tesla-death (updated July 25, 2022).

Freeman, Mike. "On Pro Football; Dream Job for Rice: N.F.L. Commissioner," *New York Times*, https://www.nytimes.com/2002/04/17/sports/on-pro-football-dream-job-for-rice-nfl-commissioner.html (April 17, 2002).

Gates, Verna. "Condoleezza Rice Recalls Racial Blast that Killed Childhood Friend," Reuters, https://www.reuters.com/article/us-usa-alabama-memorial/condoleezza-rice-recalls-racial-blast-that-killed-childhood-friend-idUSBRE98C11720130914 (September 13, 2013).

Glass, Andrew. "John Calhoun Resigns as Vice President, Dec. 28, 1832," Politico, https://www.politico.com/story/2015/12/calhoun-resigns-as-vice-president-dec-28-1832-217138 (December 27, 2015).

Goddard, Taegan. "2014 Midterms: The State of Play in Michigan," *The Week*, https://theweek.com/articles/446517/2014-midterms-state-play-michigan (January 8, 2015).

Gorman, Ryan. "20 Years After the Oklahoma City Bombing, Timothy McVeigh Remains the Only Terrorist Executed by US," Insider, https://www.businessinsider.com/20-years-after-the-oklahoma-city-bombing-timothy-mcveigh-remains-the-only-terrorist-executed-by-us-2015-4 (April 19, 2015).

Greenfieldboyce, Nell. "NASA Helps Astronauts Cast Ballots from Space," *Morning Edition*, NPR, https://www.npr.org/templates/story/story.php?storyId=91791895 (June 23, 2008).

Greenspan, Jesse. "10 Things You May Not Know About the US Census," HISTORY, https://www.history.com/news/10-things-you-may-not-know-about-the-u-s-census (May 25, 2020).

Grimshaw, Alice. "History of Early Anaheim," Orange County Historical Society, https://www.orangecountyhistory.org/wp/?page_id=225 (retrieved May 8, 2022).

Grogan, Steve. "A True Long Island War Story 75 Years Ago," LI Herald, https://www.liherald.com/stories/a-true-long-island-war-story-75-years-ago,92861 (June 16, 2017).

Hadley, Dan. "Wyatt Earp," Old West Stories (retrieved January 5, 2022).

Harris, Karen. "Katie Mulcahey and New York's Short-Lived Women's Smoking Ban," History Daily, https://historydaily.org/katie-mulcahey-and-new-yorks-short-lived-womens-smoking-ban (August 29, 2018).

Hautzinger, Daniel. "Out of the Ashes: The Birth of the Chicago Public Library," WTTW, https://interactive.wttw.com/playlist/2017/01/09/out-ashes-birth-chicago-public-library (January 1, 2017).

Higgins, Will. "Mike Pence Joins Long Line of Vice Presidents from Indiana," *IndyStar*, https://www.indystar.com/story/life/2016/07/15/indiana-no-2-vice-president-state-us/87082488/ (July 15, 2016).

Hildebrandt, Darlene. "20 of the Most Famous Photographs in History," Digital Photo Mentor, https://www.digitalphotomentor.com/20-most-famous-photographs/ (July 31, 2020).

Hill, Ray. "Harry Truman's White House Restoration," *Knoxville Focus*, https://www.knoxfocus.com/archives/this-weeks-focus/harry-trumans-white-house-restoration/ (February 4, 2018).

Hindley, Meredith. "Christmas at the White House with Winston Churchill," *Humanities* 37(4), https://www.neh.gov/humanities/2016/fall/feature/christmas-the-white-house-winston-churchill (Fall 2016).

Hodenfield, Jan. "Woodstock: 'It Was Like Balling for the First Time,'" *Rolling Stone*, https://www.rollingstone.com/feature/woodstock-it-was-like-balling-for-the-first-time-229092/2/ (September 20, 1969).

Hutto, Cary. "What Philadelphia Department Store Began Sponsoring a Thanksgiving Day Parade in 1920?," Historical Society of Pennsylvania, https://hsp.org/blogs/question-of-the-week/what-philadelphia-department-store-began-sponsoring-a-thanksgiving-day-parade-in-1920 (November 20, 2011).

Hylton, J. Gordon. "Supreme Court Justices Today are Unlikely to Die with Their Boots On," https://law.marquette.edu/facultyblog/2012/03/supreme-court-justices-today-are-unlikely-to-die-with-their-boots-on/ (March 9, 2012)

Inbody, Kristen. "Montana's Best Dinosaurs: Five Finds That Have Shaped Science," *Great Falls Tribune*, https://www.greatfallstribune.com/story/life/my-montana/2018/03/30/montanas-best-dinosaurs-five-finds-have-shaped-science/473585002/ (March 30, 2018).

Jackson, Debbie, and Hilary Pittman. "Throwback Tulsa: Gunshots, Flying Inkwells and a Spittoon Figure in Legislatures Past," *Tulsa World*, https://tulsaworld.com/news/local/history/throwback-tulsa-gunshots-flying-inkwells-and-a-spittoon-figure-in-legislatures-past/article_c96676c5-347e-5c5b-9b23-a357c66c9273.html (January 22, 2015).

Jacob, Mary K. "This Is How the White House Almost Looked: 5 Rejected Designs," *New York Post*, https://nypost.com/2021/08/12/how-the-white-house-almost-looked-5-rejected-designs/ (August 12, 2021).

Jarvis, Robin. "8 Insane Things That Happened In South Carolina You Won't Find In History Books," Only In Your State, https://www.onlyinyourstate.com/south-carolina/sc-weird-history/ (March 20, 2016).

Jefferson, Brandie. "Old Rocks, New Science: Why Apollo 11 Samples Are Still as Relevant as Ever," *The Source*, Washington University in St. Louis, https://source.wustl.edu/2019/07/old-rocks-new-science-why-apollo-11-samples-are-still-as-relevant-as-ever/ (July 18, 2019).

Jenness, Amy. "A Look Back . . . Folger Brothers: Not Just Coffee," *Yesterday's Island: Today's Nantucket* 52(17), https://yesterdaysisland.com/look-back-folger-brothers-not-just-coffee/ (August 25, 2016).

Johnson, Ted. "Ford-Carter Debate Flashback: When the Candidates Went Silent for 27 Minutes," *West Central Tribune* (September 25, 2016).

Kamcza, Randy. "Historical Analysis of the American Civil Liberties Union: 'In God We Trust' and the ACLU, 1955–1959," Bowling Green State University, https://publications.kon.org/urc//aclu/kamcza.html (June 9, 2009).

Katz, A. J. "CNN Launched 40 Years Ago Today," TVNewser, https://www.adweek.com/tvnewser/cnn-launched-40-years-ago-today/442979/ (June 1, 2020).

Keyes, Carl Robert. "Jackson's Mineral Well," Daily Advert Update, The Adverts 250 Project, https://adverts250project.org/tag/jacksons-mineral-well/ (August 17, 2017).

Kingston, Mike. "The First Thanksgiving?," *Texas Almanac*, https://www.texasalmanac.com/articles/the-first-thanksgiving (retrieved November 22, 2021).

Kirby, Bill. "Monday Mystery: Headlines Followed U.S. Sen. Hamilton Lewis Until He Vanished into History," *Augusta Chronicle*, https://www.augustachronicle.com/story/news/2021/12/20/former-augustan-and-u-s-senator-buried-honors-then-disappeared/8921492002/ (December 20, 2021).

Klein, Christopher. "7 Things You May Not Know About the Constitutional Convention," HISTORY, https://www.history.com/news/7-things-you-may-not-know-about-the-constitutional-convention (September 15, 2020).

———. "10 Reasons Why Gouverneur Morris Was the Oddest Founding Father," https://www.history.com/news/10-things-you-may-not-know-about-the-oddest-founding-father (January 24, 2020).

———. "10 Things You May Not Know About Herbert Hoover," HISTORY, https://www.history.com/news/10-things-you-may-not-know-about-herbert-hoover (October 20, 2014).

———. "10 Things You May Not Know About Martin Luther King Jr.," HISTORY, https://www.history.com/news/10-things-you-may-not-know-about-martin-luther-king-jr (updated January 11, 2022).

Kruse, Michael. "How Grief Became Joe Biden's 'Superpower,'" Politico, https://www.politico.com/magazine/story/2019/01/25/joe-biden-2019-profile-grief-beau-car-accident-224178/ (January 25, 2019).

Lacy, Lee. "Dwight D. Eisenhower and the Birth of the Interstate Highway System," U.S. Army, https://www.army.mil/article/198095/dwight_d_eisenhower_and_the _birth_of_the_interstate_highway_system (February 20, 2018).

Latson, Jennifer. "5 Times Ernest Hemingway Cheated Death," *TIME*, https://time .com/3961119/birthday-ernest-hemingway-history-death/ (July 21, 2015).

Levin, Tim. "Dodge Is Killing Its Grand Caravan Soon—See How It Kicked Off the Rise and Fall of the American Minivan," Business Insider, https://www .businessinsider.in/slideshows/miscellaneous/dodge-is-killing-its-grand-caravan -soon-see-how-it-kicked-off-the-rise-and-fall-of-the-american-minivan/slidelist /75014603.cms (April 6, 2020).

Lewis, Jennifer. "A Brief History of Coffee in the United States," Coffee or Die, https: //www.coffeeordie.com/history-coffee-united-states (November 13, 2020).

Livesay, Dakota. "Dentist Clay Allison," Cowboy to Cowboy, https://cowboytocowboy .com/dentist-clay-allison/ (August 18, 2020).

Loudenback, Doug. "Wiley Post—An Oklahoma City Hero," Doug Dawgz Blog, http://dougdawg.blogspot.com/search?q=wiley+post (updated July 11, 2008).

Lyles, Maryn. "125 Mind-Blowing Historic Facts & Trivia That Are Almost Too Weird to Be True," Parade, https://parade.com/1099930/marynliles/history-facts/ (October 10, 2020).

Malor, Gabriel. "There's Ample Precedent For Rejecting Lame Duck Supreme Court Nominees," *Federalist*, https://thefederalist.com/2016/02/13/ample-precedent-for -rejecting-supreme-court-nominees/ (February 13, 2016).

Malouse, Caroline. "5 Worst Calamities in New Orleans History," New Orleans, https://www.myneworleans.com/5-worst-calamities-in-new-orleans-history-2/ (July 25. 2016).

Maraniss, David. "Before Race Began, Clinton Resolved Pledge Not to Run," *Washington Post*, https://www.washingtonpost.com/archive/politics/1992/07/15/ before-race-began-clinton-resolved-pledge-not-to-run/696cb650-3dab-4fcc-97dd -8bdcbb4b50f5/ (July 15,1992)

Maranzani, Barbara. "Thomas Edison's Near-Death Experience Set Him on the Road to Fame," Biography, https://www.biography.com/news/thomas-edison-train -accident-young-boy-saved-telegraph (October 15, 2020).

Marini, Richard A. "The Boerne Hotel Where Polo was First Played in U.S.—Maybe," *San Antonio Express-News*, https://www.expressnews.com/news/local/history -culture/article/The-Boerne-hotel-where-polo-was-first-played-in-13169819.php (August 23, 2018).

Markoff, John. "How the Computer became Personal," *New York Times*, https:// www.nytimes.com/2001/08/19/business/how-the-computer-became-personal.html (August 19, 2001).

Martin, Lawrence. "Savannah in the Civil War—A Chronology of Key Events," Lakeside Press (March 31, 2012).

McCarriston, Shanna. "Here's Why the Lions Always Play on Thanksgiving, Explained," *Sporting News*, https://www.msn.com/en-us/autos/news/here-s-why -the-lions-always-play-on-thanksgiving-explained/ar-BB1blRq7 (November 26, 2020).

McCracken, Elizabeth. "Gertrude Jeannette," *New York Times Magazine* (December 27, 2018).

McGuire, Patrick. "15 Renowned Feats in Colorado's History," Uncover Colorado, https://www.uncovercolorado.com/famous-events-in-colorado-history/ (May 20, 2021).

McNeill, John R. "How the Lowly Mosquito Helped America Win Independence," https://www.smithsonianmag.com/science-nature/how-lowly-mosquito-helped-america-win-independence-180959411/ (June 15, 2016).

Mires, Charlene. "San Francisco, Almost the Capital of the World," https://www.zocalopublicsquare.org/2013/07/11/san-francisco-almost-the-capital-of-the-world/chronicles/who-we-were/ (July 11, 2013).

Mooney, Richard E. "William Zeckendorf and the Deal that Brought the UN to New York," *New York Daily News*, https://www.nydailynews.com/new-york/william-zeckendorf-deal-brought-new-york-article-1.2949388 (August 14, 2017).

Mouat, Lucia. "Why the UN Was Built in New York and Not in South Dakota," PassBlue, https://www.passblue.com/2013/07/18/why-the-un-was-built-in-new-york-and-not-in-south-dakota/ (July 18, 2013).

Mulligan, Hugh A. "America's Darkest Christmas—Dec. 25, 1941—The Gloom Of War Hung Over World, *Seattle Times*, https://archive.seattletimes.com/archive/?date=19911222&slug=1324437 (December 22, 1991).

Muradian, Vago. "US Navy's McCampbell Downs Record Nine Japanese Planes in One Day," Defense & Aerospace Report, https://defaeroreport.com/2016/10/24/us-navys-mccampbell-downs-record-nine-japanese-planes-one-day/ (retrieved January 7, 2022).

Murphy, Patrick. "75 Years Ago, Tarnov was Bombed in World War II Accident," *Norfolk Daily News*, https://norfolkdailynews.com/news/75-years-ago-tarnov-was-bombed-in-world-war-ii-accident/article_b6b1b094-91a4-11e8-bfd1-572cf1a2c32e.html (July 27, 2018).

Naylor, Roger. "10 Surprising Things about Arizona that You Probably Don't Know," AZcentral, https://www.azcentral.com/story/travel/arizona/2019/12/12/weird-and-fun-facts-about-arizona-things-you-probably-dont-know/4380557002/ (December 12, 2019).

Nelson, Steven. "Flashback: Debate Glitch Took 27 Minutes to Fix in 1976," *Washington Examiner*, https://www.washingtonexaminer.com/news/white-house/flashback-debate-glitch-took-27-minutes-to-fix-in-1976 (June 27, 2019).

Neumann, Thomas. "Why White House Visits by Champions are a U.S. Tradition," ESPN, https://www.espn.com/college-football/story/_/id/14870667/how-white-house-visits-championship-teams-became-american-tradition (May 1, 2016).

Nicastro, Kathie O., and Claire Prechtel-Kluskens. "Passport Applications: A Key to Discovering Your Immigrant Ancestor's Roots," *Prologue* (Winter 1993), 390–4.

Nosowitz, Dan. "Daylight Saving Time Is Actually a Good Thing," Flipboard, Popular Mechanics, https://flipboard.com/@popularmechanics/daylight-savings-time-is-actually-a-good-thing/f-8f0eddfcf7%2Fpopularmechanics.com (March 7, 2020).

O'Neil, Tim. "'You're Not Going to Believe This': A Bizarre Hijacking at Lambert 50 Years Ago," *St. Louis Post-Dispatch*, https://www.stltoday.com/news/archives /youre-not-going-to-believe-this-a-bizarre-hijacking-at-lambert-50-years-ago/ article_1aac5de6-6eb4-5245-a126-7adf324d5eb2.html (June 23, 2022).

Parkinson, Hillary. "Green Bay Packer, Detroit Lion, or US President?," Pieces of History (blog), US National Archives, https://prologue.blogs.archives.gov/2011/02 /02/green-bay-packer-detroit-lion-or-us-president/ (February 2, 2011).

Paxton, John R. "Christmas on the Rappahannock," American Battlefield Trust, https: //www.battlefields.org/learn/primary-sources/christmas-rappahannock (*Harper's Weekly*, 1886).

Petras, George, Janet Loehrke, Ramon Padilla, Javier Zarracina, and Jennifer Borresen. "Timeline: How the Storming of the U.S. Capitol Unfolded on Jan. 6," *USA Today*, https://www.usatoday.com/in-depth/news/2021/01/06/dc-protests -capitol-riot-trump-supporters-electoral-college-stolen-election/6568305002/ (January 7, 2021).

Phelps, Jordyn. "Ex-President Warren Harding's Love Child Confirmed Through DNA Testing," ABC News, https://abcnews.go.com/Politics/president-warren -hardings-love-child-confirmed-dna-testing/story?id=33060408 (August 13, 2015).

Pilkington, Ed. "Pittsburgh Bridge Collapses Hours Before Biden's Infrastructure Speech in City," *Guardian*, https://www.theguardian.com/us-news/2022/jan/28/ pittsburgh-bridge-collapse-biden-infrastructure-speech (January 28, 2022).

Pittman, Craig. "The Seven Weirdest Stories in Florida History," *Miami New Times*, https://www.miaminewtimes.com/arts/the-seven-weirdest-stories-in-florida -history-8631101 (July 28, 2016).

Porterfield, Nolan. "Pinkston, David Proctor [Dave Stone] (1913–2004)," Texas State Historical Association, https://www.tshaonline.org/handbook/entries/pinkston -david-proctor-dave-stone (June 3, 2015).

Prial, Frank J. "Truman Is Recalled Here for Warmth And Simplicity That Had Wide Appeal," *New York Times*, https://www.nytimes.com/1972/12/28/archives/truman -is-recalled-here-for-warmth-and-simplicity-that-had-wide.html (December 28, 1972).

Price, Greg. "How Much Did Trump Spend On His Campaign To Beat Hillary Clinton? Total Money Raised By 2016 Election Candidates," *International Business Times*, https://www.ibtimes.com/reporters/greg-price?page=14 (November 9, 2016).

Ratliff, Amisa. "12 Numbers to Know About the Money in the 2020 Presidential Election," Issue One, https://issueone.org/articles/12-numbers-to-know-about-the -money-in-the-2020-presidential-election/ (December 14, 2020).

Reber, Patricia Bixler. "Thomas Moore's Refrigerator, 1802 Patent," Researching Food History (blog), http://researchingfoodhistory.blogspot.com/2012/04/thomas -moores-refrigerator.html (April 13, 2012).

Riley, Christopher. "The Moon Walkers: Twelve Men Who Have Visited Another World," *Guardian*, https://www.theguardian.com/science/2009/jul/09/apollo -astronauts-walking-moon (July 10, 2009).

Ring, Wilson. "150 Years Since Death of Vt. 'Sleeping Sentinel,'" Associated Press, https://www.reformer.com/local-news/150-years-since-death-of-vt-sleeping -sentinel/article_97dd4dbb-dbc8-5b53-a7ca-480d436667c1.html (April 17, 2012).

Rosen, Julia. "November 10, 1934: Arizona Declares War Against California at Parker Dam," *Earth: The Science Behind the Headlines*, https://www.earthmagazine.org /article/november-10-1934-arizona-declares-war-against-california-parker-dam/ (December 3, 2014).

Rossell, Deac. "The Public Exhibition of Moving Pictures Before 1896," https://core .ac.uk/download/pdf/42388048.pdf (2006).

Sarris, Andrew. "I Am Happy! The Great Debaters Gives Me Hope and Joy," *New York Observer* (December 18, 2007).

Schulman, Ari N. "The Dinosaur Discoverer," *Philanthropy Magazine* (Winter 2015), https://www.philanthropyroundtable.org/magazine/winter-2015-the-dinosaur -discoverer/.

Schultz, Colin. "This Picture of Boston, Circa 1860, Is the World's Oldest Surviving Aerial Photo," *Smithsonian*, https://www.smithsonianmag.com/smart-news/ this-picture-of-boston-circa-1860-is-the-worlds-oldest-surviving-aerial-photo -14756301/ (April 3, 2013).

Sherman, Amy. "Rubio Exaggerates in Saying It's Been 80 Years Since a 'Lame Duck' Made a Supreme Court Nomination," Politifact, https://www.politifact.com /factchecks/2016/feb/14/marco-rubio/rubio-exaggerates-sayig-its-been-80-years -lame-duc/ (February 14, 2016).

Solomon, Kristine. "52 Fascinating Facts You Never Knew About U.S. Presidents," Reader's Digest, https://www.rd.com/list/facts-about-u-s-presidents/ (updated December 2, 2022).

Staff Report: "Ike Hoover Counts 40 Years' Service," *Washington Post* (May 7, 1931).

———. "Ten Years Ago in December," govinfo.gov (January 2, 1953).

———. "The Nation: Well, Thanks Anyway," *TIME*, https://content.time.com/time/ subscriber/article/0,33009,910318,00.html (July 10, 1972).

———. "Last Trolleys Rolled in the City in 1957," *New York Times*, https://www .nytimes.com/1975/07/09/archives/last-trolleys-rolled-in-the-city-in-1957.html (July 9, 1975).

———. "Message from New Hampshire," *TIME*, https://content.time.com/time/ subscriber/article/0,33009,913462,00.html (September 29, 1975).

———. "Dinosaur Eggs Discovered in Montana," *New York Times*, https://www .nytimes.com/1979/08/28/archives/dinosaur-eggs-discovered-in-montana.html (August 28, 1979).

———. "Astronaut James Irwin Dies," *Washington Post*, https://www.washingtonpost .com/archive/local/1991/08/10/astronaut-james-irwin-dies/f6a8eb51-f7b5-436d -afe6-91b0adc6e1d0/ (August 8, 1991).

———. "13 Escape Cuba in Stolen Biplane," *Tampa Bay Times*, https://www .tampabay.com/archive/1993/11/16/13-escape-cuba-in-stolen-biplane/ (December 16, 1993).

————. "D-Day Invasion/June 6, 1944: The Invasion of Normandy: By the Numbers," *Los Angeles Times*, https://www.latimes.com/archives/la-xpm-1994-05 -31-wr-64230-story.html (May 31, 1994).

————. "Frank W. Cyr, 'Father of the Yellow School Bus,' Dies at the Age of 95," Teachers College Columbia University, https://www.tc.columbia.edu/articles/1995 /august/frank-w-cyr-father-of-the-yellow-school-bus-dies-at-the/ (August 1995).

————. "Worldwide Flu Pandemic Strikes," *A Science Odyssey*, PBS, WGBH, https: //www.pbs.org/wgbh/aso/databank/entries/dm18fl.html (1998).

————. "Montana Wakes Up To Speed Limits," *Buffalo News*, https://buffalonews .com/news/montana-wakes-up-to-speed-limits/article_12946ffb-1dd2-5479-8e38 -415f527643f1.html (May 28, 1999).

————. "Amateur Gardener Grows World's Biggest Potato," *Telegraph*, https:// www.telegraph.co.uk/news/newstopics/howaboutthat/7979980/Amateur-gardener -grows-worlds-biggest-potato.html (September 3, 2010).

————. "1786: Elizabeth Wilson, Her Reprieve Too Late," ExecutedToday.com, http://www.executedtoday.com/2011/01/03/1786-elizabeth-wilson-her-reprieve -too-late/ (January 3, 2011).

————. "Jan. 23, 1973 | Nixon Announces End of U.S. Involvement in Vietnam," Learning Network, *New York Times*, https://archive.nytimes.com/learning.blogs .nytimes.com/2012/01/23/jan-23-1973-nixon-announces-end-of-u-s-involvement -in-vietnam/ (January 23, 2012).

————. "Telstar 1 Legacy: 1st Live TV Broadcast by Satellite Turns 50," Space.com, https://www.space.com/16549-telstar-satellite-first-tv-signal-anniversary.html (July 12, 2012).

————. "The First Jet Landing on a Carrier," HistoricWings, http://fly.historicwings .com/2012/11/the-first-jet-landing-on-a-carrier/ (November 6, 2012).

————. "Which President Got a Speeding Ticket on a Horse?," Ghosts of DC, https: //ghostsofdc.org/2014/03/04/ulysses-grant-arrested-speeding/ (March 4, 2014).

————. "5 Facts You Didn't Know about D-Day," VA News, https://news.va.gov /14383/5-facts-you-didnt-know-about-d-day/ (June 6, 2014).

————. "Lincoln Pardons his Sister in Law," Civil War Talk, https://civilwartalk.com /threads/lincoln-pardons-his-sister-in-law.107097/ (December 14, 2014).

————. "How 'Zoot Suit' Changed Theatre Forever," https://www.centertheatregroup .org/news-and-blogs/news/2017/january/how-zoot-suit-changed-theatre-forever/ (January 5, 2017).

————. "The Vermont Sleeping Sentinel: A Strange Civil War Legacy," New England Historical Society, https://newenglandhistoricalsociety.com/vermont -sleeping-sentinel-strange-civil-war-legacy/ (retrieved June 17, 2017).

————. "Emily Dickinson Biography," Biography, https://www.biography.com/ writer/emily-dickinson (retrieved August 25, 2018).

————. "October 13, 1957: The Edsel Show!," Mac's Motor City Garage, https: //macsmotorcitygarage.com/october-13-1957-the-edsel-show/ (September 22, 2018).

———. "The Hanging and the Hermit: The Tragic Timing of William Wilson," Hushed Up History, https://husheduphistory.com/post/612168059767095296/the-hanging-and-the-hermit-the-tragic-timing-of (March 9, 2020).

———. "10 Birthday Facts about President James Monroe," National Constitution Center (blog), https://constitutioncenter.org/blog/10-surprising-birthday-facts-about-james-monroe (April 28, 2020).

———. "Abraham Lincoln Imposes First Federal Income Tax," HISTORY, https://www.history.com/this-day-in-history/lincoln-imposes-first-federal-income-tax (August 3, 2020).

———. "August 5, 1863: Berkeley Co. Admitted to New State of WV," WVPB, West Virginia Encyclopedia, https://www.wvpublic.org/radio/2020-08-05/august-5-1863-berkeley-co-admitted-to-new-state-of-wv (August 5, 2020).

———. "Capitol for a Day" | 214 Years Ago, Kingston was Tennessee's State Capitol for a single day," WBIR, https://www.wbir.com/article/news/history/capitol-for-a-day-214-years-ago-kingston-was-tennessees-state-capitol-for-a-single-day/51-ecfb08b0-aa49-4964-a0c5-f6299ba56eea (September 21, 2021).

———. "First U.S. Soldier Killed during Vietnam's August Revolution," HISTORY, https://www.history.com/this-day-in-history/first-us-soldier-killed-during-vietnam-august-revolution (September 26, 2021).

———. "Battle of Yorktown Begins," HISTORY, https://www.history.com/this-day-in-history/battle-of-yorktown-begins (September 28, 2021).

———. "Battles of Trenton and Princeton," HISTORY, https://www.history.com/topics/american-revolution/battles-of-trenton-and-princeton (updated September 29, 2021).

———. "Flu Pandemic of 1918," Kansapedia, Kansas Historical Society, https://www.kshs.org/kansapedia/flu-pandemic-of-1918/17805 (October 2021).

———. "Archie, the First Internet Search Engine," Stackscale, https://www.stackscale.com/blog/archie-internet-search-engine/ (October 9, 2021).

———. "The History and Origin of Memorial Day in Waterloo, New York," Waterloo, New York: Birthplace of Memorial Day, https://waterloony.com/memorial-day/history/ (retrieved October 11, 2021).

———. "The Most Infamous Floor Brawl in the History of the U.S. House of Representatives," History, Art & Archives: Historical Highlights, https://history.house.gov/Historical-Highlights/1851-1900/The-most-infamous-floor-brawl-in-the-history-of-the-U-S--House-of-Representatives/ (retrieved October 19, 2021).

———. "The Louisiana Purchase: Jefferson's Constitutional Gamble," National Constitution Center, https://constitutioncenter.org/blog/the-louisiana-purchase-jeffersons-constitutional-gamble (October 20, 2021).

———. "Income Tax Day," Research Guides, Library of Congress, https://guides.loc.gov/this-month-in-business-history/april/tax-day (retrieved November 4, 2021).

———. "Biography: James Bridger," YourDictionary, https://biography.yourdictionary.com/james-bridger (retrieved December 30, 2021).

———. "CDC Museum COVID-19 Timeline," Centers for Disease Control and Prevention, https://www.cdc.gov/museum/timeline/covid19.html (retrieved January 5, 2022).

———. "John B. Meachum, Minister Born," AAREG, https://aaregistry.org/story/rev -john-b-meachum-born/ (retrieved January 7, 2022).

———. "Dave Stone—Inducted 1999," CRS '23, https://www.countryradioseminar .com/dave-stone (retrieved January 8, 2022).

———. "Benjamin Lincoln's Sword," Smithsonian's History Explorer, https:// historyexplorer.si.edu/resource/benjamin-lincolns-sword (retrieved January 11, 2022).

———. "Bourbon Street: The Complete Block-by-Block Guide," New Orleans French, https://www.frenchquarter.com/bourbon-street/ (retrieved January 22, 2022).

———. "Thomas Moore," Monticello: Research and Education, Thomas Jefferson Encyclopedia, https://www.monticello.org/research-education/thomas-jefferson -encyclopedia/thomas-moore/ (retrieved January 30, 2022).

———. "Top 10 Most Reclusive Celebrities," *TIME*, https://content.time.com/time /specials/packages/completelist/0,29569,1902376,00.html (retrieved February 1, 2022).

———. "Rocket Men," University of Michigan Alumni Association, https://alumni .umich.edu/michigan-alum/rocket-men/ (retrieved February 2, 2022).

———. "Description of Each Execution Method," Death Penalty Information Center, https://deathpenaltyinfo.org/executions/methods-of-execution/description-of-each -method (retrieved February 4, 2022).

———. "Clyde Tombaugh: A Man of Universal Wonder," Academy of Achievement, https://achievement.org/achiever/clyde-tombaugh/ (updated February 4, 2022).

———. "1,000 New Yorkers Join Klan in Opposition to Interracial Marriage," EJI: A History of Racial Injustice, Equal Justice Initiative, https://calendar.eji.org/racial -injustice/aug/17 (retrieved February 13, 2022).

———. "Bobby Fischer," IMDb, https://www.imdb.com/name/nm1648139/ (retrieved February 21, 2022).

———. "Belle Boyd: Confederate Spy In The Civil War," History of American Women, https://www.womenhistoryblog.com/2008/06/belle-boyd.html (retrieved April 15, 2022).

———. "The Beginning of the End of Slavery in Massachusetts," New England Historical Society, https://newenglandhistoricalsociety.com/beginning-end-slavery -massachusetts/ (retrieved May 7, 2022).

———. "The Great Hurricane," neworleanspast.com (retrieved May 31, 2022).

———. "First Artificial Snow Falls on Mt. Greylock," massmoments, https://www .massmoments.org/moment-details/first-artificial-snow-falls-on-mt-greylock.html (retrieved June 5, 2022).

———. "Military Naturalization During WWII," U.S. Citizenship and Immigration Services, https://www.uscis.gov/about-us/our-history/overview-of-agency-history/ military-naturalization-during-wwii (June 9, 2022).

———. "Huey Long: Life & Times | Huey Long Timeline," https://www.hueylong .com/life-times/ (Long Legacy Project, 2023).

Stamm, Amy. "How Do Astronauts Vote From Space?," National Air and Space Museum, https://airandspace.si.edu/stories/editorial/how-do-astronauts-vote-space (November 2, 2020).

Starr, Stephen. "The Creationist Astronaut Who Tried to Find Noah's Ark," OZY, https://www.ozy.com/true-and-stories/the-creationist-astronaut-who-tried-to-find -noahs-ark/72047/ (October 6, 2016).

Steponaitis, Cookie. "Making History Happen From Inside The Vergennes Jail: The Tale Of Matthew Lyon," *Valley Voice*, http://www.vvoice.org/?module =displaystory&story_id=1944&format=print&edition_id=211 (retrieved June 2, 2022).

Stilwell, Blake. "17 Wild Facts about the Vietnam War," We Are the Mighty, https:// www.wearethemighty.com/lists/vietnam-war/ (December 16, 2021).

Stockdale, Charles, and John Harrington. "35 Musicians Who Famously Told Politicians: Don't Use My Song," *USA Today*, https://www.usatoday.com/story /life/music/2018/07/16/35-musicians-who-famously-told-politicians-dont-use-my -song/784121002/ (July 16, 2018).

Stuart, Reginald. "Iacocca Named Chrysler Chief," *New York Times*, https:// www.nytimes.com/1979/09/21/archives/iacocca-named-chrysler-chief-bergmoser -exford-aide-is-president.html (September 21, 1979).

Trickey, Erick. "In the Darkest Days of World War II, Winston Churchill's Visit to the White House Brought Hope to Washington," *Smithsonian Magazine*, https://www .smithsonianmag.com/history/darkest-days-world-war-ii-winston-churchills-visit -white-house-brought-hope-washington-180961798/ (January 13, 2017),

Trimble, Marshall. "Opening Shots in Arizona's Pleasant Valley War," True West Blog, https://truewestmagazine.com/article/opening-shots-in-arizonas-pleasant -valley-war/ (June 6, 2018).

Tucker, Neely. "Thomas Jefferson: A Man of the Pasta," Library of Congress Blog, https://blogs.loc.gov/loc/2019/12/thomas-jefferson-a-man-of-the-pasta/ (December 2, 2019).

Vale, J. Allister, and John W. Scadding. "Did Winston Churchill Suffer a Myocardial Infarction in the White House at Christmas 1941?," *Journal of the Royal Society of Medicine* 110(2) (2017), https://journals.sagepub.com/doi/10.1177 /0141076817745506.

Van Riper, Frank. "Ford to City: Drop Dead in 1975," *New York Daily News*, https: //www.nydailynews.com/new-york/president-ford-announces-won-bailout-nyc -1975-article-1.2405985 (October 29, 2015).

Waddell, Bill. "Death Toll Rises as Rescue Efforts Continue in Wake of Historic Tornado Outbreak," Accuweather, https://news.yahoo.com/nighttime-tornadoes -wreak-havoc-across-033409584.html (December 10, 2021).

Wadler, Joyce. "PUBLIC LIVES; Mrs. Seuss Hears a Who, and Tells About It," *New York Times*, https://www.nytimes.com/2000/11/29/nyregion/public-lives-mrs-seuss -hears-a-who-and-tells-about-it.html (November 29, 2000).

Walker, Micah. "John Dingell's 4 Children: Who They Are, What They Do," *Detroit Free Press*, https://www.freep.com/story/news/local/michigan/2019/02/08/john -dingell-kids-death/2812203002/ (February 8, 2020).

Wall, Mike. "Voting from Space: How Astronauts Do It," Space.com, https://www.space.com/34643-how-nasa-astronauts-vote-from-space.html (November 8, 2016).

Wallechinsky, David, and Irving Wallace. "First Artificial Snow from a Natural Cloud," Trivia-Library, https://www.trivia-library.com/a/first-artificial-snow-from -a-natural-cloud.htm (retrieved June 5, 2022).

Wallenfeldt, Jeff. "10 Things You Need to Know About the Hamilton-Burr Duel, According to Hamilton's Burr," *Brittanica*, https://www.britannica.com/list/10 -things-you-need-to-know-about-the-hamilton-burr-duel-according-to-hamiltons -burr (retrieved February 18, 2022).

Wang, Jennifer. "Donald Trump's Fortune Falls $800 Million To $3.7 Billion," *Forbes*, https://www.forbes.com/sites/jenniferwang/2016/09/28/the-definitive -look-at-donald-trumps-wealth-new/?sh=3bbc594847a5 (September 28, 2016).

Wicentowski, Danny. "The Final Flight of Martin McNally," *Riverfront Times*, https://www.riverfronttimes.com/news/the-final-flight-of-martin-mcnally-3137418 (January 11, 2017).

Wilk, Tom. "240 Years Ago, Lancaster was the U.S. Capital—for 24 Hours," *Philadelphia Inquirer*, https://www.inquirer.com/philly/opinion/commentary/ historic-lancaster-united-states-capital-day-20170925.html (September 25, 2017).

Williams, Christian. "Super Station's Super Man," *Washington Post*, https://www.washingtonpost.com/archive/lifestyle/1979/02/11/super-stations-super-man /416b0082-6659-45ad-a1af-5bc77e84895e/ (February 11, 1979).

Williams, Matt. "History of Challenges: The Orteig Prize (1919–1927)," Hero[x], https://www.herox.com/blog/428-history-of-challenges-the-orteig-prize-1919-1927 (retrieved October 16, 2021).

Willis, Dail. "1st to Die in Del. Gallows in 50 Years Could Be Last—Couple's Murderer Picks Death By Hanging," *Baltimore Sun*, https://www.baltimoresun .com/news/bs-xpm-1996-01-24-1996024027-story.html (January 23, 1996).

Willis, Derek. "The 2012 Money Race: Compare the Candidates," *New York Times*, https://www.nytimes.com/elections/2012/campaign-finance.html (November 26, 2012).

Woestendiek, John. "Again, a Cause Celebre," *Baltimore Sun*, https://www .baltimoresun.com/news/bs-xpm-2001-07-27-0107270131-story.html (July 27, 2001).

Wright, David. "Trump Defends 'Brilliantly' Using Bankruptcy Laws," CNN, https://www.cnn.com/2016/06/22/politics/donald-trump-defends-bankruptcy-history/ index.html (June 22, 2016).

Zentner, Joe. "Okie Faces & Irish Eyes: John Steinbeck & Route 66," *Irish America Magazine*, https://www.irishamerica.com/2007/06/okie-faces-irish-eyes-john -steinbeck-route-66/ (June/July 2007).

WEBSITES CONSULTED

army.mil
businessinsider.com
emilydickinsonmuseum.org
geneautry.com
npshistory.com
princeton.edu
roadsideamerica.com
santaclausind.org
usacitiesonline.com
waimea.com
whitehouse.gov
Video
Neufeld, Michael J.: "Wernher von Braun and the Nazis," *American Experience: Chasing the Moon*, PBS (May 20, 2019).

About the Author

For thirty-one years, Mike Henry taught American history to students at all levels of the educational spectrum from elementary school to college. His technique of using the events of the past to show how they impact our lives in the present made him a popular classroom instructor and guest speaker. After the inception of *No Child Left Behind*, he averaged a success rate of more than 80 percent on mandated testing where the majority of his students were at or below the poverty level.

Mike is a two-time award winner of *Who's Who Among America's Classroom Teachers*. Following his retirement, he wrote *Black History: More Than Just A Month* which was published in 2012. The book has become popular among those wanting to learn more and for educators of African American history.

What They Didn't Teach You in Your American History Class was released in 2014 and nominated for the James Harvey Robinson Prize. Its sequel, *What They Didn't Teach You in Your American History Class: The Second Encounter*, debuted in 2016. These works are for those who are interested in learning about the fascinating backstories that are not included in most history texts.

In 2015, Mike introduced his *American History for Kids* series. The first volume, *Tell Me About the Presidents*, was nominated for the Grateful American Book Prize. All of his works are published by Rowman & Littlefield.

The follow-up effort is titled *Christmas with the Presidents*. It tells how our nation's leaders spent their holiday seasons ranging from the simple to the elaborate and even heroic. The book is a fun read for children and their parents.

The writer's election year (2020) work was *That Tuesday in November*. As always, Mike's book is filled with backstories of little-known events of the people and happenings that are connected to the nation's most historically changing elections.

"True education begins with reading," said the author. "Once that takes place, learning can happen with any subject matter."

Mike and his wife Pamela, who is also a retired educator and coeditor of his books, reside near Dallas, Texas.